Praise for Eddie Ensley's
VISIONS: THE SOUL'S PATH TO THE SACRED

"*Visions* clearly speaks to the current yearnings of Christians in a post-modern world. Moving us beyond the prism of rationalism, Ensley frees us by opening ancient and forgotten windows of transcendent realities."

ROBERT E. WEBBER
Myers Professor of Ministry, Wheaton College

"In his new work, *Visions*, Eddie Ensley has again succeeded, as he has done before in many of his writings and conferences, to connect us to the presence of the sacred in our ordinary world. He reminds us that through the whole of human history there have always been 'visions,' perceptible signs of the divine, and they continue to occur today. . . . [Ensley] guides us in a rewarding journey of rediscovery of the very 'footprints of God' in the world of nature as well as in the world of our daily lives."

BISHOP RAYMOND W. LESSARD
Former bishop of Savannah

"This wonderful, life-giving book invites us to see that whatever 'heaven' means it's closer to us than we've allowed ourselves to believe."

WILLIAM J. O'MALLEY, S.J.
Fordham University, author of God—The Oldest Question

"The author makes two fascinating contributions to our thinking and experiencing. First, he shows that visions are the 'natural and normal' confluence of the human and the divine. Second, he demonstrates how visions must be subject to the scriptures and tradition of the church. This distinguishes the book from most others in the field of spirituality."

NEELY D. MCCARTER
President emeritus, Pacific School of Religion

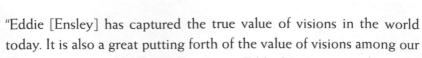

"Eddie [Ensley] has captured the true value of visions in the world today. It is also a great putting forth of the value of visions among our indigenous peoples of the Americas. . . . Eddie has, in a very clear way, shown the visions for what they are, with the need for correct interpretation of visions of modern-day life."

JOHN S. HASCALL, O.F.M.
Native American spiritual leader (Ojibwa)

"*Visions: The Soul's Path to the Sacred* continues Ensley's quest to learn and share more on little-known areas of Christian spirituality. An extraordinary study of visions in the Christian tradition."

VINSON SYNAN
Dean, Regent University School of Divinity

"Mysticism is natural to the human, and perhaps to all beings. Part of the inner life of all of us is the capacity for vision, an intuitive seeing that has its source in the divine reality, but is innate to us. . . . Eddie Ensley illuminates this point in his compelling account of the nature of visions and the beautiful examples he presents. His treatment is really a higher level of understanding of an elusive dimension of experience. It is a step forward, and this book is destined to be a classic."

WAYNE TEASDALE
Author of The Mystic Heart *and professor of theology,*
Chicago Catholic Theological Union

"I am honored that Eddie Ensley considers me his mentor, but I can hardly take any credit for the powerful witness to God's work that Eddie offers in this captivating book. I see *Visions* in continuity with the great apologetic tradition of the fathers of the church and pray that many people will be led from visions to the gift of faith, which is of things unseen, and to the grace and peace that Eddie has found in full communion with the Catholic Church."

CARDINAL BERNARD F. LAW
Archbishop of Boston

"Eddie Ensley wrote the now charismatic classic *Sounds of Wonder* years ago and went on to have a profound influence on many souls. I met him more than twenty years ago and was deeply impressed by his life and his work. *Visions* is a continuation of that extraordinary life and work. In a time of seemingly endless streams of mediocre religious words and books, Eddie's work reaches deeper into the stream of orthodox Catholic Christianity to bring the living water of Jesus and the Spirit to all people in a most extraordinary way."

JOHN MICHAEL TALBOT
Folksinger, recording artist, and founder of The Brothers and Sisters of Charity

---

"Eddie [Ensley's] words and shared experience awaken the reader to the interconnectedness of creation. His words remind the reader of what our elders called 'original instructions.' Original instructions are the road map to the source of our being, guiding those who are lost in confusion home to the magic lake wherein we may see our original face reflected. These original instructions also carry the song of our ancestors' accumulated wisdom, which assists in 'retuning' our hearts and minds to that original sound for the skillful application of spiritual vision in our daily lives."

DHYANI YWAHOO
Author of Voices of Our Ancestors:
Cherokee Teachings from the Wisdom Fire

VISIONS

VISIONS

THE SOUL'S PATH TO THE SACRED

EDDIE ENSLEY

LOYOLAPRESS.
CHICAGO

LOYOLAPRESS.

3441 N. Ashland Avenue
Chicago, Illinois 60657

Interior design by Kathy Kikkert

Library of Congress Cataloging-in-Publication Data
Ensley, Eddie.
     Visions : the soul's path to the sacred / Eddie Ensley.
          p. cm.
     Includes bibliographical references (p.).
     ISBN 0-8294-1427-4
     1. Visions. 2. Spiritual life—Catholic Church. I. Title.
     BV5091.V6 E67 2000
     248.2'9—dc21   00-021261

Printed in the United States of America
00 01 02 03 04 / 10 9 8 7 6 5 4 3 2 1

This book is dedicated to six people whose presence in my life made this book possible:

His Eminence Cardinal Bernard F. Law, my lifelong mentor
Fr. Gerard Schreck, my pastor, who believed in me when I found it hard to believe in myself
Fr. Douglas Kent Clark, whose wisdom and candor help guide my life
My cousin Dhyani, who helped me remember
Rhea White, who believed in the book when I had a hard time believing in it
Robert Herrmann, whose constancy, patience, and care teach me the meaning
of unmerited grace

C O N T E N T S

acknowledgments ix

part 1 · touched by god

1. we all see visions 3

2. the light makes a promise 23

3. what are visions? 39

4. the medicine stories of christianity 51

5. how visions come to you 69

part 2 · a new way of seeing

6. seeing life with new eyes 85

7. trips to the horizon 99

8. finding the remembering spot 117

9. remembering visions 135

part 3 · the healing power of visions

10. god's therapy 157

11. the light returns 175

12. help for our grieving 191

13. visions to heal our wounded world 209

part 4 • the role of visions in life today

14. walking in balance with visions 229

15. spiritual emergencies 247

16. visions and the new millennium 263

notes 277

contact the author 285

A C K N O W L E D G M E N T S

Many people played a critical role in the writing of this book. Steve Wilburn, my old classmate from Belhaven, helped me find just the right publisher. Rhea White, Judy Esway, and Dr. Barbara Fleischer of Loyola Institute of Ministry, along with Steve Wilburn, believed in the book when I found it hard to believe in it. Their excitement made this book possible. My editor, Jim Manney of Loyola Press, got in the trenches of writing with me daily, becoming more than a colleague, becoming a brother. LaVonne Neff and Vinita Wright of Loyola Press contributed not only their skills but their hearts. My agent, Loretta Barrett, offered me both professionalism and friendship. I thank the many people who read the manuscript as it emerged, guiding and helping as they read. Among them are the "gang": Vicki and Wayne Scheer, Rosanne Maltese, Jerry and Pat Johnson.

My cousin Dhyani Ywahoo, Cherokee elder, helped shape the memoir sections. Dr. Michael Garrett of the Eastern Band of Cherokee encouraged me along the way. Deacon George Foster promptly gave the kind of feedback that kept the project going during the vital, final stages.

The comments of Fr. Tom Francis, O.S.C.O. lifted me up when the workload of the book grew especially heavy. Others who contributed through reading parts of the emerging book are my cousin Helen Young, Dr. Neely McCarter, Bishop Raymond Lessard, Steve Patton, and Deborah Keswani.

Kattee Dugas and John Quillen provided listening ears and supportive hearts during the hectic time of writing.

My mother, my aunt Margaret, and my other aunts and cousins loved and supported me as always and were graciously understanding when work on the book meant I had less time to spend with them.

PART 1

touched by god

Thou art like silence unperplexed,

A secret and a mystery

Between one footfall and the next.

Most dear pause in a mellow day!

Thou art inwoven with every air.

O pause between the sobs of cares;

O thought within all thought that is:

Trance between laughters unawares:

Thou are the shape of melodies,

And thou the ecstasy of prayers!

—ALICE MEYNELL

Visions are moments when "the human is embraced by

the transcendent Other," as the Catholic theologian

von Balthasar put it. Visions are happening every-

where, all the time, to all of us. Some of them happen

for our healing. Some of them are quite subtle and

fleeting. Some of them are given to us for the sake of

others. Visions come in many forms and sizes and

shapes, but they are always with us. We human

beings are made to experience the sacred that

surrounds us. All we need to do is watch and listen.

we all see
visions

BENEATH THE CLUTTER OF OUR EVERYDAY BUSYNESS IS A YEARNING. Sometimes it is quiet, hardly noticeable. Sometimes it throbs like a toothache. This yearning is built into the very cells of our bodies and inhabits the textures of our souls.

It is the quest for mystery. Our finite world is bordered by the infinite, a limitless horizon that sometimes invades and draws us intimately near.

Those invasions of mystery, those graced moments, can sneak up on us unexpectedly. Perhaps you are running along the beach. You cease to be aware of the movement of your muscles or the splashing of your feet in the water. The sound of the breaking waves stills and calms your mind. You seem one with the sea, the beach. You feel connected. Your fears leave you for a moment. And sacred mystery rushes in, closer to you than the blood that surges through your veins.

Sometimes the encounter is more vivid. You see the sacred light, hear the eternal sounds, greet loved ones now passed over into the holy.

Quiet or vivid, the experience you are having is what our spiritual ancestors called a vision.

Such moments take us out of the ordinary and help us glimpse the limitless. Such moments can comfort, give hope, and reveal fresh possibilities. They are as human as our breath and our heartbeat.

Because *visions* is a pointer word—a word like *God* or *love* or *prayer* that points into mystery and eludes precise definition—it has been used in many ways throughout the centuries. Some use the word *vision* to describe extraordinary experiences in which a person sees sacred scenes vividly. Others use it in a more fluid way, as a word for all sacred encounters, whether subdued or vivid. It is in this broad, fluid way that I use the word. I mean it to describe everything from a mellow warmth we feel when singing a hymn or looking out over God's ocean to the ecstatic meetings that seers at Lourdes or Fatima are said to have experienced. All our meetings with the holy, whether subdued or vivid, can mend us and transform us and deserve our prayerful attention.

A WOMAN'S STORY

I am listening to a middle-aged woman describe a healing vision that illuminated her spirit when her spirit was dead. She is a Catholic of Native American descent, as I am. The words come slowly, carefully, during a healing retreat for Native people in Canada. Five hundred years of genocide and dehumanization have left terrible wounds on my people's souls, and I have heard appalling stories of pain and anguish during this weekend. This is one of the most agonizing.

Years ago, when the woman was young and living on a reserve, a teenage nephew she especially loved killed himself. He stole beer from her cabinet, got drunk, and drove off the road. The woman blamed herself. She fell into a profound depression that counseling and medication could not touch. Her marriage failed. Her children chose to live with her husband. For years she lived in the misery of this tragedy, which mirrored the anguish of her people.

One day she was driving to the grocery store. A tingling filled her ears, ringing inside and out. Fear overcame her. She knew she was moving into the unknown. She pulled off the road into a clump of trees and leaned back in her seat.

She felt herself whisked out of her car, carried on a journey to a place of unspeakable splendor and brilliance. The awareness of *Gitche Manitou*—the Great Mystery, the Great Spirit, whose reality words cannot approach—washed over her.

Above her head she sensed a presence. When she looked up, she saw the hand of a healer holding an eagle feather above her. The healer sang an ineffable chant that touched her hidden, lonely places with loving-kindness, carrying a power that strengthened her heart.

She turned to see which great healer held the eagle feather—and beheld her nephew. Beside him stood Christ.

After she returned to everyday awareness, she wept for a long while in the car, finally able to grieve for her nephew. Cleansed by this period of grieving, she rested in a stillness that was all-encompassing.

The vision marked a turning point for her. She began to rebuild her life. This took time and much hard work, but she was able to begin anew because God had broken through her depression and guilt. She was healed by the vision of Christ's boundless love.

A PRIEST'S STORY

A priest friend is about sixty-five years old and the author of several significant scholarly books. He is describing a vision that happened during his vacation.

He was consumed by a desire to write a best-seller. Away in the mountains, he couldn't enjoy skiing, his favorite sport, because his mind kept turning over ways to make his next book a best-seller. Then, standing on a slope, he looked at the bright blue sky and the towering mountains. For a moment, in a wordless, imageless way, he caught an inner sight of eternity.

In that instant, he realized that his wanting to write popular, long-remembered books was a way of trying to win a type of immortality, the immortality of living on in the memories of readers. When he felt eternity in that moment, he knew that eternity is a gift, God's gift. It isn't something we can achieve by building monuments and accomplishing great deeds. My friend turned to his skiing with pleasure. He let go of his struggle to achieve immortality through books.

VISIONS ARE GIFTS

A woman in her late twenties approaches me after I have given a talk at a parish mission. I am exhausted, perhaps a little sick. She says that she wants to tell me something. Reluctantly, I agree. I can hardly bear to hear the story of the family problem or personal crisis I'm sure is coming.

She tells me about her nine-year-old son, who died of leukemia a year ago. Her husband couldn't deal with the illness. He left six months before the boy died. But the woman isn't telling me a tale of misery. A different kind of story emerges.

Toward the end of his life, her son told her, "Mama, I like it when I fall asleep, because every time I go to sleep I go to be where Jesus is. There's light everywhere, and all the children laugh and play." Each night, her son told her more about the land of light where Jesus lived. That world her son journeyed to in his sleep became, as he put it, "more real than when you're awake."

One night not long before the end, her son raised himself up slowly and painfully in his hospital bed and said, "Mama, I know I'm going to die soon. I'm going to be with Jesus and play in the light."

She encircled his thin frame in her arms and wept, saying the only thing she could say: "I love you."

"Don't be sad, Mama. We'll still be in touch. Someday you will be with me."

He asked her to step back from the bed and bend down so he could touch her.

"I live much of the time where it's bright and where Jesus is. I'm going to touch you now, and you can feel what it's like to be where the light is and where Jesus is."

The nine-year-old put both of his hands on her head, like a priest or rabbi giving a blessing. He held his little hands firmly on her head. She felt an indescribable brightness, a comfort, and a joy.

Two days later, the boy died.

Several times in the next few weeks, when the woman was in a state between waking and sleeping, her son came to her with the brilliance of a holy light around him, letting her know that he was OK.

Now the woman tells me that the story is for me, not for her. She knows I am tired and that I am struggling for the inspiration to do the mission well. She has told me the story of her son to encourage me.

She asks me to lower my head. She places her hands on my head in silent prayer, the way her son placed his hands on her. I feel a stream of brightness pass through me. I feel as though Jesus himself is touching me, rejuvenating me. A cleanness and a refreshing grace wash over me.

The vision was a gift—for me.

VISIONS HAPPEN ALL THE TIME

What these people experienced are visions—moments when "the human is embraced by the transcendent Other," as Catholic theologian Hans Urs von Balthasar put it. Visions are happening everywhere, all the time, to all of us. Some of them happen for our healing, as the Native woman in Canada was healed. Some of them are quite subtle and fleeting, as was the priest's brush with eternity on the mountain-top. Some of them, like the dying child's vision, are given to us for the sake of others. Visions come in many forms and sizes and shapes, but they are always with us. We human beings are made to experience the sacred that surrounds us. All we need to do is watch and listen.

Men and women in the past understood this better than we do. They were not burdened by the rationalist culture we inherited from the Enlightenment, a culture that regards visions as extraordinary exceptions to the rigid "laws of nature." Our ancestors understood the subtle interrelationships of flesh and spirit more accurately than we do. They looked for visions in their daily lives. When they received visions, they knew what do with them.

This wisdom about visions is preserved by Native people and oth-ers on the fringes of our mainstream culture. This was obvious at a healing gathering of Native people I helped lead in Canada. People poured out stories of pain and stark anguish, followed by stories of exquisite healing. Person after person spoke of how visions of the hal-lowed presence that surrounds us all broke into their lives, bringing fresh possibility where hopelessness had resided. They talked natu-rally of visions as if they were just an ordinary part of life—like the wind, the touch of a friend, or sunlight breaking through gray clouds. They have preserved what the so-called advanced world has lost: the realization that visions mend souls, mend families, and mend cultures.

WE ARE YEARNING TO KNOW
THE SACRED AGAIN

We in the rationalist West are gradually recovering this sacred knowl-edge. Long-lost treasures are being found again. We are on the verge of a healing discovery as great as any of the startling medical discov-eries of the past century. It will be not a discovery but a *recovery*—the recovery of something long known but long lost to us, a lost healing art. It is a reality at the core of our psyches, built into the structures of our bodies. This reality is the ability we all possess to respond with soul-mending visions to the touches of the beneficent mystery, the mystery we call God, that borders all of our existence.

Like all things human, the recovery of our knowledge of visions carries risks. In our time, one of these risks is the tendency to excess. Certainly the desperate search for spirituality found nearly everywhere in contemporary society testifies to both the consuming hunger for the sacred and the dangers that the search entails.

Talk of mystical experiences extends throughout popular culture. Books on near-death experiences become best-sellers. TV shows and movies about angel encounters and all sorts of meetings with wonder have become commonplace. Several years ago, a recording of ancient Christian, Latin hymnody, titled simply *Chant,* sold tens of millions of copies worldwide, hitting the top of the charts and becoming a true golden oldie.

The New Age movement churns out hundreds of books every year touting mystical experiences and visions—some of them certainly bogus and many others sounding outrageous. Millions of people, unattached to the traditions of churches or synagogues, consult tapes, books, seminars, and CD-ROMs about mystical experiences in sometimes desperate efforts to taste the sacred.

Much of this spiritual activity is completely detached from the historic spiritual traditions. These traditions possess wisdom, knowledge of what the human race has learned about its relationship with God. We need these spiritual traditions to guide us. The freelance, free-flowing passion for "spirituality" that is detached from community and tradition will ultimately disappoint and confuse us.

But the historic religious traditions are also yearning for mystery. They too have been affected by the rationalist suspicion of spiritual experience. Believers want more. Within the Christian tradition, the worldwide Pentecostal movement, which emphasizes visions and spiritual experiences, continues to grow at a record pace not only in

Pentecostal denominations but also within traditional religious bodies such as the Catholic and Episcopal Churches.

Stories of new appearances of the Virgin Mary seem to appear every week. Tens of millions of people have visited Medjugorje, in remote Bosnia, the site of reported appearances of Mary. As one priest friend put it, "Everybody's mother is seeing Mary." Stories of miracles multiply within the Catholic Church and other Christian denominations. Modern culture, both within and without historic spiritual traditions, seems to be on a spiritual quest of monumental proportions.

It is no surprise that the Jewish tradition shares with Christians and Native Americans an openness to visions. Interest in visions is burgeoning in synagogues. One rabbi, Gershon Winkler, regularly engages in what he calls "Jewish vision quests" in the wilderness of New Mexico, seeking a direct encounter with God. The son and grandson of ultrareligious rabbis, he is deeply rooted in his Jewish heritage. He has written on Jewish mysticism, and he calls for a return to the silences of the wilderness, saying, "All of our inspired prophets and teachers in ancient times received their inspiration and their supernatural capabilities . . . in the wilderness."[1] The great Jewish thinker Martin Buber gathered many of the old "holy stories" in Judaism, many of which involved visions. And listen to the wisdom of a Rabbi Kook:

> Each time that the heart feels a truly spiritual stirring, each time that a new and noble thought is born, we are as though listening to the voice of an angel of God who is knocking, pressing on the doors of our soul, asking that we open our door to him that he might appear before us in his full majesty. . . .
>
> The holy men, those of pure thought and contemplation, join themselves, in their inner sensibilities, with the spiritual that pervades all. Everything that is revealed to them is an emergence of light, a disclosure of the divine, which adds life and firmness, abiding life and spiri-

WE ALL SEE VISIONS

tual firmness, which gives stability to the whole world with the diffusion of its beneficence.[2]

VISIONS USED TO BE NORMAL

It would be easy to dismiss all of this as just another fad that has engulfed our fickle, affluent, and media-driven society—a fad that will quickly be eclipsed by another fad. But history suggests that dismissing such spiritual hunger and discovery would be a mistake. Our contemporary hungering for the spiritual is an effort to recover something that human beings have always had. In fact, the spirituality boom looks like something new only by comparison. Human beings in the past did not seek after visions the way we do today. They didn't have to. Visions were a normal part of their lives.

The research of acclaimed cultural historians paints a vastly different history of Christian and Jewish societies than our textbooks taught us. Our ancestors in faith viewed visions as a natural part of life, as common as the sun's life-giving rays. People told their visions to one another around campfires, on pilgrimages, as they washed laundry in the backyard. Troubadours sang of visions. Preachers reminded people that visions could touch their lives. Synagogue leaders told stories about the visions of the healing rabbis. Average people experienced visions frequently. The visions healed—and telling them and hearing them healed too.

Some of the evidence for this comes from thousands of depositions that are finally being studied by scholars. The accounts show visions and wonder as a normal part of village and farm life in the Middle Ages. These are not legends, invented stories, or manufactured saints' biographies. They are the actual words of common people taken down soon after their wondrous experiences. These reports are reliable, firsthand testimony about the inner spiritual lives of people who lived centuries ago.

The visionaries include many of the great figures in Christian history. Historical sources long ignored by scholars reveal that most of the key figures in the Christian past, and many in the Jewish past, experienced vivid visions and allowed those visions to powerfully affect their writing and work. These visionaries include the great Christian leaders who decided the basic tenets of belief formulated at Nicaea and other councils of the early church.

Some names? The list of ancient visionaries includes the saints Augustine, Anselm, Ambrose, John Chrysostom, Gregory of Nyssa, Teresa of Ávila, Hildegard of Bingen, and many other major religious figures, together with some of the most sophisticated thinkers of all time. For example, St. Thomas Aquinas, known for his powerful logic and encyclopedic knowledge, regularly took time alone, seeking visionary insight with sobs and tears, waiting for a moment of ecstatic spiritual insight that came as a gift from beyond.

Talk of visions went underground, at least in polite company, with the rise of modern science in the sixteenth and seventeenth centuries. Intellectuals and opinion makers came to view visions as an embarrassment rather than a human reality to be celebrated. We treat visions as the Victorians treated sex. People still have visions and learn from them, just as Victorians had sex and continued to populate the world. But talking about it was frowned upon. That embarrassment is just now beginning to melt away. We are once again seeing visions as a long-suppressed but essential human reality. And we're talking about it.

WE ARE DESIGNED TO EXPERIENCE VISIONS

Some might reason that our ancestors had visions because they expected to have them. They found what they were looking for. Let's turn that supposition upside down. Perhaps human beings are *made* to experience the sacred. This, in fact, is a reality indicated by research in several fields.

Neuroscientists are discovering that our bodies may be built for visions. Researchers at the University of California, San Diego brain and perception laboratory are finding compelling evidence that "the human brain may be hardwired to hear the voice of heaven." Other studies suggest that our brains respond uniquely and intensely to sacred words such as *God*.[3]

Social scientists report that people have visions all the time, even though the visions can't be discussed in many circles. Visionaries are found in the suburbs, not just in the pages of the Bible, among Native Americans, or in biographies of saints.

Rev. Ben Johnson, a Lutheran minister with a doctorate in theology from Harvard, and sociologist Milo Brekke surveyed two thousand Christians in mainline churches in St. Cloud, Minnesota. They found that 30 percent had seen dramatic visions, heard heavenly voices, or experienced prophetic dreams. Johnson told a joint meeting of the Society of Biblical Literature and the American Academy of Religion, "Two centuries after the intellectual world has said that these kinds of things do not happen, they show up among almost a third of the population in a conservative Midwestern city."[4]

Other researchers tell us that the majority of people report mystical or paranormal experiences. One study by Andrew Greeley put the figure as high as 60 percent.[5] The University of Chicago's National Opinion Research Center found that 42 percent of Americans report contact with deceased loved ones and 67 percent claim to have had moments of extrasensory perception.[6] In my own experience, almost everyone reports some partly remembered sacred moment—once they feel safe enough to talk about it.

Common sense suggests that phenomena this widespread point to a widely shared human ability—in this case, the ability to perceive the sacred.

In fact, we are on the threshold of a great breakthrough in the way we understand faith and spiritual consciousness. Three realities are becoming clear to us.

Visions are natural. They are not miracles—inexplicable interventions of the supernatural into our workaday natural world. They are natural manifestations of the fullness of reality.[7]

Visions are human. They come from our humanity just as much as they come from God.

Visions can transform, heal, and brighten our lives.

LET'S RETURN TO REALITY IN ITS FULLNESS

We have all been trained to think that a chasm separates the natural and the supernatural worlds. The natural world is the realm of physical reality, science, reason, and sure knowledge. The supernatural world is the realm of wonder, the spirit, angels, and God. When the chasm is occasionally breached—when we touch God or hear an angel or experience ineffable wonder—it's a "miracle."

Rudolf Bultmann, the Protestant biblical scholar, represented the prevailing view early in this century when he triumphantly declared that truly modern human beings who flick on electric lights could not believe in miracles.

Our ancestors were wiser. The fullness of reality is far more complex and subtle than the picture presented by our crude rationalism. Before the Enlightenment, no one would have defined a miracle or a vision as a breaking of a fixed natural law. Even the most startling miracle was natural. Miracles were any sign that provoked wonder and awe in human beings. In the mind of a great theologian like St. Augustine, everything was both natural and miraculous. Rain, snow, and wind were everyday miracles, manifestations of God's mystery. When human beings became accustomed to these ordinary miracles, they needed special signs to open them to the wondrous that always surrounded them. These signs were seen not as contrary to nature but as part of it, arising from secondary causes we could not see.

As Augustine most eloquently said, "God himself has created all that is wonderful in this world, the great miracles as well as the minor marvels I have mentioned, and he has included them all in that unique wonder, the miracle of miracles, the world itself."

The naturalness of visions dovetails with Augustine's view that we are created for God and that we are restless until we find him. It enforces the deep intuition of so many of us that all finite creation is possessed with a yearning for the infinite.

Popular spirituality loudly asserts, "Genuine visions are from God." I agree. But after forty years of studying visions, I maintain that they are deeply human as well.

All historic religious traditions include visions. Within the Sufi tradition of Islam has evolved a beautiful understanding of visions. Religious experiences helped Anwar Sadat, a Muslim, endure his time of imprisonment and played a role in his becoming a peacemaker. Hindus have visions; Buddhists have visions. Wherever humans search, with pure hearts, for the sacred, according to the light they have, there are visions.

My life has been enriched by the world's spiritual traditions. Gandhi has inspired me toward peacemaking. The current Dalai Lama has moved me by his call for all of us to develop hearts of compassion. What I have learned from these faith expressions has helped me become a better, richer Christian. My own Catholic tradition strongly believes in dialogue with all religious traditions. The Vatican appoints special representatives to dialogue with the world's major traditions.

Just as other spiritual traditions have helped me become more solidly Christian, I believe the Jewish and Christian traditions, which I have studied intently for thirty years, contain wisdom that can enrich people everywhere, not just Christians and Jews.

John Courtney Murray once said that to be truly universal a person had to be truly particular. Because I know the Western traditions so well and have researched them for so long, and because I am of Native American descent, reared somewhat in that spiritual tradition, this book will draw primarily from Jewish, Christian, and Native sources.

But I know that, just as I have been enriched by traditions outside Western spirituality, the wisdom concerning visions within Western traditions can also enrich people outside them.

It is in that spirit I speak from what I know best, what is most particular to me, with the prayer that in being faithful to my own particularity, my words may become truly universal.

This ubiquity of visions in all historic sacred traditions reinforces their humanness.

To say that visions are human does not detract from God's work that they accomplish within us. Rather, it affirms that work. Christians believe that God became fully human in the Incarnation. Jesus was completely and authentically human; he was completely and authentically God. The beginning words of John's Gospel remind us that God communicated to us most fully by becoming human. Through Jesus, God made our humanity the language in which we can truly speak of God. Therefore, humanity, graced and elevated by God, becomes our best language for communicating about God.

It's no surprise, then, to point out that visions come from our human imagination, from the cells of brain and body. Our memories help give birth to visions. The culture and heritage in which we were raised color them. Our emotions become conduits of the sacred. The humanity of our visions in no way diminishes their godliness. Embracing visions helps us become more fully, more authentically, human—and therefore more like Jesus, who was human in the most complete and authentic form.

Indeed, we are fashioned to see God. As human beings, we have a deep desire for this mystery and an ability to be open to it and receive it. We are always addressed by love. At the innermost center, the human being is oriented toward receiving this love. As theologian Karl Rahner put it, "The capacity for the God of self-bestowing personal Love is the central and abiding existential of man as he really is."

You may be wondering: Even if visions are natural and human, can they be good for us? The answer is a resounding yes. Visions do transform us. Not only have I observed the healing effect of graced spiritual moments in my own life and the lives of many others, I have read the results of studies that actually document the transforming power of visions. Ralph Hood, professor of psychology at the University of Tennessee, gave a variety of psychological tests to individuals reporting mystical experiences. The results showed that they measured significantly better than average on tests indicating mental health. As author Phillip Berman summarized Hood's results, Hood "concluded that mystical experiences are neither pathologic nor escapist, but actually lead to healthier and more stable personalities."[8] Dr. Hood himself wrote, "It is clear that the person reporting mystical experience may be described as one with a breadth of interest, creative and innovative, tolerant of others, socially adept, and unwilling to accept simple solutions to problems."[9]

Studies by medical researcher and physician Melvin Morse find similar conclusions. Using scientific methods, with control groups, Morse gave a battery of tests to people reporting visionary and mystical experiences. He found the results dramatic. People who had had these experiences were transformed in significant ways. They possessed less fear of death, gave more to charity, and showed more zest for living.[10]

The loud message of both tradition and modern research is that visions hold the potential to lead us on a powerful journey of healing, both for ourselves and for those we care about. Visions open us to the one who can mend our wounds, change us, and send us out into the world with a relish for living and loving that mirrors the transforming whirlwind of God's own inner dynamic of life.

Our capacity for visions is part of that all-so-human, holy hunger for the limitless. That hunger is God's gift to us.

These three discoveries—that visions are natural, that they are human, and that they transform us—are the keys to the spiritual revolution that will unfold in the years ahead. They are also the keys we need to learn how to use visions constructively to grow closer to God.

VISIONS REQUIRE WISDOM AND BALANCE

Visions bring risks. They can mislead us. We can make mistakes with visions, as we can with everything else.

A woman once told me about a compelling dream she had. She was surrounded in light as she took the habit of a nun and joined a cloistered convent. The woman took the dream literally. Even though she was a divorced mother with two rambunctious teenage daughters, she wondered whether the dream meant that she should turn her daughters over to their grandmother and join a convent.

I explained that the vision was about enjoying the fruits of prayer in her busy life, perhaps by cultivating silence in her noisy home whenever she could. The woman agreed, but her initial mistake is a good example of how easy it is to mislead ourselves when we are dealing with visions.

The landscape of contemporary spirituality is littered with mistakes in following visions. Some people follow self-appointed leaders who claim direct visionary contact with God; the followers relinquish their precious gifts of self-direction and human dignity, reverting to spiritual infantilism. Some naively believe that all the information in stories of near-death experiences is literally true and that they now know the geography of heaven. Others uproot their lives to follow cult leaders or because they think that fearful visions of worldwide catastrophe are literally true.

Problems of this kind lead many people to reject the visionary and the transcendent. Secularists lament the return to a new superstition. Theologians sound similar alarms, worrying that these spiritual dramas distract people from the truly central realities of faith.

The answer is not to reject visions but to learn how to discern and work with them. This is precisely why I wrote this book. Visions are not hot lines to heaven. They are human responses to the holy, and they are fallible as we are fallible. What is missing is the ancient wisdom for understanding them, for working with them and using them to help inspire and heal our lives.

YOU HAVE VISIONS, BUT DO YOU KNOW IT?

You have visions already. I wrote this book to help you recognize them and grasp their power in your own life. Visions are a central reality of life that our society and our churches have been neglecting for a long time. What's needed is the wisdom to tap their healing power and spiritual potential. I call it walking in balance with visions.

This book will also help you dispose yourself to the sacred. We have visions, but most of us have trouble recognizing them. The visionary side of our humanity has atrophied in a culture that is suspicious of the mystical, experiential aspects of being human. This book will help you awaken the part of you built to sense the sacred. It will use stories and meditations and prayers and writing exercises to help you recapture your nearly forgotten moments of astonishment. It will enable you to discover your unique pathway to experiencing the transcendent.

My background is unusual. I am a Catholic of Native American descent who is both a retreat leader and a student of religious history. For twenty years I have been researching our religious past and publishing my findings, also leading retreats within the Catholic Church and other Christian churches, as well as among other persons of Native descent. This book grows out of that work.

My own identity as a Catholic of Native American heritage brings these influences together. I am of Cherokee descent. My grandfather taught me the Cherokee way of harmony—"walking the beauty road," he called it. This means living all parts of life, family, and nature in balance and compassion. In Cherokee tradition, visions enhance the harmony we all seek. They are woven into the fabric of the whole.

I am also a lifelong Christian and a Catholic since my early adulthood. I have a master's degree in religious studies along with four years of graduate work in theology and psychotherapy. I have read widely in the religious history of Christianity and Judaism, seeking knowledge about how human beings have encountered God. I've been published in the field of church history for twenty-five years.

At first glance it may seem surprising that I am both Christian and Native in my outlook. Actually, these two spiritualities are complementary in many respects. Both take the world seriously. Both view God as holy mystery. The majority of Native healers are also Christian. The early Baptist missionaries to Oklahoma, far more flexible than many of their successors, encouraged the Cherokee to keep their ancient spirituality along with their Christianity. A high percentage of Cherokee medicine persons are also Baptist ministers or deacons (or married to Baptist ministers or deacons). The sacred ceremonial dance sites are often on the grounds of a Cherokee Baptist church.

Black Elk, the Sioux medicine man and perhaps the most quoted Native visionary, was also a Catholic. He is said to be responsible for four hundred of his tribespeople entering the church. On visits to North America, John Paul II has participated in ancient Native American spiritual ceremonies such as the pipe ceremony and the smudging ceremony. He has urged us Christian Native Americans to keep alive our Native spiritual teachings and practices.

Like John Paul II and Mother Teresa, I am touched and inspired by many spiritual traditions because I am secure in my own. I am a Catholic, rooted in and at ease with my faith. In Jesus, infinite mystery became human and touchable. The Incarnation means that the Mysterious Other did not absorb us but embraced our cultures, our imaginations, our whole world. This includes all that is true in our spiritual traditions. Because of the Incarnation, all truth wherever found, all beauty wherever experienced, can be the embrace of God. The Incarnation brings me into the inner, very human, earthly processes of spiritual experiencing.

This book is full of stories. One of the stories is my own. Like so many others, I've experienced the awesome power of a sacred glimpse. I have seen visions open up a brand-new future where no future existed. One little boy went on to fulfill his dreams despite brain damage because one evening a light from beyond drew near and embraced him and gave hope to his soul. I know that story well. I was that little boy.

v i s i o n   j o u r n e y

It is an ancient Christian and Native American custom to offer a prayer at the beginning of a journey. Here is such a prayer for the journey you are starting with this book. Pray it now, saying the words in your heart or speaking them softly. Call on God's protection and help to be touched by the graced moments that will enable you to touch the sacred that surrounds you.

Prayer

Dear God,
you are near me when I doubt you,
you are close to me
when the chatter of everyday frustrations
closes for a while
my awareness of your nearness.
You bound my world
and soften my day,
soothe and comfort me,
when I can no longer comfort myself.
You are the mender of my soul,
the one who can set my feet
on the pathway of beauty.

I am beginning a journey,
a time of rediscovering the ways
you have interrupted my life,
the times you slowed my breathing
and quieted my heartbeat,
made the day like new,
and brought eternity to me for a moment.
Like most lives,

mine is filled with forgetting,
and often I have forgotten
the times of your nearness.

Remind my heart of my visions,
large and small.
When I sleep, when I go about the day,
when I speak,
and when I am finished speaking,
when I pray,
and when I am finished praying,
remind me of your wonder.

Make my heart docile now.
Clear my mind and make it ready
to begin a fresh journey with you, to you,
a journey of remembering,
a journey of touch,
a journey in which I widen my soul
to the holy,
that I may live and love in this world
as you live and love,
that I may touch with your touch.
May my life convey your nearness,
my words impart your healing.

the light makes

a promise

I WAS BORN BREECH FASHION, FEETFIRST, IN 1946, BEFORE THE DAYS WHEN modern imaging could predict the baby's position and doctors could avoid problems by performing a cesarean section. The umbilical cord wrapped around my neck three times. The doctor used heavy forceps. He told my mother that she would have received a dead baby if the delivery had taken a few more seconds.

The whole family rejoiced that I seemed to be normal. I began to talk even earlier than the age-appropriate time, and I eventually walked. My family believed they had experienced two miracles—the birth of a child against impossible odds, and the birth of a child who was not disabled, which was a common result of such a traumatic birth.

They were wrong about the second miracle. My birth left me with brain damage and learning disabilities. These effects of cerebral injury took years to manifest. In those days, people didn't know how to watch for the subtler signs of damage. If a child could talk and walk, that was enough.

A head injury at age two reinforced the birth injury. At five I could talk and understand even better than my peers, but I couldn't dress myself. I easily forgot how to exit rooms or houses. My eyes could see, but the part of the brain that processes visual-spatial information wasn't working right. Physical tasks of any complexity left me blank, even nauseated.

Even at age thirteen I experienced difficulty getting dressed and ready for the day. My parents had to coach me through each step, from brushing my teeth to buttoning my shirt.

My ease with words and complex thought caused people to think I was bright. But I simply could not perform basic school tasks. I learned to read well but couldn't learn to write properly. Problems with short-term memory at times kept me from understanding teachers' verbal directions. My problems with visual memory and organization left me bewildered. If I put down a piece of paper or some other physical object, often I would forget that it existed. It was common for the whole classroom to become a blur of noise and sound. Everything around me turned into a mess, like the little cloud that accompanies the Pigpen character in the "Peanuts" cartoon.

Teachers in those days knew little about the kinds of nonverbal learning disabilities I possessed. My scrawled and messy handwriting was only partly legible part of the time. The teachers lectured me in front of everyone else when they returned papers. Often, when I knew the subject backward and forward, there would be an F on the top of my paper and "Careless!" or "Lazy!" red-lettered across it.

I could not play sports or do things well with my hands. And it seemed that all the children knew that my parents still coached me in dressing, even though I was now a teenager. Because of my confusion in using my body, other children made fun of me. Some teachers even encouraged this taunting. It would wake me up, they thought.

One teacher once told me, "You're no good; you're no good at all."

I tried with all my might. I appeared normal. My limbs moved. I was not confined to a wheelchair. I could talk fluently. I didn't know why I couldn't do the simple things others could do. It was years before my brain damage was diagnosed and the source of my problems identified. When I was a teenager, I thought I was lazy. I assumed everyone else was like me, except they had fortitude and could do all the normal things people are supposed to do—dressing themselves easily, playing baseball, writing legibly. To me, these were mountainous, confusing tasks.

One way to handle it was to say worse things about myself than others said about me. Then their words would hurt less. I found some relief by taking the eraser out of a school-issued pencil and pressing the hollow copper tube against my upper leg or my arm until I felt a sharp pain. I would push it in and whisper the mantra, "You're no good at all." I had less to fear. Nothing others said about me would be worse than what I said to myself.

Like other boys, I dreamed of adventure. I fantasized that one day some miracle would make my problems go away. I would swim the Panama Canal or the strait of Dardanelles like my hero, the true-adventure writer Richard Halliburton. I yearned to be a great writer like him or like Alan Paton, a South African writer I admired.

Once, in class, I said that I wanted to be a great explorer like Richard Halliburton. One of the girls, one of the cute ones I had been eyeing, piped up and said, "But, Eddie, how can you find your way through the Andes when you can't locate the end of the hall?"

The class roared in appreciation of her wit.

When no one was looking, I pressed the pencil against my flesh until I winced hard and said the words again, "You're no good at all. You're no good at all." For a while the emotional pain diminished.

At home, after school, the strain of the day caved in on me. I could often hear the sounds of other children playing in the neighborhood, doing normal things. I peeked at boys playing football in the street and dreamed I could be one of them. At age thirteen I dreamed of what it would be like to have a friend, what it would be like to go out to recess without laughter centering on me.

A VISION STARTED MY JOURNEY

One day I managed to get the old record player playing and put on some of the music that I loved. I played Beethoven's Pastoral Symphony and then Schubert's Unfinished Symphony. The music often took me away from the hurting.

As Schubert's symphony finished, the silence brought me again to face the day's happenings. I reached into my pocket to pull out my steady painkiller, the pencil that had no eraser. But that day the pencil fell out of my hand, and my head began to spin. I felt myself go light.

I was spinning and going somewhere, yet staying in the same place. The room twirled. I twirled. The pain began to flow from me. I became aware of a light, a light I saw not with my eyes but with my heart. That light filled the room, and in the light I saw a gentle, somewhat bluish figure surrounded by a white brightness. The seeing was richer than eyes can see, and the feeling richer than normal feelings can sense. The light was all warmth. And the warmth of the light spoke to me, but without words.

I asked the light, "Who are you?"

"I am the one who dries the tears of little boys. . . . I am the one from whom people hide their faces."

"They hide their faces from me too," I responded, speaking to the light not with words but with the communication of the heart.

"I know, and that's why I came. I am here to cradle you."

The light extended limitlessly, and in my heart I could flow out with the light into that eternity, or so it seemed. I had tasted little peace for months. Now I felt the exquisite softness and ease of the light. It was as though the light were massaging me, like my father had massaged me when I was sick, using the old methods of touch to drive away sickness.

"Who are you?" I asked again.

"I am the one who helps little boys dream and helps them fulfill them."

"I'm not a little boy. I'm a teenager, thirteen years old."

I sensed humor in the light; you might say the light smiled. "I think you are still a little boy."

"But," I said, "I'm a teenager and I'm a sinner."

"Why are you such a sinner?"

"Because I'm lazy and I can't do things."

"You've done more than you know."

I felt so at home with the light that I dared to ask, "Will I ever be an explorer?"

"Oh yes."

"Will I find the lost treasures Richard Halliburton looked for?"

The light smiled again and said, "I don't know about that, but you will uncover gleaming treasures as valuable as these, and you will be an explorer."

"Will I ever write books like Alan Paton or Halliburton or Dickens?"

"You will write as many books as you wish to write, and many will feel the warmth."

"What will I write?"

"I will show you."

Then the light touched my chest. The best way to describe it is to say it was like a hand that passed over the area of my chest and gently encompassed the whole area of the heart, though it was more than this.

The light continued, "I plant in your heart now; I plant with love. This message will always be in you. You cannot understand it now, but bit by bit you will. And you will speak it aloud as you understand. For now I have planted this treasure within you, and you will come to know it as you grow. I will come to you at different times; I will always be near you even when you cannot see or feel me."

I heard a whisper even with my physical ears, "The stone which the builders rejected has become the chief cornerstone." Then, "Read Isaiah 53."

And I began to have a sense of the identity of the light. When I was smaller, in kindergarten, and I came home from carrying the hurt of the day, my mother often picked me up in her arms and carried me to her special rocking chair. As I poured out my little-boy tears, she sang me a lullaby. In a way that can only be hinted at in words, the light sang me a lullaby. I heard the sound without ears, yet it was sweeter than sounds heard with ears.

I asked the light, "If you leave me now, is there a place I can go and find you?"

"I am always near those from whom people hide their faces. Find them and you find me. . . . I am the one who hides that you may find me."

The light that gathered in the room formed a figure, like that of Christ risen. This was, of course, a seeing with the heart, not a bodily seeing. Christ pressed his palms to mine. The fear for the future, the shame of the past—all gathered in me and passed through my palms into his. I touched the wounds with body and hand. All the pain of my heart and body collapsed into his wounds and body. His breath swept over me like wind, not breath. The warmth of it radiated through my hands, my arms, my shoulders. The fragrant aroma filled every part of me with sweetness.

He asked me to stretch out my palm in front of my face and blow. I felt the warmth on my hand. He then asked me to touch my heart with my hand. My heart, too, sank into the warm radiance. He told me to remember that I could always blow warmth on my palm, then place it over my heart and be reminded of his comfort.

THE VISION CAME TRUE

Most of what the light predicted came to be. The vision of the light when I was thirteen triggered in me a passion to understand visions and spiritual experiencing. I became a writer. I have spoken to hundreds of groups throughout the world. I spent four years in graduate school, studying theology, psychotherapy, and ancient languages. I became an explorer. I never overcame my clumsiness, so I never swam the Dardanelles or explored the hidden passageways under Jerusalem. I hunted instead through books hidden away in libraries, finding buried wisdom of Native American, Jewish, and Christian wisdom keepers richer than any treasure made of gold.

Struggle still remained a part of my life. My disability did not go away. Another head injury in an auto accident in 1971 added more difficulties. I thought they were due to a character problem or an emotional disorder, so I masked and hid these difficulties as much as possible.

I discovered the real reason for my visual-spatial problems in 1991. I went to a friend, a clinical psychologist with a background in head injury, and poured out the story of my daily difficulties. I told him of my frustrations with simple daily tasks. I told him that I could speak with great assurance, without notes, to a crowd of several thousand but became frightened and confused if I had to pack clothes into a suitcase. What could be wrong with me?

His answer was not one I expected. He suggested that the cause was likely physical in origin. He gave me some pen-and-pencil tests that are preliminary screening devices for brain damage. I showed a strong positive. I told him my history of birth injury and closed-head injury. He said that was more than enough physical trauma to account for things. His suspicion was confirmed by intensive medical testing and diagnosis at Roosevelt Warm Springs Institute, a premier institution for rehabilitation with a strong specialty in head injury. The testing showed significant visual-spatial dysfunction and right hemisphere dysfunction.

Several of the clinicians got together to question me after the diagnosis. One said, "We've never seen anyone finish high school with your level of impairment, much less college, much less write books for national publishers. How did you do it?" I thought for a moment, smiled, and said, "I had help."

And I did. I had lots of help, help from family and loving friends. I didn't tell the clinicians that my visions helped too, but that was surely the case. Along with Scripture, sacrament, and many close friends, visions drenched me in the love of the one who is always there to encourage and comfort. Over a period of two years as a patient in the Institute of Head Injury Rehabilitation Division, I was taught many ways to cope with my disability and work around it.

Some of the ways spiritual experience has come to me may seem remarkable. But God comes to each of us in remarkable ways. Visionary literature can move others, enrich them, speed them on their journey. So can scholarly talks, a good liturgy, a good painting, sacred music. Each of us contributes what he or she has. This is what I have, and it is only in this spirit that—as part of this book—I tell my story of my own visions. My prayer is that their rhythms and metaphors will help connect readers to their own unique ways of experiencing.

I have had many visions. I have seen my room filled with an utterly bright, dazzling holy light. At times, I have seen the holy figures from memory and tradition as clearly as my hand in front of my face.

I struggled a long time before deciding to write of my visions. I finally realized I could not help people grow comfortable with their own religious experiencing unless I was comfortable enough to share mine. As I have mentioned, statistics say that most of us have dramatic visionary moments once or twice in our lifetime, plus many moments of more subdued sacred encounter. Other statistics say that about 5 percent of us frequently experience the more vivid visions. I probably fall in that 5 percent. That's really a large club, but not particularly an elite one. That's more people than play the piano well or are good at golf. I felt that sharing my history might help this group grow comfortable with the normalcy of their experience.

You may be wondering what role my neurological condition has had on my religious experiencing. Do you have to be brain damaged to see vivid visions? Actually, a lot of people, few with histories of brain damage, are especially sensitive to spiritual experience and frequently experience visions. Yet, in my case, I can't dismiss the possibility that my struggle to live with my disability—along with the deep needs for reassurance and comfort that go with it—has made me more sensitive to subtle streams of inner reality that are really in all of us.

I think I am especially sensitive to visions. Perhaps a better way to put it is that I am unusually prone to respond to God in highly imaginative ways. This does not mean that I am more closely connected to God than anyone else or that my sensitivity to visionary experience is a greater or higher or deeper gift than the abilities of others. Each of us is uniquely gifted to respond to God. Some of us are equipped to write music, tell stories, lead organizations, study, and serve others in response to the God who loves us and sustains us. I happen to be equipped to sense the visionary quality of God's presence, but that does not make me holier or even a better Christian.

If we think about it, even vivid visions are not that unusual. Great artists often see the painting on canvas before they paint it, real and vivid as life. Sculptors see the image that will emerge in the raw stone. Many architects can look out over a landscape and with eyes open see the building they will be designing, even as they view the present landscape. Composers often say that they hear the music in their minds, emerging unbidden, before they actually compose it. Vivid visions of the sort I describe in my own life are simply a version of this process. When the imaginative and the creative get caught up in that which is ultimate and sacred, utter vividness can emerge.

So having even bright visions of holy light and hearing holy sounds is not as exceptional as it sounds; it's the part of us that dreams and creates being caught up in that which is truly ultimate, truly Holy.

Having visions does not mean that I am less fallible than others. No matter how vivid spiritual experiences become, they are not direct sightings of God. "We see in a mirror, dimly," as St. Paul wrote. Pop, my Cherokee grandfather, put it this way: "The angel tells it right, but none of us hear angels all that good."

Nevertheless, we all have some ability to hear the angels. The mirror may be fogged, but all of us can see something in it. Visions, even dramatic visions, are meant to be a normal part of our spiritual experience. What's needed is help in awakening our natural style of sensing the holy so that each of us can take ownership of our own style of sacred seeing.

Later I will introduce some techniques for awakening your unique style of sacred experiencing. But first I want you to understand that you surely have the ability to see visions.

WE'RE EQUIPPED WITH A GOD SENSOR

All of us can see visions? That's the kind of claim that strikes many people as dubious. We instinctively ask what science has to say about it. Stories of visions, like my story of the light, are all well and good. Survey data indicating that the majority of people do in fact experience the sacred may be interesting and suggestive, but it's still "soft science." What do the hard scientists say?

Quite a lot, in fact. Neurologists are finding solid indications that our bodies may be "hardwired" to experience God.

Research by Eugene d'Aquili and Andrew Newberg at the University of Pennsylvania suggests that "beatific visions" can be observed through brain scans and other tools of scientific research. They described religious experience in terms of "eruptive overflows" and "reverberating circuits" involving the prefrontal cortex and various lobes of the brain. In a talk entitled "Why God Won't Go Away" Newberg suggested that "transcendent reality may be hardwired into the human mind." The part of the brain that translates sensory data into emotions "generates a sense of religious awe," he said. These findings have been confirmed by other neuroscientists at New York University and the University of California, San Diego.[1]

In an article summarizing this research, Robert Hotz said, "Already there is evidence suggesting that the human brain may be naturally calibrated—by experience or by design—to spirituality. . . . An essential element of the religious experience of transcendence may be hardwired in the brain."

Materialists might claim that pinpointing a physical location in the brain for religious awe and religious visions reduces God to a material cause. But this is a nonscientific conclusion. It is more reasonable to surmise that if our brains are built to perceive the holy, then there *is* a holy. Nancy Murphy, a philosopher of science and religion at Fuller Seminary in Pasadena, suggested that these findings mean "God must have some way of interacting with human brains." In her view, they shed light on "one of the most difficult and pressing theological questions now—how God acts in the brain."

John Haughey, a Jesuit theologian at Georgetown University, called these new discoveries "wonderful knowledge." He wisely cautioned that the full interplay of mind and spirit can never be understood in purely physical terms but that "we can acknowledge the dependency of mind on body without having to imply that mind is reducible to chemistry."[2]

Melvin Morse, who has studied near-death visions and mystical experiences of all sorts, summed up the growing body of evidence this way:

> After examining thousands of case studies [of visions and mystical experiences] and even after having had a death-related vision of my own, I can say without a doubt that the brain *both* creates visionary experiences and detects them. . . . Just as we have a region of our brain devoted to speech and one that helps us regain our balance when we trip and almost

fall, we have an area that is devoted to communication with the mystical. It functions as a sort of sixth sense. In short, it is the "God sensor."[3]

Morse's idea of a built-in human "God sensor" helps us maintain a balanced view of our visions. Some people locate the source of every
vision, conversion, spiritual coincidence, or happening in the supernatural, while, in fact, the capacity for visions is built into our minds
and bodies. God has given us a yearning for him. He has also given us
the means to satisfy this yearning.

AWAKENING YOUR GOD SENSOR

It may be normal for us to have visions; however, it's not always easy.
In fact, experiencing the sacred is difficult for most people today, who
have been raised in churches that distrust spiritual experience and
educated in schools that relegate it to the realm of the irrational, paranormal, and miraculous. Visionary moments pass by unnoticed.
Transcendent occasions are forgotten. We do not perceive the touch
of the sacred. We don't know what to do when these moments come.
Our God sensors need training.

Providing this training is one of the purposes of this book. Each
chapter ends with guided reflections, meditations, prayers, and writing exercises to open your heart to God's touch and to help you allow
that touch to enable you to live a commonsense, everyday life that is
encompassed by the sacred.

These guided visions will help you recapture your nearly forgotten
moments of astonishment. They are not techniques for manufacturing
artificial feelings of wonder and awe. They are among the oldest and
most reliable methods for getting in touch with God—devotional techniques and approaches to prayer that, in many cases, have been sorely
neglected for a long time. The guided visions are a return to features of
our Christian past that served generations of believers very well.

It's worth going into this history in more detail.

Today, when people want to experience healing of soul, they are likely to visit a psychotherapist. In fourteenth-century Europe, they went to church.

The church would be packed with worshipers of all social classes. The priest or other meditation leader guided the people into colorfully depicted scenes roughly based on the life of Christ. They imagined these scenes in vivid detail. They gave expression to their pain, let the scenes soften their hearts, and cried tears of joy. According to cultural historian Denise Despres, people typically expressed their feelings spontaneously, saying deeply felt prayers and amens in the manner of modern spontaneous prayer meetings. People spoke to Christ, and Christ spoke to them.

These were guided visions. Ordinary laypeople were taught to use their imaginations to penetrate their hearts and connect to the key events in salvation history. In the words of Despres, these meditations "provided daily life with a conscious pattern of redemption."[4]

Other features of Christian life contributed to this vivid imaginative quality of daily faith. People attended mystery and miracle plays that depicted scenes from Scripture, dramatized visions in the lives of ordinary people, and showed God's intervention in ordinary lives. People witnessed dramatic depictions of Christ and Mary speaking to ordinary people in their own language.

The great Gothic cathedrals of medieval Europe often induced a visionlike experience. Abbot Suger's luminous words describe the effect that a visit to a Gothic cathedral could have on a visitor:

> These temples of grace had powerful ability to transform that which is
> material to that which is immaterial. . . . It seems to me that I see myself
> dwelling, as it were, in some strange region of the universe which nei-
> ther exists entirely in the slime of earth nor entirely in the purity of
> heaven; and that, by the grace of God, I can be transported from the
> inferior to that higher world.[5]

Guided visions seem to have flowered among the Franciscans in the thirteenth and fourteenth centuries, but the form is much older than that. The sermons of the church fathers frequently asked listeners to place themselves imaginatively in the presence of Christ or a Gospel scene in a way that simulated a vision. In the fourth century, St. Cyril of Jerusalem used guided visions to assist in the instruction of those preparing for baptism. Here's an example of Cyril's catechetical instruction:

> Even now, I beseech you, lift up the eye of the mind: even now imagine the choirs of Angels, and God the Lord of all there sitting, and His Only-begotten Son sitting with Him on His right hand, and the Spirit present with them; and Thrones and Dominions doing service, and every man of you and every woman receiving salvation. Even now let your ears ring, as it were, with that glorious sound, when over your salvation the angels shall chant, Blessed are they whose iniquities are forgiven, and whose sins are covered: when like stars of the Church you shall enter in, bright in the body and radiant in the soul.[6]

A remarkable guided vision comes down to us from the time of St. Ambrose, St. Augustine's mentor and one of the giants of the church in the fourth century. In a sermon, Ambrose described the scene of the woman washing the feet of Jesus with her tears, then urged the listeners of his sermon to enter into the scene with their own wounds and receive healing:

> Show, then, your wound to the Physician that He may heal it. Though you show it not, He knows it, but waits to hear your voice. Do away your scars by tears. Thus did that woman in the Gospel, and wiped out the stench of her sin; thus did she wash away her fault, when washing the feet of Jesus with her tears.[7]

These guided visions, cathedrals, evocative sermons, and visionary plays stimulated the imagination—one of our most powerful mental and spiritual faculties. As Despres beautifully put it:

> No faculty is more essential to a sacramental religion than the imagination. The intangible mysteries of the Trinity, of the Resurrection, or of transubstantiation elicit visual responses from all neophytes, whether they are adults probing a new theology or children memorizing a catechism. As medieval theologians from Augustine to Bonaventure were quick to point out, sight is our primary means of cognition, and the imagination is central to the process of conversion.[8]

Metaphor, poetry, the nonverbal, enliven the part of brain built for sacred experience, medical researchers d'Aquili and Newberg contend in their recently released book that probes the biology of religious experience. But genuine religious imagination always points to something ultimate. Newberg and d'Aquili strongly assert:

> The road to God is paved with many stones: metaphor, poetry, music, ritual experiences, prayer and meditative experiences . . . relative as they are, they point to that which is "really real." Metaphor does not point to more metaphor, nor does religious poetic language point to more poetry. That which gives religious poetry and metaphor its meaning is real in an absolute, ultimate, and unconditioned way.[9]

Abraham Heschel describes this way of visionary praying within the Jewish tradition:

> It is through reading and feeling the words of the prayers, through the imaginative projection of our consciousness into the meaning of the words, and through empathy for the ideas with which the words are pregnant, that this type of prayer comes to pass. Here the word comes first, the feeling follows.[10]

The guided visions in this book are efforts to restore this link between visualization and the inner transformation, conversion, and healing that God wants for us. They help repattern our lives, in our inmost selves.

v i s i o n   j o u r n e y

Our first guided vision is an exercise in writing. Few of us regularly share our visions in comfortable gatherings of family and friends, as our ancestors did. Today most of us are more comfortable writing our thoughts. Writing is an excellent way to begin to tune up our God sensor.

Writing

The technique in this exercise is sentence completion. I have found it to be a very successful way to help others get their hearts stirring. To use the technique most effectively, write quickly without conscious thought. Do not judge what you are writing. Write what comes into your mind; reflect on it later.

Complete the following sentences three different ways:

"If I drew a picture of my own 'disability,' I would draw . . ."
"If hope had sounds, they would be . . ."
"I was surprised by comforting hope from beyond when . . ."

C H A P T E R 3

what are
visions?

WHILE WRITING THIS BOOK, I OFTEN THOUGHT THAT I HAD SET OUT TO
do something impossible. Books are works of the intellect. Authors
employ words and the tools of logic and analysis to describe and
define their subjects. But visions, by definition, are beyond words and
logic. At the very least, the task is paradoxical. The question, What
are visions? points out the problem. A definite answer eludes us. Yet
answers are possible, even though they are more like hints and riddles
than the kind of tangible statements we are accustomed to.

The answers are real because visions are real. Our experiences of
the sacred provide real knowledge of God and ourselves. If words fail
us when we speak of them, if language about visions so often seems
vague and unsatisfying, it's because we are touching the great mystery
of who we are.

The first person who taught me how to talk about visions was my
Cherokee grandfather.

In his later years, Pop would spend hours roaming the woods at the top of the bluff above the river or walking on the riverbank. He would look at the rocks or plants. Often he would appear to be doing nothing, just gazing at the landscape or water. When I was a young boy, I would follow him. I have a vivid memory of my grandfather standing motionless on the top of the bluff, letting his eyes soak in all that came to him.

Once, I asked him what he saw when he looked. I still hear his answer, rhythmic with Cherokee and Appalachian intonations: "I see the dirt, the trees, the water, the skies."

"Why?" I asked him. "Why do you look so long?"

He paused, took his pipe out of his mouth, swallowed, then slowly said, "If you look a long time, it will all shimmer, and you will see the glory."

I have no doubt that Pop saw the glory. He was telling me what a vision is. A vision is when life shimmers and we see the glory. Visions are perceptions of God's splendor, the glory that knits and ties all things together.

I'm amazed at how similar the language is between Pop and Jewish writer Rabbi Samuel Dresner:

> God did not forsake the world after having created it. His love for His creation manifests itself in His constant effort to reach down to it. At Sinai His voice broke through the curtain which man had painstakingly erected. Never again was it heard so clearly and so decisively, but the effort on His part to speak to His creatures never ceases. Saintly souls of all ages have caught echoes of the beyond. . . . This outpouring from heaven to man is called . . . shefa, and may be likened to the rays which emanate from the sun, ceaselessly reaching out to brighten the darkness of the world . . . which endlessly and lovingly flows from heaven.[1]

VISIONS BRIDGE A GAP

Visions are a bridge between God's splendor and our natural, tangible world. They are not "extras" in our spiritual journey. They are essential. They help resolve a paradox at the heart of Christianity.

The problem is this: God is "other." "If you can comprehend it," the ancient saying goes, "it isn't God." Yet we *can* comprehend at least something of God. The God who is "other" can be experienced in our finite world. I believe that visions are one of the most important and most common ways that this comes about. They are ways God speaks to us and we speak to ourselves about the glory hidden in and permeating the world around us.

Still, the whole business of visions is hard to pin down. We have to learn how to be comfortable with a partial understanding of something that is obviously so important. We have to be patient. And when it comes to comprehension, we have to be satisfied with metaphors and stories to do a lot of the heavy lifting.

An ancient Buddhist metaphor is one of my favorites. "The sun comes up and first shines upon lofty peaks. Then it turns to the other mountains. It shines upon hills and valleys and finally, the world's great earth. When the bright sun appears in the world, the blind man is unable to see it. However, his body relaxes and he experiences pleasure."

We are like the blind man. We cannot see the light in its fullness. But we can sense it and relax in its warmth.

VISIONS HAVE THEIR OWN LANGUAGE

The entire reality of transcendent experience cannot be captured in a single, all-encompassing definition. But we can learn much about visions by focusing on one important aspect of them. The aspect I would like to single out is language. In many ways, visions are ways we speak to ourselves and to each other about realities that are beyond words. In many cases, visions literally give us words with which to say the unsayable.

I saw the language of visions speak loudly and powerfully on a retreat I led for high school students from a parochial school. As on many required retreats, the students were initially more interested in being away from school than in encountering the sacred. But the atmosphere quickly changed the first night. A ninth-grade girl began to weep during a particularly moving song before supper. Her parents were in the midst of divorce. Her friends at her table comforted her, took her aside, and listened. Soon other students began to behave toward one another in life-giving ways, different from their inter-actions in the normal school environment. Something wonderful hap-pened that often happens on youth retreats: they began to give the retreat to one another.

Saturday morning, I put my talk aside and said, "Let's just talk about some of the ways God has touched our lives." To my surprise, they responded, vying with one another for a chance to speak. They spoke of the times God had comforted them after a death in the family, how God had come to them in nature, in worship, or in prayer. Their words carried more wisdom than do many adult testimonies.

At the end of that morning's session, one normally shy ninth-grade boy stood up and said, "You know, it's as though a golden cord of God's light has passed through each of our hearts and tied us all together."

The boy was speaking in the language of visions. He articulated a transcendent reality we were all experiencing—using a metaphor that some members of that group will probably remember when they are sixty years old. The boy had an encounter with God that day. God gave him a vision that enabled him to speak to himself and to others about the things of God.

Visions often function this way. They help us communicate with our-selves. They are a bursting forth from within of a language that helps us remember our encounter with God. Like the language of our dreams, it is not a language that we consciously make up or choose but a language that spontaneously emerges from our preconscious depths. Modern studies in brain physiology strongly suggest that our brains are designed for mystical experiences and visions. God, it would seem, built into our very bodies an ability to form languages of feeling, symbols, stories, and sounds that convey to us the touches and interruptions of God's grace.

Christian mystics often speak of the encounter with God as "heavenly discourse." "The Word has often come to me," St. Bernard would say of his brushes with God. The Word is a word. Jesus, the Word made flesh, comes in visions to give us words to speak and to cherish.

We can speak these words to others as well as to ourselves. They can change our speech and knit us to one another. That is how visions often function in older societies that are not so saturated with the media and cerebral abstractions. Visions are a gift of connectedness. They smash our isolation from God, one another, and all of creation, as well as our inmost selves. Visions provide tapestries of light that connect our inner and outer worlds, that tie us together as human beings.

Jesus' parables used this type of language. He shocked his hearers, revealing a whole new reality of insights, conveying truth from depth to depth. Used in this sense, visions communicate from God's depths to our depths, and from our depths to the depths of others.

FATHER FRED'S STORY

One man I know who learned the language of visions is Fr. Fred. His story will help you see what visions can say.

Fr. Fred was proper, formal, educated, but he was also a man whose very presence exuded the warm, the holy, and the sacred. He was the kind of friend who always listened and never judged. Well dressed for every occasion, he perfectly fit the role of middle-aged cleric.

Fr. Fred had spent most of his professional life in the chancery, the headquarters of his diocese. Holding advanced degrees in systematic theology and canon law from Rome, he had spent most of his career as a diocesan administrator and adviser to the bishop and his staff.

Then an unexpected change tossed Fr. Fred into another world entirely. He was appointed pastor to the largest parish in the diocese.

He possessed no anxiety about getting along with people. What frightened him was giving sermons. Preaching and public speaking were his weaknesses. He did poorly at using words to inspire people or transform their lives. People's attention wandered whenever he preached. Some snoozed. His problem, of which he was keenly aware, was that all his training had led him to be overly cerebral. His talks were filled with abstractions and lofty ideas, but these did not touch the hearers.

Fr. Fred attended a prayer seminar that I gave in his diocese. He listened intently when I spoke of the great meditations and prayers of Bonaventure and Anselm, great preachers who combined erudition and education with the ability to touch the simplest soul with their words. Bonaventure and Anselm helped people exercise their spiritual imaginations through what were essentially guided visions.

I led the group through Bonaventure's meditation on the fountain of eternal, bright, and healing light. I read some of Anselm's prayers that help people envision Gospel scenes and tie their own inner images of hopes and sorrows to those scenes.

These exercises had an electric impact on Fr. Fred. He realized that his education had taken away his imagination. He began to practice some of these meditations at home, eventually using Scripture to craft homemade imaginative meditations for himself. He began by imagining God's sacred presence as light surrounding the hurting people who came to him for counseling or the penitents who came to him for the sacrament of reconciliation.

One day a man came to him confessing an adulterous affair. The man was broken, sorrowful to the core. Behind him, Fr. Fred saw the image of the thief on the cross. A new depth of love and compassion welled up within him as he told the man of Christ's enormous love for him, the same love that Christ showed to the thief who repented on the cross.

That was the beginning of seeing with new eyes. Instead of analytically seeing the world in parts, Fr. Fred came to see events tied together, with sights, sounds, tastes, feelings, and movement, full of stories and drama, of plotlines that revealed the holy.

He told those stories when he preached. Often, while he was preaching, Christ would seem so real that Fr. Fred could all but feel his warm, assuring touch on his shoulder.

One Sunday during his homily, Fr. Fred told a story about a parishioner who drew very close to God as she neared death. He saw something he never dreamed he would see in his congregation: tears in people's eyes. He realized that his sermons now carried a power that moved people and altered their lives. Such is the power of the language of sacred vision.

To cultivate your visions, listen to the language of your surroundings. What is being said to you in the events of your daily life, your encounters with other people, your dreams and hopes, your insights?

In my experience, most of these moments, unlike my vision at age thirteen, are not especially dramatic. At times, the sacred invades us, lights flash, and bells ring. Most people experience dramatic visions from time to time. But this isn't the ordinary way. More frequently, we find ourselves moved by a special story someone tells us, or we are touched by a memory, a Scripture passage, a work of art, or a piece of music. Something is being *said* to us. What is it? It's the classic still, small voice by which God spoke to Elijah (1 Kings 19:11–12 KJV).

We can hear and understand the language of visions because it is part of that special capacity to taste and know God, a capacity that God has built into us. The language is within our own selves, in the language of metaphor and in our capacity for imagination.

WE CAN MISUNDERSTAND OUR VISIONS

We also possess the ability to *misunderstand* the language of visions. It takes time and training to be able to read correctly the messages that visions send us. This is something I learned in the immediate aftermath of the vision that came to me when I was thirteen.

The morning after the vision, I awoke relaxed. My breath was deep and at ease. I stretched out, then let both arms hit the bed with joy.

I nearly floated to school that day. The fifth-period teacher left the room, the familiar spitball hit the back of my head, and muffled laughs came from all directions. But this time a peacefulness came over me, for I knew that all the hurt and pain would be transmuted. I glided through the next few days. Rather than stumble along with my head turned down to avoid looking at people, I peered directly at them. All my problems would go away; I could play ball like the others. After all, hadn't magic come into my life?

I thought that, after I had been touched in such a manner, my life would be a dream from here on. The things that had always seemed impossible now seemed possible. I could picture myself joining the football team when I got to high school. I could hear the cheers. I smiled at one of the girls I liked to eye in class. I didn't see flat rejection in her eyes. She giggled and turned away a moment, but her face didn't say no. From now on, I would lead a charmed life. I would be a famous writer and explorer.

Saturday morning I got the chance to show the world the change that had taken place in me. A group of boys gathered to play a game of football. With my new confidence, I walked fearlessly into a scene I would have shunned before. I volunteered to play. The boy organizing it had been a friend from my grammar school days and had generally been good to me.

I could feel my limbs grow newly limber. I was sure that whatever had happened to me had cured my clumsiness. Now I could handle the football. I could run. The other boys were changed by my ease. No one made fun of me. No one pointed. My confidence said, "I'm a boy who can do what all boys do."

We lined up to be picked for the team. I was picked last, as I knew I would be, picked by the friend whom I had known since grammar school. We started to play.

But the clarity and focus that I was sure would come didn't materialize. My visual-spatial confusion remained. I didn't know which team had the ball. I just piled in. Then I picked up a loose ball, wrapped my arms around it, and ran. Finally, I would be the hero.

Then I looked back to see who was chasing me. No one was. My teammates looked disgusted, and the other team was laughing. It took a moment until I heard someone screaming, "You went the wrong way."

I left. I went behind the school to be completely by myself. I hurt too much to cry. The vision had injected my life with new hope. And in one football scrimmage that hope was gone.

I wondered, for a brief moment, if there even was a God. If God did exist, God was the master of disguises.

My life returned to its previous confused and lonely state. As usual, when I crossed the halls of the school, I avoided as many eyes as I could. I still had all the problems I'd always had. I still didn't know what was wrong with me.

But something had changed. At night when I would be falling asleep, or in the morning when I would be waking up, a hope would settle in my chest that had previously been absent. One night in particular I felt the old pain tie up my chest. I remembered the vision. I put my palm in front of my mouth and blew warm air on it. I placed my hand on my heart. The presence came again in a subdued way. God may be the master of disguises, but God comforted me still. I had that at least.

v i s i o n   j o u r n e y

We all experience visions, but most of us have lost touch with them. It's easy for those experiences to become buried under the busyness of daily life. Our schools, and even our churches, have given us no place to tell our wonder tales and be changed by the tales of others. We have no place to process our trips to the horizon.

This book can be such a place. Try to use it that way. Most chapters end with a writing exercise. Read over what you wrote every time you pick up this book. Reflect on it. Pray about it. I think you will soon find that you are remembering your wonder, dreaming your dreams, and seeing your visions. The theologian Hans Urs von Balthasar put it this way: "This bursting forth of riches from the innermost center is eternally a surprise." Look for this eternal surprise.

In the last chapter you wrote about a time you were met with comforting hope in the midst of crisis. I asked you to do this quickly, to short-circuit the "inner censor." Were you surprised at what you wrote? Now, just as quickly, write another vision (remember, the less vivid visions can mean just as much as the vivid ones). Begin now.

The visions of your lifetime are waiting to come to the surface. Now is a good time to stop a moment and acknowledge that process.

Writing

As in the exercise at the end of the last chapter, complete the following sentences three different ways. Write quickly without thinking. Then reflect on what you have written. The first sentence begins with "A vision is like . . ." One woman completed the sentence this way: "a balloon floating up from my heart, rising through the clouds, bursting, becoming one with the sunlight and air." On reflection, she came to see it as the yearning of her heart to become one with God.

Complete the following sentences three different ways:

"A vision is like . . ."

"If awe could be drawn in a picture, I would draw . . ."

"A bright early memory is like . . ."

"During the first vision I can remember, I saw . . ."

"If the Creator were speaking to me right now, I might hear these words . . ."

the medicine

stories of

christianity

WHEN I WAS A BOY, I SAT ON THE FOOTSTOOL IN FRONT OF MY GRAND-
father Pop's chair, listening to his stories of growing up in the
Appalachians. He told stories told to him: fables of animals,
accounts of holy times and holy workings, stories of how the world
came to be. Many of them were what native peoples call "medicine
stories"—stories that heal by evoking the holy. My grandfather died
when I was thirteen. I remember only a few stories plus many fragments. What I remember most vividly is the sense of presence I felt
when he told the stories. I felt surrounded by my ancestors who had
gone before us. With the tone of his voice and the quality of his
remembering, Pop summoned the sacred presence that had guided
the ancestors.

The Christian people have their own medicine stories—stories of
healing and hope preserved through the centuries by people telling
them and retelling them and instructing their children to remember

them. In this way, visions abided with God's people as they continued their walk through the ages.

I have studied these medicine stories of Christianity for many years. Some of them are like buried treasure, hidden away in archives and libraries, a neglected part of our history. Many of them are well known. In fact, they surround us. The writer of Hebrews was thinking of medicine stories when he wrote:

> Therefore, since we are surrounded by so great a cloud of witnesses, let us also lay aside every weight and the sin that clings so closely, and let us run with perseverance the race that is set before us, looking to Jesus the pioneer and perfecter of our faith, who for the sake of the joy that was set before him endured the cross, disregarding its shame, and has taken his seat at the right hand of the throne of God. (Hebrews 12:1–2)

These stories of the holy cloud of witnesses that surrounds us testify that visions are from God. Millions of Christians throughout the ages have had visions. And visions have played an important role in formulating and preserving the key doctrines of our faith. Visions are more important than we ever guessed.

ORDINARY PEOPLE HAVE VISIONS

Thousands of pages giving accounts of the sacred rest on the shelves of academic libraries, buried away. As we read them again, they shake the foundations of our rational world and change forever how we understand our history. They have the potential to affect our understanding of the spiritual life as much as the Dead Sea Scrolls influenced our understanding of the Bible.

These stories tell us that visions did not end with the time of the apostles but played a mighty role in the Christian faith, transforming and enlivening the world through the greater part of Christianity's history. They depict visions lighting up not just the lives of saints and mystics but the lives of ordinary people as well.

A friend once said to me, "Wouldn't it be wonderful if we had video-tapes of people at different times in history, telling of their visions?" In fact, we have something very much like it, at least from the Middle Ages to the early modern period. These records are court depositions, often under cross-examination, about thousands of purported incidents of wondrous happenings—visions and miracles—at shrines in Europe. Some of these incidents are supported by ten or more eyewitness depositions. People speak eloquently in their own voices about dimen-sions of reality that have grown dim in today's world.

These accounts provide immediate access into people's lives, fami-lies, emotions, and faith and remind us that God is the giver of visions.

Keeping accounts of shrine-related miracles was not new; this prac-tice dated back to at least the fourth century. What was new was tak-ing down the firsthand testimony of individuals who saw visions or believed they had experienced cures. Ecclesiastical courts took these depositions as part of the process of the canonization of saints. The hearings were very tough. The inquisitors asked hard questions and were looking for fabrication or fraud. In addition to these depositions, scribes wrote down visions and purported cures in miracle books at certain shrines. A large number of such accounts survive.[1]

These accounts demonstrate that people experienced their spiritu-ality in community, not just as individuals.

For instance, if someone was injured in a village, parents, friends, and passersby surrounded them. They took off their shoes and stock-ings to kneel barefoot and bare-legged upon the earth. They wanted physical contact with the earth when they called upon the mystery called God, much as Moses took off his shoes when meeting God's presence in the burning bush.

People usually prayed by lifting their heads and raising their arms toward heaven in the ancient posture of Christian prayer. Sometimes they formed a circle, joining their hands and encircling the injured or ill person in a vortex of shared healing prayer. They then prayed or chanted two of the most basic biblical prayers, the Ave and the Our Father, as well as the creed that restated the central tenets of their faith. Tears and expressions of great anguish frequently accompanied their prayer. Family and neighbors spent long periods, hours or days, saturating the injured or ill person with their tears and prayers. Later the person believed cured or the person's family made pilgrimages to a shrine, where the event was recorded, or they gave their deposition in an ecclesiastical court.[2]

Visions were often part of the healing process. Sometimes the afflicted person would be told in a vision to visit a certain shrine dedicated to a particular saint. Pilgrims accompanied one another on the road, praying for one another, gathering their hearts together into a sacred reality. At the shrine, people prayed day and night, readying themselves for God's touch. After what was often an average of nine days, many saw a vision—often of light or a saint—usually at day-break. The seeking of a vision at the shrine was called incubation.[3]

The story of Anne, a fifteen-year-old girl, is typical of the thousands of shrine accounts. Anne's vision marked a physical cure. Her leg had been crippled in an accident; she could move only by dragging herself along the ground. When Anne was fifteen, a woman pulled up her dress to survey the extent of her injuries; she found pus, putrefaction, and a twisted limb. In the late spring of 1303 her father eventually begged the money to buy a wheelbarrow so that he could cart her from their home in London to the healing shrine of St. Thomas at Hereford. There the family prayed day and night, embracing Anne with their prayers, seeking a vision that would herald a cure.

One night, as Anne lay sleeping in her stepmother's lap, she saw in her dream a kindly man with snow-white hair carrying the Eucharist. He gently anointed her twisted foot with a pure white liquid. Entranced by the sight of this healing man, Anne raised her arms and shouted, "St. Thomas, have mercy on me!" Smiling, the man gently made the sign of the cross on her forehead and disappeared.

Anne stirred in her stepmother's lap and announced that she could walk. After staggering at first, she did, according to the firsthand accounts.

A canon at Hereford asked the family to stay for a week to investigate the miracle. Afterward, Anne and her family left the wheelbarrow at the shrine as an offering and walked home to London and personally thanked those who had contributed to the purchase of the wheelbarrow that made their pilgrimage possible.[4]

The archives contain thousands of stories such as this one. Sometimes there was no cure. A person would recover at a shrine just long enough to make peace with God and reconcile with the significant people in his or her life before dying. At other times, the gift was a gift not of physical healing but of God's comforting presence. Whatever the vision, transformation of life often resulted. Some pilgrims took the sacrament of holy orders, becoming deacons or priests or entering religious life. This incubation of spiritual encounter led to a better sense of a person's identity before God and a greater connectedness to the community. Pilgrimage and visionary incubation became a way of knitting society together around the sacred.

Both in the patristic era and in the Middle Ages, as medievalist Benedicta Ward put it, "miracles formed an integral part of everyday life. . . . [They were] closely woven into the texture of Christian experience."[5]

This heritage remains in the expectant crowds of Lourdes and other Marian shrines and in shrines such as Santiago de Compostela, which has attracted pilgrims for centuries. Protestants show the same impulse in certain revival movements and pilgrimages to certain churches, such as Brownsville Church in Pensacola, where miraculous events are said to occur.

VISIONS AND HEALING OFTEN GO TOGETHER

We might well wonder, Did all these healings actually occur? The

answer is not easy. Benedicta Ward says that there are no signs of
fraud in the early shrine documents. The people who recorded them
believed them, and they believed that what they had witnessed and
recorded was true. There is no way we can go back in time and find
out exactly what happened. As Ward puts it, "All that can be said is
that here are events that caused wonder and awe and were interpreted . . . as signs of the action of God in human affairs."[6]

Since they lived in a world in which all good things could be seen
as both miracle and natural, even the body's natural recovery could be
recorded as miracle. They believed in the efficacy of long saturation
prayer, hour after hour, for the sick and injured. They believed that
incubating a vision through praying and sleeping, night and day at
shrines, disposed them to healing.

These beliefs begin to make a lot of sense in light of recent medical research. Serious research carried on at prestigious medical insti-
tutions is providing startling documentation on the power of prayer
and spiritual experience to speed up the natural processes of healing.
These studies indicate that more than mere suggestion is at work;
some studies involve patients being prayed for without knowing it.
For instance, in a ten-month study of 393 cardiac patients in San
Francisco, a research cardiologist divided the patients into two
groups. One group was prayed for by others, without knowing they
were prayed for. The other group received no prayer. The findings
were staggering. Patients who received prayer were five times less
likely to need antibiotics and three times less likely to develop fluid
on the lungs. As medical researcher Dr. Larry Dossey wrote, "It was a
randomized, double-blind experiment in which neither the patients,
nurses, nor doctors knew which group the patients were in."

Dossey details over 130 other scientific experiments on the efficacy of healing prayer, with similar results. In his book, *Healing Words*,
Dossey asserts, "The evidence is simply overwhelming that prayer
functions at a distance to change physical processes in a variety of
organisms, from bacteria to humans."[7]

Equally startling is the role of visions in contemporary spontaneous recoveries. Researchers have long known about and been puzzled by spontaneous healings of incurable or serious illnesses that defy easy explanation. It is believed, for some unknown reason, that the body's immune system becomes suddenly and intently focused on ridding the body of disease. An intense spontaneous focusing of body and, often, mind take place. Some of those cures come at healing shrines such as Lourdes. Many happen randomly to people with no particular religious affiliation. When these spontaneous events happen, some researchers note that they are sometimes accompanied by a vision—usually of light—that is unexpected. Dr. Melvin Morse, a medical researcher who has studied the healing power of visions, writes of an instance in which a woman was so disabled by arthritis she could hardly move. One night as she and her husband lay in bed, as the woman put it, a ball of light "came through the window and hovered above our bed. My husband watched it too, and both of us were too frightened to run. It was there for a couple of minutes and then it just went away." Afterward the arthritis went away. Dr. Morse later confirmed that "her arthritis did indeed spontaneously disappear."[8]

Larry Dossey, M.D., in a medical journal, describes contemporary cases of spontaneous remission of illness accompanied by visions in dreams. Remarkably, Dossey seems unaware of this long medieval tradition of dream visions and healing. He's finding healing through dream visions not because he's looking for it but because his research of spontaneous cures leads him in that direction. He describes one case in which the editor of a prominent medical journal suffered for a year with severe, unrelenting bronchitis that interfered with all of her life and work. One night, in a dream, her father, who had been dead for years, appeared to her, expressed unconditional love for her, and said, "Remain aware of those who have come before you. . . . Don't forget they have much to teach you." Her father was surrounded by light as he spoke. The woman felt her body immediately pass through a "physiological transformation." The bronchitis abruptly disappeared and did not return.

He tells another story of a man diagnosed with an incurable brain tumor who had been told to get his affairs in order and prepare for death. Each day he anointed himself with water from Lourdes and prayed. One night Mary, plainly dressed, came to him in a dream. The man said, "It was the most unusual feeling I have ever had. It was not a sexual love, but one that resembles a mother's love for her child. I did not believe it was possible to feel such deep love and warmth." He awoke, deeply at peace and free from the anxiety that had weighed on him for the two years he had had the tumor. "I went into the MRI chamber on August 22, 1994, with Mary's love still warm in my heart. Later that day the results showed that the tumor had virtually disappeared."[9]

Highly acclaimed novelist and professor at Duke University, Reynolds Price, tells the remarkable story of a vision that came to him in the depth of depression when he was suffering from a ten-inch-long cancer in his spinal cord that paralyzed him. Not active in church or particularly religious at the time, Price tells how he was

> transported, thoroughly awake, to another entirely credible time and place. I was lying on the shore of the Lake of Galilee with Jesus' disciples asleep around me. Then Jesus came forward and silently indicated I should follow him into the lake. Waist deep in the water, I felt him pour handfuls down the long fresh scar on my back—the relic of unsuccessful surgery a month before. Jesus suddenly told me, "Your sins are forgiven." . . . I asked him, "Am I also cured?" He said, "That too."

Following surgeries were successful, to the surprise of Price's doctors. Though partly paralyzed, Price lived and for fifteen years has actively promoted the Jesus whom he believed cured him in both heart and body, translating part of the New Testament and writing a novel about Jesus that became a cover story for *Time* magazine. Price wasn't looking for a healing vision and apparently knew nothing of the long Christian history of visions in relationship to physical healing.[10]

It is fascinating to compare these modern accounts of spontaneous remission of disease with the accounts of the spontaneous healings recorded at the medieval shrines. Like the woman Morse describes, people healed at old shrines often experienced visions of light, sometimes seen by several people at once.

Could it be that, instead of raw superstition, there was a medical type of sacred wisdom going on in the practice of incubating healing visions through pilgrimage and sleeping and praying day and night in shrines? Could it be that body and soul were so focused that the body's natural healing ability was moved into action by the touch of grace?

Such questions, hundreds of years afterward, are impossible to answer accurately. But I suspect that here we have grace building upon the natural. Because people were saturated by prayer and love, their bodies' healing potential could be marshaled; they disposed their whole selves to the holy. Somewhere, in the midst of it all, was God's presence and care.

Studying these thousands of accounts of shrine healings may well help us as we rediscover again the power of prayer and sacred experience to speed our body's natural processes toward healing.

Still, I must add a word of caution. While I have seen prayer enhance so many people's comfort and recovery during illness, I know that we are dealing with mystery. If someone is not healed, it does not mean that the person or those praying for the person have failed. There is no reason for guilt. We are dealing with the mysteries of God's providence, the delicate interrelationships of flesh and spirit. Healing comes in God's timing, in God's will, and is always surrounded by mystery. Still, we are discovering once more the power of the sacred to enhance the natural.

GREAT THEOLOGIANS HAD VISIONS

There's an even greater surprise in the documentary record of

Christian history. The greatest theologians of the church were just as prone to see visions as were ordinary Christians on pilgrimages to shrines. These towering figures include the saints Thomas Aquinas, Gregory the Great, Augustine, Macrina, Ambrose, Anselm, Hildegard of Bingen, and many others—those who shaped the core of the faith. Their visions influenced their thinking, which shaped not only the course of Christianity but also human thought itself.

Augustine of Hippo, whose work was so formative to Western thought, provided us immediate access to the workings of his inner life in his *Confessions*, arguably the most famous of all spiritual auto-biographies.

Visions, dreams, and subtle but varied encounters with the sacred played a key role in Augustine's narrative. He looked back on his spiritual journey with the mellowing touch that memory grants, as he recounted how his heart was transformed. Augustine was candid about his times of confusion, the upheavals of his youth, his bereavement and inner agony, and his yearnings. His work became a forthright, tell-all document that resembles late-twentieth-century books in the author's willingness to bare his soul. Albert Outler described the book as "a deliberate effort, in the permissive atmosphere of God's felt presence, to recall those crucial episodes and events in which he can now see and celebrate the mysterious actions of God's prevenient and provident grace."

Augustine's mother, Monica, influenced his life more than any other person. She wept and prayed for his change of heart and coming to faith. Just as, in the shrine accounts, tears and grieving paved the way for moments of astonishment and vision, Monica's expressed anguish before God paved the way for comfort and vision.

Of his mother's anguish over the profound darkness in which Augustine found himself, he says that she "wept to you on my behalf more than mothers are accustomed to weep for the physical deaths of their children. . . . Lord, you heard her and despised not her tears when, pouring down, they watered the earth under in every place she prayed."

Monica's yearning readied her for a vision: She saw "a bright youth approaching her, joyous and smiling, while she was grieving and bowed down with sorrow." When she told the bright youth about Augustine's confusion, the heavenly youth showed her Augustine standing with her as a person of faith.

As he recounted this story, Augustine broke out into prayer to God: "You truly hear her. For what other source was there for that dream by which you consoled her." Augustine closed his account of her vision with this famous and timeless prayer:

> Where did this vision come from, unless it was that your ears were
> inclined toward her heart? Omnipotent Good, you care for every one of
> us as if you cared for that person only, and so for all as if they were
> but one!

In answer to his mother's prayers, Augustine was baptized by Ambrose in Milan on Easter of 387, along with his son, Adeodatus.

The climactic moment of Augustine's spiritual pilgrimage was a vision he and his mother, Monica, shared at Ostia. In one of the most sublime passages in all of visionary literature, Augustine described their meeting with eternity's hallowed Lover. In the villa they were using at Ostia, Augustine and his mother leaned out the window, talking pleasantly together, the garden lying before them.

> We were in the . . . presence of Truth . . . discussing together what is the
> nature of the eternal life of the saints: which eye has not seen, nor ear
> heard. . . . We opened wide the mouth of our heart, thirsting for those
> heavenly streams of Your fountain . . . that we might be sprinkled with its
> waters according to our capacity and might in some measure weigh the
> truth of so profound a mystery. . . . We lifted ourselves with . . . ardent
> love. . . . We gradually passed through all the levels of bodily objects, and
> even through the heaven itself, where the sun and moon and stars shine
> on the earth. Indeed, we soared higher . . . marveling at your creation.

> Then with a sigh . . . we returned to the sounds of our own speaking.
> . . . But what is like to Your Word, our Lord, who remains . . . without
> becoming old, and "makes all things new"?

Augustine and his beloved mother came near to touching "that eternal wisdom which abides over all." A wisdom that can "so ravish and absorb and envelop its beholder in these inward joys that his life might be eternally like that one moment of knowledge which we now sighed after."[11]

Augustine eventually became a presbyter in Hippo (a town in North Africa) and then bishop. While serving as bishop, he recorded many of the "innumerable" visions and miracles he witnessed or heard about from his congregation.[12]

One of the church's greatest theologians is St. Cyril of Jerusalem, who gave so many catechetical lectures that he has been called the patron saint of religious education. In the fourth century, he told those preparing for baptism that visions were an expected part of the life of faith, affirming that God is the author of our visions:

> For, when enlightened by faith, the soul has visions of God and, as far
> as is possible looks upon God and ranges round the bounds of the uni-
> verse, and before the end of this world already beholds the Judgment,
> and the payment of the promised rewards. You should therefore have
> that faith in Him . . . so that you may also receive from Him that faith
> which works things above human beings.[13]

Other church fathers indicated that visions and dreams were an expected part of the conversion process. One was Gregory of Nazianzus, one of the most influential theologians in the church's history. Along with his close friend Basil, Gregory vigorously defended, explained, and expounded the Trinitarian faith of Nicaea. The church so valued him that, along with canonizing him, they gave him the special title *Theologus*, "Divine." The only other person to have received this title was the apostle John.

Gregory told part of his story at the funeral of his father, Gregory the elder, who died in 374 at the age of one hundred. His father came to faith through the prayers and loving witness of his wife, Nonna, much as Augustine came to faith through the prayers and visions of his mother, Monica. Gregory the elder's son recounted the role that visions played in his father's conversion:

> For the salvation of my father there was a concurrence of the gradual con-
> viction of his reason, and the vision of dreams which God often bestows
> upon a soul worthy of salvation. [At my father's baptism] as he was
> ascending out of the water, there flashed around him a light and a glory
> worthy of the disposition with which he approached the gift of faith; this
> was manifest even to some others, who for the time concealed the won-
> der, from fear of speaking of a sight which each one thought had been
> only his own, but shortly afterwards communicated it to one another.[14]

Visions played a role in Gregory the younger's own conversion. On a voyage to Greece from Alexandria over the Parthenian Sea, a danger-ous storm came over the boat. The passengers were gripped by a ter-rible fear of death. Not yet having made a profession of faith or been baptized, Gregory felt a special inner terror. Like many people in times of danger, he cried out in prayer along with his shipmates. Without his knowing it, the boat's danger had been communicated to his parents in "a nightly vision." At a distance, his parents aided him by calling upon God and, as he put it, "soothing the waves by prayer, as I afterwards learned by calculating the time after I landed."

At the time the boat was in the worst danger, a boy on board, as Gregory told it, "thought he saw my mother walk upon the sea, and seize and drag the ship to land with no great exertion."[15]

This event played a great role in Gregory's decision to be baptized and move into public Christian ministry. In a poem he wrote, "And God summoned me from boyhood in my nocturnal dreams."[16]

Gregory gave vivid and passionate explanations of the Trinity, which became indispensable to the triumph of orthodox Christianity against all the forces that besieged it. Here again, a vision played a substantial role. One night Gregory dreamed that, in a humble way, he sat at a throne teaching, with many people coming to hear him. From his mouth, in the dream, these words poured out: "The Trinity alone ought to be adored."[17]

Gregory, in addition to having been honored with the title "Divine," was a member of a group called the Cappadocian Fathers, along with Basil the Great and Gregory of Nyssa. This group's tireless efforts and theological thought firmly established orthodox Christian belief. In all of them, as Morton Kelsey's study shows, "one finds the conviction that God speaks through the medium of dream-visions."[18]

Athanasius, the paramount promulgator of Christ's divinity and humanity in the controversies that raged in the mid-fourth century, strongly believed in the power of visions: "The soul transcends the natural power of the body . . . imagines and beholds things above earth, and even holds converse with the saints and angels."[19]

One of the most surprising visionaries in Christian history is Thomas Aquinas, the brilliant systematic theologian whose intellect is considered one of history's most powerful and influential. Yet Aquinas regularly experienced visions. Tears and astonishment gave birth to his thought.

Above all else Aquinas became a theologian of love—*caritas major omnium,* "love above all." The French Thomist and novelist Jacques Maritain summarized Aquinas's vision of faith this way:

> He constructed on this Gospel teaching an unbreakable theological syn-
> thesis in which he shows how Love . . . has an absolute practical pri-
> macy over our whole individual and social life, and constitutes the very
> bond of perfection; how it is better to love God than to know Him.

Aquinas left no spiritual confessions, but his earliest biographers and the records for his canonization reveal the central role that visions played in his personality and thought. Aquinas employed a highly personal, even visionary, methodology for theology. He showed us how to interpret the Gospel with the total personality.

Bernard Gui's biography of Thomas, written from the testimony of eyewitnesses soon after Thomas's death, portrayed Thomas as a man of deep and fervent prayer.

Gui said that during his celebration of Mass, Thomas "was utterly absorbed in the mystery, and his face ran with tears."[20] At night, when he awakened to go use the latrine, he took time on returning to his cell to prostrate himself in prayer. Gui wrote, "He never set himself to study or argue a point, or lecture or write or dictate without first having recourse inwardly—but with tears—to prayer for the understanding and the words required by the subject."[21] Prayer brought Thomas the understanding of "holy mysteries." When yearning to get his message right, he "prayed first and then wrote down what the Spirit moved him to write."[22]

Thomas himself put it this way: "I dare speak of nothing except of what Christ has done in me." For that reason when he preached to ordinary people, he spoke simple words that had "a warmth in them that kindled the love of God." One Lent in Rome he preached of Christ's death so profoundly that his hearers were moved to tears. On Easter he preached so that they were carried away in joy and a woman who was hemorrhaging was said to be cured.

People often observed Thomas in trancelike, ecstatic contemplation. He could become so absorbed in prayer and thought that he would lose track of his surroundings. Gui recounted an incident when Thomas, teaching in Paris on Paul's writings, came to a particularly difficult passage. He ordered his secretaries out of the room, "fell to the ground and prayed with tears; then what he desired was given him and it all became clear."[23] He put his whole body into the struggle for visionary clarity, just as ordinary folk knelt on the ground and wept at shrines.

Once Thomas was wrestling with an obscure text in Isaiah. He mulled it over for days but couldn't get anywhere with it. He prayed and fasted, begging God "for light to see into the prophet's mind." Finally, one night, his close friend Reginald heard sounds from

Thomas's cell, as though Thomas were talking with several people. The voices then went silent, and Thomas summoned Reginald, asking him to bring a lamp. He then dictated a commentary on Isaiah for an hour. When he finished, he told Reginald to go to bed and take what sleep the night still offered. Reginald refused, saying he wouldn't leave the room until Thomas told him whom he had been speaking to. Reginald persisted until Thomas, with tears running down his cheeks, said that his company had been the apostles Peter and Paul, whose holy presence had helped him resolve his questions about the passage in Isaiah.[24]

In the last year of his life, while visiting his sister in her castle at San Severino, Thomas became "rapt in ecstasy" for nearly three days. Reginald tugged at him to bring him back to everyday awareness. When Thomas came to, he said, "Reginald, my son. All my writing is now at an end; for such things have been revealed to me that all I have taught and written seems quite trivial to me now."[25]

vision journey

We have seen how God's splendor breaks into mundane, everyday life. Augustine struggled with selfishness and lack of direction. Yet his life was touched and redirected by a sublime, transforming glory. Thomas Aquinas was a practical, logical theologian, yet his work was fueled by visionary ecstasy. Ordinary Christians in the Middle Ages frequently experienced visions that led them to love, service, and healing.

Our vision journey involves seeing the holy in the midst of the ordinary. Say this prayer, slowly and reflectively. Then complete the writing exercise.

Prayer

Lord, your touches have reached places in my heart
that no one else has ever reached.
May your touches, your visions,
always move my life in the direction of your life,
passing on to others the presence
with which you have gifted me.
May I not so much tell others of my visions
as live my visions.
And may I always allow all my visions to become teachers
that teach me to care for all those you care for.
May all my visions become one vision,
a burning, consuming vision of compassion and redemption
that so fires my heart
that I spend and lose and give my life away,
for the sake of all those for whom you gave your life.

Writing

Quickly describe a time someone told you a story that left you with a sense of holy presence.

Describe a time that a vision or religious experience helped you serve others and love them better.

CHAPTER   5

how visions

come to you

IT'S HELPFUL TO KNOW THAT ORDINARY CHRISTIANS HAVE COMMONLY experienced visions for most of the last two millennia and that some of the greatest thinkers of the church were animated by close encounters with the sacred. But we all want to know how we can personally experience visions here and now. That's what this chapter is about. It's time to take a close look at the ways we can enhance our sensitivity to the holy presence that surrounds us.

For me, reading about visions, listening to others' visions, and telling my own visions have made me more sensitive to these moments of transcendence. I was fortunate to grow up around a grandfather from an oral Native American culture that prized visions as a living, presenced reality. I was especially blessed that my grandfather mentored my soul for the first thirteen years of my life. I have also uncovered and learned from countless visions in my work as a researcher and writer. Perhaps most important, I have learned to tell my visions. These tellings involve many intimate moments, including moments of pain and anguish, as I share in this book. This has not been easy. But it has been necessary for me to get in touch with my own personal rhythm of sacred encounter.

Much of what follows is intended to help you discern your own visionary style. I will offer some techniques that have worked for me and that have proven successful with large numbers of people I've worked with in retreats, missions, and private counseling. I will freely illustrate these guided visions with visionary experiences of my own.

But the purpose of all this is to help you discern *your* style of sacred experiencing. This is an individual matter. Some people experience visions vividly, some less vividly. Vividness is not what is important, but rather learning to sense and be open to God. The guided visions that follow employ techniques involving sound, memory, visual imagination, and imagery from pop culture. Some are likely to appeal to you more than others. Try them all and use the methods that offer the most promise for cultivating the visionary side of your nature, which I imagine could use more attention than you have given it so far.

As you embark on this journey, remember that visions are a combination of sacred touch and inner response. The touch of God is the experience of an endless caring, an endless mystery that can become more intimate to us than we are to ourselves. The touches of God are beyond the telling. The telling comes from within us.

God touches you, but the part of you that is built to experience the holy provides the sensible content of the vision. That part allows you to remember the vision, share it, and use it. Genuine visions are always part us and part God. Though the content of visions might seem to come straight from heaven, it comes from our inmost center. These are our own vibrations at the touch of the Eternal Artist's hand.

The goal is to enter into the ebb and flow of sacred experience that is right for you, that fits with your personality and your history. Your inmost center, where God dwells, intuitively knows the kind and flow of sacred response that is right for you. The goal of reflecting upon sacred touch in your life is learning to trust this inner core—the wisdom God has planted in your unique personality.

The aim is to experience God, not as someone else does, but as you do.

FRANK'S STORY

Frank is a man who discovered his own way of experiencing God. He fell a long way—and found God at the bottom of his personal pit.

Frank was an Episcopal priest. He was rector of a large, wealthy church in the Northwest. He had married his college girlfriend, a sophisticated young woman from a prominent family. They had one teenage son. To observers like me, he had a magazine-cover family and a wonderful parish. His sermons were educated and spellbinding. His parishioners called him the bright new star in the diocese, sure to be made a bishop someday. His wife mastered the art of being a fine hostess.

Then, suddenly, his wife left him. She had fallen in love with someone else. She insisted on divorce and won custody of their son. The vestry of this priest's very proper church did not want a divorced man as pastor. In order to stay in ministry, he moved away and took a job as a hospital chaplain in the Southwest—a move that greatly upset his son. But Frank wanted to get as far away as he could. Uprooted and transported to a totally different location, he handled everything the only way he knew how: by being professional, plowing through, getting his work done, losing himself in comforting others—all the while feeling nothing. The weeks and months went by in numbness.

Frank's sense of bewilderment deepened. He even lost touch with his own need for comfort. His relationship with his son became strained. His son blamed Frank for leaving the area.

One night, it all came to a head with his son. The boy yelled at Frank over the phone, saying, "I just finished playing a baseball game, and you weren't there." Frank's response, a wooden-sounding promise of an adventurous summer spent together in his new home in the Southwest, only angered his son further.

But Frank couldn't respond appropriately. He told me that his personality, even his voice, had become wooden. His emotional state was numb. His world, so rich in spiritual meaning just a few months earlier, had been pulled apart.

That evening, right after his son's call, Frank went into the hospital chapel to pray. There hung an Eastern Orthodox icon of Christ looking down upon Mary, who stood at the foot of the cross.

As Frank looked at the Christ in the icon, Christ's eyes engaged his. Quietly as he sat there, he mumbled, "I thought it would be forever." In the recesses of his heart, he heard a voice, without words. It was Christ's voice coming from the icon, looking down at Mary and saying, "And she thought it would be forever too."

Frank reflected on the fact that the world had indeed fallen apart for Mary. Her dreams for her son, the wonderful promises of the angel, had ended in seeming failure at the foot of the cross.

Frank wept for a long time. He wanted it to be forever, but it couldn't be forever, anymore than it was forever for Mary or for Christ himself. Frank emptied out his tears before the icon, and when the tears were emptied, he rested in a love that surrounded him.

Afterward he called his son back. This time his voice was breaking, and this time he cried as he spoke to his son. Frank spoke from the heart about how much he missed his son. He told him that he wished he could make it all OK but that he couldn't. For the first time since the divorce, his son heard emotion in Frank's voice. His son could feel the deep caring of his father. Frank told the boy how they'd go hiking in the desert when he came down for the summer, and he talked about the fun they would have. This time he knew he had gotten through. His son's voice broke too as he said, "I miss you, Dad. I miss you so much."

Frank connected again with his son. The vision didn't make everything all right, but it opened the way for newness.

Frank's pathway to the sacred was the icon. In the quiet, with no clanging bells or dazzling lights, he experienced moments of grace. No angels swooped down; nothing had the character of the paranormal. Yet what happened to Frank in the quietness reached beyond the heavens.

ANCIENT TRADITIONS USED GUIDED VISIONS

The guided visions in this chapter and elsewhere in the book are rooted in an ancient tradition. During the Age of Faith, great saints such as Bonaventure wrote meditations to help people in times of sorrow and grief. These meditations drew on the imagery of the saints' own visionary experiences. They blended wonder and therapy, images of caring and light with images of deep contrition and repentance. The goal was to carry the meditator on a powerful journey of healing. Interestingly, similar meditations to elicit compassion and love are found among Tibetan Buddhists.

The early forms of guided meditations were meant to be spoken aloud, and people responded verbally, often in a communal setting. The guided meditations here are adapted to a literate and individualist audience. You will most likely participate in these exercises by yourself—in a quiet place when you can count on an hour or so of uninterrupted time. They also call for a written response.

Some basic principles of sacred writing can loosen our inhibitions as we probe the realm of the sacred.

Grammar and punctuation don't matter. When you use writing in prayer, you can't care very much about the rules of grammar, spelling, and punctuation that you learned in school. Your writing is for you. You're not trying to impress anyone. An excessive concern for "doing it right" can inhibit the freedom that you are trying to achieve in these exercises.

The process is more important than the content. Remember that what you write is less important than your actually engaging in the writing. It doesn't matter if what comes out is beautiful or cumbersome. The very act of writing starts a process of paying attention to the hidden streams of your being. Paying attention, not the final product, is what's important. Ten years from now, it can be wonderful to read what you write today. But even if you lose it tomorrow, the most important work is the process of looking at your heart, which writing assists in doing.

Write when you want to. Books on journal writing usually extol the benefits of daily journaling. That's a wonderful ideal, but the reality is that most of us can't or won't write in our journals every day. Then we feel guilty—another obstacle to writing.

It is far better to write when you want to. Practice it now; return to it when you are next ready for it. Let yourself fall in love with writing as a means of prayer. When you are dealing with spiritual matters, it is better to fall in love than to set yourself new and burdensome rules and resolutions.

Let your imagination run free. Be creative. No rules apply, except to write from your heart. I include some creative suggestions for using writing that will open you up to spiritual experiencing. Use a separate journal, for once you start you will need lots of paper and time to finish the work of your sacred sight.

Writing is a useful tool for most people, but you don't have to write as you go through these guided visions. You can write later or not at all. You can answer these questions in your own thoughts or words if you prefer.

Here's a suggestion: If you answer mentally, physically reinforce your answers. Say the answers out loud or at least move your lips. If you are going through a numbered list, physically touch your thumb to a finger for each item, much as you would touch a rosary bead to physically reinforce prayer. This is an ancient method of spiritual practice that should help the exercises penetrate your inner self.

v i s i o n   j o u r n e y

The first guided vision will help you reawaken your ability to sense the sacred. We all have this ability, but in most of us the talent to feel the touch of God has fallen into disuse. This exercise is based on a vision I had some years ago that helped me greatly.

Guided Vision: The Harp

In the vision, I clearly dreamed I saw standing in front of me a beautiful, small harp like the psalmists used. The voice of the Creator said, "Take this; embrace it." As I embraced the harp, it merged with me.

Then I heard the words, "Ready yourself for the melody of the touch of my hand upon the strings of your soul."

I came to see that dream as God's call for me to prepare my heart for the rhythmic movements of his Spirit.

To begin this vision journey, find a comfortable spot. Begin to relax. Put on some sacred music that eases you. Begin to let the love of God come over you. Tell God the thoughts of stress or pain that distract you now from awareness of God's nearness. God is near. God is always kindly bent to ease us, kindly bent to hear our frustrations.

Begin to pray, slightly moving your lips and tongue. Name some of the struggles reverberating inside you. In naming them, give them over to God.

Prayer

Dear God,
here are some of the struggles in my life now.
(Name those struggles as they come to you.)
I release them into your caring hands.

Thank you, God, for hearing me,
for taking up in your caring
the worries and strains
that can hold me so tightly inside.
Make my heart ready for meditation,
ready to see, to hear, to hold, and to remember.
Amen.

Imagine the warm, healing light of God surrounding you, filling you, calming you.

Have a sense of an ancient harp standing in front of you. You do not need to visualize it vividly; just having a sense of it is enough.

The harp sounds a holy sound,
a holy music.
It is a music that soothes, exquisite in its inspiration,
that carries you Godward.
You know its sound,
for you have always carried that sound within you,
heard it in your infancy,
heard it in dreams long forgotten.
It is God's sound and your sound,
both at once,
your music and God's,
your unique reverberation of the holy.

Pause a moment and you will hear the harp's sound as the wind of God's Spirit touches the strings.

Now that you have listened for a while, embrace the harp, letting it merge with you.

Hear from within you the sound of the melody wedding itself to your body, attuning you, balancing you, reviving your rhythms of the holy.

Guided Vision: Remembering Stories of Wonder

Even in these modern times, we are still being touched by wonder stories. Movies such as *It's a Wonderful Life, The Robe, The Razor's Edge,* and *Brother Sun, Sister Moon* touch us with sacred metaphor. Remembering some of these stories can unlock memories and dreams we have long forgotten. Awareness of the ways wonder has touched you in the past can help you sense the ways wonder touches you in the present.

Be alert to movements of the Spirit as you go through this vision. If at any time you feel a stillness, a fullness of being, pause and rest in the graced moment before going on.

Take a moment and let your heart grow calm. You might put on some music that stills you.

Sense God's love,
like an unseen cloud, gathering around you,
easing you,
quieting your mind.
Let the warmth of God's nearness flow to your arms,
your legs, your heart.
Grow relaxed and calm in God's nearness.

It's time to remember now,
time to journey into the past,
to discover how wonder has touched you,
how love has moved you,
how God, in the past, has entered your soul.
Let some of the sacred sounds
that in the past have conveyed God's touch
reverberate in your soul again.
Listen,
remember,
hear again the sounds that have brought God.

Pause a moment.
Now it is time to see again,
to follow again, some of the sacred stories
that have moved your heart into a process of healing.
Remember the scenes, the sounds, the memories
of stories you have seen in movies or on television,
have read or heard,
that carried you into a place of mind and heart
where God is near.
Now it is time.

Writing

Answer the following questions. Write quickly to bypass the mental censor and access your feelings.

What images from these movies most touched you?

What sounds?

What stories?

What do you feel as you remember?

Look at what you have written. Do you feel an "at-homeness" in remembering these stories and images? These memories can give you clues about your style of sacred experiencing. Investigate these clues with more writing.

Which of your early brushes with the holy were like those in the movies?

Complete the following sentences three different ways:

"If I had to draw a picture of my style of sacred experiencing, I would draw a picture of . . ."

"If I had to pick out a piece of music that was like my rhythms of sacred experiencing, I would pick . . ."

"Of visions I have heard about, the one that most resembles the way I experience God is . . ."

Guided Vision: Dialoguing with Symbols

We each have certain symbols, metaphors, or pictures that mediate the holy for us. A good way to understand our unique style of experiencing the religious is to engage in a dialogue with these symbols. The following exercise will help you do this. It's a simple exercise. You will be asked to quickly name a symbol that personifies the holy for you in a personal way. Then you will speak to the symbol and let the symbol reply.

This is how I carried out the exercise myself. My symbol of the holy is the cross.

Eddie: Cross, why do you mean so much to me?

Cross: Eddie, I mean so much to you because I have been with you from your earliest memories. When they read you stories about God, I was there on the book. When you saw them pick up the songbooks they sang from in church, I was there on the cover. Many of the songs they sang were about me. Later I came to mean that God loved you, for I held the Redeemer. I held the one who could look on your deepest failing, your most hidden sin, and take it as his own. I met you in the moments of dread in your life, for then you knew that your God had tasted dread more painful than your own. My presence, the memory of me in your heart, told you that pain embraced God and gave a way into God, who raises even the dead.

Eddie: Cross, when did you become closest to me?

Cross: I became closest to you when, imprinted on the host, I was taken into your very body. I have thus become part of you—intimate, always present.

Eddie: Cross, what can you show me about my future?

Cross: I will show that you will be conformed to me. Your life will know more loss. Your life will know more pain. You will lose those you know. You will lose your health and your life. But I will always cling to you and will always invite you to cling closer to me. I bore the Redeemer, and I will bear you, through the lonely place, through the silent and somber place of passing through death to redemption. I am always here to draw you near to the one I bore.

The dialogue went on much longer in my journal. It brought me to understand more about the role that suffering has played in drawing me close to Christ. Later I dialogued with the empty tomb, with the Eucharist, and with other symbols that mediate the holy to me. This is an exercise you can return to often.

Now it's your turn. Use symbols that come to you.

Quickly write the first symbol that comes to mind that mediates the holy. You can return to this exercise many times to work with some of the other symbols that mediate the holy. For now, write the first one that comes to mind.

Start a dialogue with this symbol. First ask the symbol, "Why do you mean so much to me?" Then quickly write the first response that comes to you. After that, you're on your own. Ask any questions that come to you, such as "How do you bring God near?"

Guided Vision: Dialoguing with God

Another devotional technique, used by Thomas à Kempis and others, is to engage in a written dialogue with Christ or God. Like the dialogue with symbols, the individual asks a question of Jesus or the Father and writes a reply as if it were coming from God.

These replies are by no means supernatural. Rather, the writer attempts to engage the hidden part of himself or herself that seems to be most in touch with God. These dialogues have never been viewed as a replacement for Scripture, sacrament, or church guidance.

Protestant writings have also used this devotional form. An excellent example is the famous evangelical hymn-poem "I Come to the Garden Alone," a blend of imaginative meditation and dialogue with the part of us that is near God. In the poem, Jesus walks with the hymn writer (really with anyone who sings or listens to the hymn) and talks to the person and "tells me I am his own."

Begin a dialogue with Jesus, God, or the Holy Spirit. Here are some starter questions:

You: Why did you so move me?
Jesus: (Fill this in quickly, letting the "knowing" part of you answer.)
You: How are you like my style of sacred experiencing?
Jesus:
You: Since you are so like me, remind me of a vision of my own, like
      yours, that I have forgotten.
Jesus:

Continue in this same vein as long as you wish. Remember if you are hurried, or just wish to, you can carry on these dialogues in your head, then come back later and fill in the spaces. You can also answer these questions many times and see how your answers change.

Quickly answer, If the Creator were speaking to me now, I expect I would hear . . .

a new way of seeing

And on the glimmering limit far withdrawn, God made
Himself an awful rose of dawn.
—ALFRED, LORD TENNYSON

We need visions because our vision is too limited. We

see poorly. We pay attention to certain aspects of

reality and ignore others. The underlying, mysteri-

ous, luminous significance of so much of the world

goes unnoticed by people trained in an either/or,

black-and-white, empirical mentality that prizes rea-

son and distrusts ambiguity and spiritual suggestion.

Our memories are filtered through this limited,

circumscribed mentality—personal memories, family

memories, and the memories of our communities. This
impoverishes our imagination and greatly restricts our
view of what we can do and experience and hope for.

— The renewal of visions in our time is giving us
new eyes, a new way of seeing.

seeing life
with new eyes

DAN WAS A FIFTY-NINE-YEAR-OLD MAN WHO WAS DOWNSIZED OUT OF AN editorial job at the local newspaper. At his age, he had no job prospects. He lost his sense of identity and much of his pension. Most of all, he saw his dreams die. For weeks, his inner world became a pool of nausea and fear. He just wandered around town on the bus during the hours he used to work.

One afternoon he fell into a reverie as he ate lunch on a park bench across from the now-closed grammar school he once attended. As he half dozed, he saw his old school bathed in a soft, celestial luminosity. The scene rekindled forgotten memories of his schoolboy dreams for a successful life. He felt the hand of a holy presence touch the back of his shoulder, and a warm shiver raced through him. He heard the words, "Dreams may fade, but God is always near."

Dan believes that this was the vision of an angel. It left a burning imprint on him that helped him readjust to his new situation. He began to view life as more than accomplishments. He used his new-found time to reestablish his relationship with his siblings and took time to garden with his wife, discovering her in a brand-new way. The simple acts of daily walking through life began to speak of the eternal. His life got a new footing.

Lisa was a young woman holding a near 4.0 grade point average at a top Catholic college. Reluctantly she decided to help at a men's shelter. She hoped it would look good on her résumé for medical school.

Walking back to the dorm one afternoon after working at the shelter, she saw, in her mind's eye, the face of one of the men at the shelter. Lisa's thoughts centered on his eyes. They spoke of an exquisite sorrow and longing and possessed a haunting familiarity. Suddenly she realized that she saw the eyes of Christ in that man's gaze. She changed her life's direction. She took a year off to work with a medical mission in Central America and changed her career goal to an occupation that involved working directly with the poor.

A friend told me a story about a friend of his, an agnostic Jewish attorney who fell into a near-suicidal depression on the third anniversary of his fourteen-year-old daughter's death. He had recently left his wife; the turmoil of the daughter's loss was too much for the relationship to bear. As he awoke one morning, his daughter appeared to him in a brief instant, more vivid than life. She was bathed in soft light that, in the father's mind, could only be God's light.

That moment of vision led him on a spiritual journey that changed him. He became involved with a synagogue and spent genuinely life-enhancing time with his remaining child, a young boy. He made sure this son had a bar mitzvah, an event he himself had never had. Life slowly began to take on a soft richness as he made room for the spiritual in his life, getting to know God again.

The common thread in all these stories is that wonder intruded, and wonder changed the way each of these people looked at life. Wonder gave them a new way of seeing.

These three people didn't look upon their visions as proof for God or as an anointing to be spiritual leaders or heroes. They didn't live their lives for their visions, trying to convince everyone they met that something utterly supernatural had happened. Rather, they let their visions help them live; they allowed the visions to transfigure how they viewed the world. Their visions helped them uncover the wonder that had always been around them, just waiting to be found.

Stories like these, which I hear everywhere, convince me that by ignoring visions, we ignore a mighty means of transformation. Each of these people allowed the vision and the wonder to become sacramental. These visions pointed them to God's activity in every part of their lives.

WHY WE STOPPED TALKING ABOUT VISIONS

Several centuries ago, church and society stopped talking about visions and wonder. Many thinkers turned away from their ancestry in faith and grew ashamed of the Western religion's long history of wonder. Visions still happened. Miracles still brought people to awe, but opinion makers—the philosophers and writers, even the theologians—grew ashamed of these stories. Tales of the holy became private and were generally banished from educated discussion.

This change marked one of the great shifts in the history of faith. When we stopped talking about visions, we lost touch, to a great extent, with the power of wonder to uncover for us God's marvelous doings in every particle of our reality. This has impoverished our understanding of who God is. By recovering our sense of the sacred, we will come to see God in a new way.

A fundamental change in how society viewed reality arrived with the dawning of the Enlightenment toward the end of the sixteenth century and the beginning of the seventeenth. The Enlightenment brought the beginnings of modern science. The early version of the

scientific method envisioned the world as machinelike. All that critical observers had to do was figure out how the machine worked.

Great figures disparaged the long history of the marvelous, within
both church history and the Bible, in the name of tough-minded
empiricism. Hume, the great philosopher, saw miracles as a sign of
"nature disjoined." Jean-Jacques Rousseau saw miracles as the main
obstacles to religion. He railed, "Get rid of miracles . . . and the whole
world will fall at the feet of Jesus." In our own century, George Bernard
Shaw echoed Rousseau:

> Miracles are the main obstacle to the acceptance of Christianity,
> because their incredibility (if they were not incredible they would not
> be miracles) makes people skeptical as to the whole narrative, credible
> enough in the main, in which they occur, and suspicious of the doctrine
> with which they are associated.[1]

Thomas Jefferson, an ardent inheritor of this tradition, eclipsed even
Rousseau in his disdain for wonders. Jefferson took a King James New
Testament, cut out all the miracles and visions with scissors, and then
had it reprinted in an edition that became known as the Jeffersonian
Bible. In a sense, many historians and theologians have followed
Jefferson's model, giving us a sanitized version of our church history,
one without the miracles and visions. Most contemporary texts that
tell of Augustine, Aquinas, Anselm, and many other great figures in our
spiritual and theological past never mention the critical role that
visions played in the formation of their thought and personal life. Most
pass over the massive references to visionary wonders in the original
sources and give us a Jeffersonian view of our spiritual past, with miracles and visions discreetly excised. The same goes for general histories
of the church. They cover the era of the Fathers and the medieval period, usually without mention of the visions that crowd the original
writings. A core part of our history is almost completely ignored, not
because it is hidden away in lost, arcane manuscripts, but because of

the embarrassment of scholars who refuse to study it and bring it to the attention of other scholars and the general public.

For example, the histories of spirituality will tell you about St. Benedict as the founder of Western monasticism, particularly about his rule, which provided the basis for ordering the common life of monks. But how often have you heard about Benedict the visionary mystic?

Gregory the Great, in his collection of wonders, related the following story of St. Benedict:

> The man of God, Benedict . . . rose early up before the time of matins
> . . . and came to the window of his chamber. . . . Standing there, all of a
> sudden in the dead of the night, as he looked forth, he saw a light,
> which banished away the darkness of the night, and glittered with such
> brightness, that the light which did shine in the midst of darkness was
> far more clear than the light of the day. Upon this sight a marvelous
> strange thing followed, for, as himself did afterward report, the whole
> world, gathered as it were together under one beam . . . was presented
> before his eyes. . . . The venerable father stood attentively beholding
> the brightness of that glittering light. . . . The world was gathered
> together before his eyes.[2]

Benedicta Ward, the great scholar of medieval religion, called this vision something more than just a miracle. It was a bringing of the "perspective of heaven" to the totality of creation. She continued, "This ability to see reality in its totality as created and re-created by God removes miracles from the realm of simplistic wonder tales." Rather, they signal "the ending of time in a single moment of redemption to which all things will be related."[3]

Most of us today categorize visions with miracles. And we tend to understand miracles in a simplistic way: stupendous, supernatural interventions in how the world works. Moving beyond a simplistic interpretation of the wondrous can open new doors for us in understanding not only visions but our whole world.

The doctrine of the Enlightenment held that all reality was comprehensible by rational examination and study. Many scholars who took these rules seriously soon debunked the miracles of the Bible and moved on to attack the core beliefs of the Christian faith. Believers fought back ferociously. Enormous energy was diverted from living and proclaiming the gospel to warding off attacks on the faith. In doing so, believers made a mistake that often happened in fierce fights over ideas. The defenders implicitly accepted the same playing rules as the attackers. As contemporary theologian George Wilson put it, attackers and defenders of orthodox Christianity adopted the same definition of truth: "that life was intrinsically decipherable, that certitude can be reached on nearly everything, if we just put our minds to it."[4]

The rationalists of the Enlightenment claimed that reality could be put under a critical microscope, be broken down into precise, definable parts, and eventually be thoroughly understood and explained. Unfortunately, believers accepted this same definition of reality.

As a result, today when we think of a miracle, we think of an event that breaks a law of the universe. Skeptics claim that this can't happen; nothing can bypass the universe's rules. Believers say that it can, that God does sometimes break the laws of nature. Skeptics say that apparent miracles and visions have natural explanations. Believers counter that God causes them to happen on occasion for God's own purposes. Both sides implicitly share the same view of the universe: clockwork governed by set laws.

This shift in perspective has had several grim consequences. Visions and miracles were once common in the lives of Christians. Believers under the sway of the Enlightenment began to see them as rare. When they did happen, they were stupendous events—God's intervention in the world's clockwork.

Miracles became something they had never been before the sixteenth century: evidence. Visions, usually classed with miracles, were no longer viewed as precious human happenings, both natural and wondrous at once, the results of humans being touched by the holy. Now they were seen as uncommon, mighty proofs of the faith. They became part of the long-running argument between skeptics and believers.

Perhaps the most serious consequence of adopting Enlightenment mentality was that it changed the way believers saw God. If miracles rarely happened, and if they were signs of God's interfering with nature's clockwork, then God was somewhat detached from the world. He was on the outside, occasionally interfering in the workings of the machine he had set in motion. Believers would argue that God did in fact exist and that supernatural events were proof of his existence. Skeptics denied this claim. But both skeptics and believers tacitly agreed that God wasn't much of a factor in the day-to-day running of ordinary life.

This supernatural view of visions and miracles robs them of much of their sacramental power to remake our souls and remake our world. But changing to a new way of seeing can have an even more fundamental effect on us. It can give us a new way of seeing who God is.

OUR ANCESTORS' VISIONS CHANGED THE WORLD

In her groundbreaking work, *Miracles in the Medieval Mind*, Benedicta Ward brought us some magnificent tools that can help us break out of the mental and spiritual boxes in which we've trapped ourselves. These tools can help us unleash the true miracle within visions. Her book takes us back on a journey in time, to the way our ancestors in faith viewed miracles.

While people reported miracles in abundance throughout the early centuries of the church, we find no major treatise or theoretical work on miracles from the time of Augustine to the time of Thomas Aquinas. As Ward put it, "The events called by this one word ('Miracula') permeated life at every level, but they were woven so closely into the texture of Christian experience that there was no incentive to examine or explain the presuppositions that lay behind them." Ward suggested that this belief in miracles came not from naïveté "but from a more complex and subtle view of reality than we possess."[5]

The crucial difference between their understanding of the world then and our understanding of it now can be found in the word *sacramental.* Our ancestors lived in a sacramental universe—one in which everything was both miracle and natural. Augustine pointed out that because we human beings become used to the natural, everyday miracles, certain signs that stand out from the ordinary provoke in us once again an awe of God's world. These special and unusual signs of God's presence did not happen by God's breaking fixed natural laws. Rather, as Ward put it, miracles drew from "the hidden workings of God within a nature that was all potentially miraculous." When people prayed for miracles, they in effect prayed for the "'hidden causes' to be manifest."[6]

Today we put the emphasis on the miracle itself breaking a law. Augustine and others in the early church put the emphasis on the psychological awe provoked within humans. In fact, the working definition of *miracle* used during the formative years of the Christian faith described any event that provoked holy amazement. Miracles did not oppose the way the world worked but were inherent in the world's workings.[7]

As William McIntosh summarized Augustine, "St. Augustine, anticipating Rousseau's brand of tough-minded empiricism, asserted that miracles do not contravene the laws of nature but rather that they occur at a level beyond human understanding of those laws." The idea of something being "beyond nature" was simply inconceivable to Augustine. He wrote, "For how can an event be contrary to nature when it happens by the will of God, since the will of the Creator assuredly is in the nature of every created thing? A wonder, therefore, does not occur contrary to nature, but contrary to what is known of nature."[8]

Thomas Aquinas made the point more succinctly: We experience wonder when an effect is obvious but its cause is hidden.[9]

The thinkers of the Age of Reason hated hidden causes. Believers tended to go along with them. Believers tried to define God precisely, attempting to make the faith comprehensible in minute detail. Thus emerged a God, somewhat apart from the world, who occasionally intervened with rule-breaking, stupendous events. People attempted to define the meaning of these stupendous events and to show exactly how they contravened the laws of nature. Thinkers attempted to domesticate God by making God utterly explainable.

In the older view—the view of Scripture and of thinkers such as Aquinas and Bonaventure—all our language and ideas are inadequate for God's mystery. God sustains the world at every instant. For Aquinas, every created thing "would collapse were God's power at any moment to leave the beings he created to be ruled by it." William Placher, a Protestant scholar, said, "In a world where God sustains everything at every moment, what distinguishes miracles is our inability to understand their causes and the wonder that results, not the fact that God acts in them but not elsewhere."[10]

As Augustine most eloquently said, "God himself has created all that is wonderful in this world, the great miracles as well as the minor marvels I have mentioned, and he has included them in all that unique wonder, the miracle of miracles, the world itself."

Von Balthasar, recapturing this original understanding of the world, asserted, "The world is a monstrance of God."

Ward summed up the point well. The idea of miracle as God's interference with how things work is "a narrow and modern concept, which had little meaning before the sixteenth century at the earliest."

Many of our misunderstandings of visions come from this view of visions as miracles that break natural laws. All too many people who hunger after vision accounts are really looking for evidence to bolster their faith. Unfortunately, a compulsive need to prove one's faith more often comes from a lack of faith, not the presence of it. In the older view, visions were not evidence of the holy but manifestations of the holy, a lived experience that rendered the whole world wondrous and alive with God's sustaining presence. There's a huge difference between visions as proof and visions viewed in a sacramental manner, as heralds that manifest wonder. Proof helps us understand. Sacraments help us see. Seeing is charged with life in a way that understanding can never be.

If we make this shift of seeing, visions can reemerge as a common reality that energizes our lives with the world-changing impact of the holy and the utterly mighty incomprehensibility of God's Spirit. We can talk about visions in church, in religious education, and in all parts of our lives. We can openly tap, once again, their power to change a culture.

Today we find science itself in the grips of change. The very idea of the detached, impartial, critical observer—the keystone of the older view of science—has fallen by the wayside in today's scientific quarters. The moment we observe something, we enter a relationship with it. We change, and what we observe changes. Even an observed electron behaves differently from one that is not observed. Many scientists now look for a methodology based on a web of interrelatedness and context, rather than the discredited methodology of detached observation. Leading thinkers have begun to see the world as far more mysterious than was ever thought before, as an alive world, interrelated, and not a machine. And if it is not a machine, it is more a world of splendor, even of miracle. It's more God's world.

All of this means that the old visions and miracle tales, which once only received an academic sneer, can be a means of recovering the sacredness of our world.

Despite blocking off from our memory many bright streams of tradition, the Enlightenment also brought much good. Modern medical science resulted from the technology that came from the Enlightenment. The diagnostic methods that helped in the discovery of my disability came from the scientific method. All of critical methodology is not bad. A degree of critical methodology gives us perspective, the ability to decide without being overwhelmed, to see the world with as little prejudice as possible. While we rediscover forgotten riches from the period before the Enlightenment, we must not forget that that period possessed its problems also. Some people were overly superstitious, closed to new discoveries such as the earth revolving around the sun. The key is balance. As we inch back behind the Enlightenment to discover fresh ways of seeing life, we must do so carefully and with balance.

CAN YOU GET A MESSAGE FROM A SACRED TORTILLA?

I have often given retreats in the Southwest of the United States to primarily Hispanic audiences. At almost every retreat, some pure-hearted soul pulls me aside and wants to show me the picture of a miracle. He or she shows me a picture of a tortilla full of brown spots. "Do you see the face of Christ in the tortilla?" I am asked. Usually I don't see anything but random brown spots. At first, when this began to happen, I had to repress my laughter. I would quickly change the subject.

Halfway through a retreat in which I had already seen two sacred tortillas, an insight hit me. I saw how much God remains a part of all aspects of life for these Hispanics. They see the Divine in the ordinary things of life. A simple activity such as baking bread holds the potential to be a window on the eternal. For them, the world of nature, the world of our daily lives, is not flat but charged with the sacred. Their simplicity reminded me again that the holy is all around us. We can see it if we will but open our eyes. These people remember what most of the rest of the world has been all too busy forgetting.

God has left footprints throughout this world. God's touch and God's breath show in all that God has created. This vast universe, this earth, all creation, our human bodies, our human minds, the animals, the winds, the weather are all radically dependent upon God's sustenance. The world is different from God, but made by God. God has not become the same as the world; rather, God has wrapped the world in embrace. The world of which our senses partake is drenched in mystery—finite and limited, yes, but resting in eternity and pulled toward consummation. For most of humanity's history, almost every culture, at every time, has seen the world as hallowed, a pointer toward the divine. Some times and cultures saw this more purely than other times and cultures. However fogged or pure the sight, our ancestors knew the world as sacred.

Then something happened that had never happened before. Humans no longer saw themselves as created, dependent upon the holy, but saw themselves as manipulators of creation. The world of science and technology caused a change in seeing, a change that reached beyond science. God's creation now began to be viewed as lifeless material to be exploited for profit—bought and sold as an economic commodity.

Society's worldview banished the sacred from creation. And in doing so, it exiled the sacred from the human heart, mind, and body. Our manipulations of creation brought about startling new things, but we paid for them by losing our view of the holy.

And sometimes it takes sacred insights of pure-hearted people, in old cultures that never fully exiled God from the world, to remind us of profound truths.

All our visions lead us to one vision. All our moments of astonishment lead us to one abiding astonishment. That vision is a vision of a new world, fresh and made alive by God's breath, rushing toward the time when creation will be refashioned, mended, and healed. When we look at each other, when we view the rain, the sky, and the soil as translucent and shimmering with the harmony of the God who makes and remakes creation, we move from visions to vision.

Early accounts of the praying saints, the hermits, and the monastics often depict wild bears, wildcats, and animals of all sorts coming to them tame and docile as infants. The original hope of paradise, the primordial harmony, was being restored through their visions. Some of the early accounts of Benedict and the other monastic saints say that at their deaths their skin was as soft, pink, and fresh as a new-born's. They tasted that vision of completion and consummation, so that while in the midst of this wounded and complicated world, even their flesh was being re-created.

v i s i o n   j o u r n e y

Freshness, newness, awe—these are some of the words that come to mind when we think of wonder. Children are masters of wonder—something we adults often get failing grades in. For toddlers and young children, the world is so new that it sparkles. A child can pick up a stone, see the sun glistening from it, and squeal with delight. A child intuitively knows that this world is sacred and that we are all tied in with this world.

When we are adults, such moments sneak up on us and brighten our world again as special, graced moments. Everything looks magical for an instant. Retreats often prepare us for such moments. So do vacations. Perhaps a long night of driving, when tiredness takes away the adult filters of our lives, will open us to the utter newness and sacredness of our world. God built miracle and awe into our world, not because God is the same as the world, but because God loves it and is entranced with its beauty despite all it faults. Surprise and healing are the bright bits of wonder with which God seeded creation.

God built us for miracles and built miracles into our world.

Augustine ultimately believed in only one miracle—the world itself, created by God and re-created by Christ. All the inspiring and unusual happenings in the world serve one purpose: to cause people to see the world afresh. Augustine said it best: "God himself has created all that is wonderful in this world, the great miracles as well as the minor marvels I have mentioned, and he has included them all in that unique wonder, the miracle of miracles, the world itself."

Writing

Write quickly.

"The earliest memory I have of looking upon the world with wonder was when . . ."

Quickly describe a scene during the last year when the veil was lifted for a moment and you saw everything about you transfigured by the sacred.

Complete the following sentences three different ways:

"I most see the wonder and sacredness of God's world when I . . ."
"The best way to dispose myself to wonder is to . . ."

Quickly write a short prayer, thanking God for the sacredness of creation.

Take time to slowly read and pray your prayer several times.

trips to the horizon

THE LATE EIGHTIES WERE FOR ME A TIME OF TRANSITION IN MY FRIENDSHIPS and in my work. My disability had not yet been diagnosed, and the constant frustrations I faced in doing simple tasks weighed down mightily on me.

I began a plunge into intensive prayer. I had had periods of intensive prayer before, and now I returned to the intimate and familiar routine of spending hours a day in stillness. I prayed ancient Christian meditations, eased into the sacred hush with the Jesus Prayer. I danced and chanted the Native American sacred rhythms. My whole being became a quest, a seeking for a new season of life that was yet to be born. I thought that if I prayed long enough I would reach a moment bursting with healing and release. My disability would disappear, and I would become the one thing that had always eluded me—a normal person who could groom himself and organize his desk with ease.

The yearning for magic, like a dream of winning the lottery, has never fully left me. The sober side of me, though, learned long ago that there is no magic. There is grace, but there is no magic. And grace isn't magic.

In the midst of this all-consuming yearning, several periods of visions came to me over the course of two years. In those graced spans of brightness and visitation, the hallowed became more tangible and clear than our everyday savoring of reality. I saw, tasted, touched, and felt the holy and pure in ways that nearly defy translation. All words I use to tell of those periods merely attempt to re-create these experiences. The attempts become, in one sense, creative artistry, giving form—story and words—to that which was beyond form. This is also true of the other accounts of visions I give in this book. Our experience of God can lie so far beyond our daily reality that metaphors and other means of crafting words are all we have to express that which defies expression.

Perhaps those times came because God needed my attentiveness. Perhaps because of the difficulties in my life, I tuned in more closely to the larger reality beneath the stream of everyday reality. And in tuning in, I glimpsed the visions that, really, we all have.

At one point in that season, I had a session of clear dreaming while sleeping seated on the floor, braced against the wall of my office. I dreamed a dream of Christ coming to me. I dreamed clear wakefulness. In this dream, I could see him vividly with my physical eyes, and I saw with more than my eyes too. Christ put out his hands, palms facing upward, and gestured for me to put my palms in his. Contentment and peace flowed from those hands to mine, passing through my hands to my arms and my whole being. His touch, firm and persuasive, invited my returning love.

"The time is coming," he said, "to tell your stories."

A burning passed through his hands into my body, warming, comforting my very bones. In his hands I felt the caring and at least a portion of the strength I would need if I said yes and began the telling. A time of telling my stories with all their anguish and their graces, telling my visions and the long story of the church's visions, would be my next season.

Then the dream ceased. I shook my head, stretched, and came to true wakefulness.

One night during this time, I fell asleep easily, knowing I would be awakened. For weeks, I had been in a period of visions. I tasted the joy and puzzlement of those days of being bathed in the sacred, even as I longed for my life to return to its more ordinary course. In the middle of the night, as I expected, the light came to me. The dark room filled with familiar, warm light that charged my lungs, my eyes, my body, my soul with mystery, creating a safe haven of love around me.

My eyes filled with a dazzling, a welcoming, beyond my ability to describe. Acceptance, loving-kindness, and compassion's own heart washed through me. I saw, tasted, and touched with abilities far beyond my physical senses. In a way, I saw through to eternity in that light.

Fear filled me—a holy fear. Then awe replaced the fear. The sweet agony of divine encounter grew. My eyes closed, but I could see the gentle form of the light even through my eyelids, cradling me, resting me, suspending me in eternity for a moment.

Even then I knew, as I had known in other encounters, that my difficulties would still face me after the vision ceased. So I asked the sender of light, who is light beyond light, a question. I asked without words, in the heart's language.

"Will you show me the way to be whole; will you make it all right?"

I was met with silence.

I asked more strongly, and again, the answer I received was silence.

I rested there, near suspended, enveloped in light.

"Help me," I begged, "to wake up in the morning and be whole."

After a long pause, the answer came in the wordless language of the heart: "I love you."

"Promise me," I begged, "that everything will be OK tomorrow."

Another long pause, and then: "I love you."

I asked yet again.

This time the answer changed: "I love you, and you are lovable."

But still I asked, "Please heal me; please make me whole."

I opened my eyes in the now-softening brightness of light. The light brushed aside my question again, and a somewhat playful answer came, changing the subject: "I see myself in your eyes, and you are beautiful."

I had to respond to this statement. But the statement itself helped me answer from my own heart: "I see myself in your eyes too, and you too are beautiful."

Then the light, in the language of wordless communion, gave a closing message: "I see myself in the eyes of all things created, and I find them beautiful."

I opened my eyes, fully awake now, and pressed my hand into the wood of the bedstead to test my wakefulness. I saw the light, dazzling brightly, as it shined onward into eternity.

Then something happened that I cannot find words or sounds or pictures to describe. All I can say is that I walked *into* the light, walked just a little bit into eternity, and the light shimmered and I shimmered in it.

My life returned to its normal course. I greatly welcomed the subsiding of this time of visions and the return to the everyday. My difficulties remained. No magical cure came my way, no instant opening of doors.

But I knew that I had inched close to the horizon. I did not pass it, but tasted it, and the world shimmered. I also inched close to the horizon of my life and work. I was brought to the place where I could almost see the next direction of my life unfold. A new season was to be born, a time of finally letting go of my stories, telling my anguish, even inching, finally, toward telling my visions.

I had come close to two horizons—the unspeakable horizon of God, which can draw us so close, and the horizon of the next season of my life. Really though, both those horizons are the same because they are both God's.

My life returned as always to my normal struggles. I still wrestled with my unique set of insecurities. The rough and uneven parts of my personality could still hurt others. Yet symbols of hope grew inside me. I felt the pull of a yet unrealized future, but my life was still in this world, this life. My visions, too, emerged from this world, this life.

Vivid as these visions were, I know they were also my stories. On a level deeper than conscious thought, part of me crafted these encounters from the images of Jesus I had always known as a Christian, from the memories of visionary literature I had read, from sacred pictures I had viewed in books or museums or on walls. God was also in that preconscious crafting, that inner artistry. I cannot separate my human, fallible role from God's role in these visions.

There is a part of us that both creates visions and detects them. The mystery of coming to the horizon was a blend of both creating and detecting. Part of me sensed God; part of me—an inner, hidden part—formed images of the wondrous to let that sensing permeate me.

WHAT VISIONS ARE—AND ARE NOT

My understanding of this trip to the horizon differs from some of the popular ideas about visions. Many spiritual people think that visions are God's marching orders, pictures from heaven, clear divine instructions. In this view, God's saints or angels directly transmit celestial information to the receiver. Visions function as highly privileged and authoritative divine communication that eclipses other ways of knowing.

I find a core of truth in that popular understanding of visions. God can and does communicate with us all the time, in visions and in many ways besides visions. And yes, religious experience can seem more real, more immediate, than the ground beneath our feet. But that intensity and immediacy can also be fleeting.

This commonly held perception of visions contains two ideas that can confuse us. The first idea is that visions are a type of heavenly dictation or picture show. In this scenario, the visionary listens and takes down God's words, sees God's pictures and writes down the description. The message is God's message—an unambiguous message straight from heaven.

The second idea is that visions are a type of hot line: A chosen few have this hot line, and the rest of us don't. An elitism can come with this viewpoint. It is true that some individuals live such heroic and God-infused lives that the clarity and heart-piercing quality of their visions speaks uniquely to us. But even then their visions can blend the human and fallible with the transcendent and sacred. Remember, the apostle Paul said that we "see in a mirror, dimly." Benedict Groeschel, a Franciscan priest and expert on spirituality, pointed out in his book *The Still Small Voice* canonized saints whose predictive visions were not literally fulfilled.

Over the last twenty-five years I have listened to thousands of stories of visions. Most of the time visions revitalize and transform. But some people end up more confused than helped. That confusion almost always comes through making the visions more supernatural than they are.

We don't possess unmediated and absolutely clear divine guidance. God comes to people in their history, in their culture, in the midst of their ambiguities. Eternity intervenes in time—saving, rescuing, and entering the stream of events in the life of Israel and the life of Jesus' followers. Jesus did not present the disciples with a set of scrolls that fell from heaven accompanied by undeniable cosmic miracles everyone in the world could see. Instead Jesus taught the mysteries of the kingdom by how he loved the rejected, embraced the outcasts, and turned the disciples' view of this world upside down through puzzling parables.

Visions play a secondary role; they help us interpret life. The visions and prophetic words of Israel's prophets interpreted and made fresh God's mighty deliverance in Israel's history. They were not the story, but the background music to the story. The same is true with the visions of the Gospels and the book of Acts. They shine light on the story, but they are not the story.

Biblical faith tells us that it is in the midst of life's distressing messes and unexpected glories that God breaks in. Our laughter, our crying, our doubting, our faith, our stories all form the context for God's coming to us. Biblical faith tells us that we meet God in the midst of this stuff of life. We have moments when reality shimmers with God's underlying presence, but even those moments contain uncertainties.

Visions are those moments that serve as pointers, and they guide us in two directions: toward God, who is the author of all graces, and toward daily living. Visions tie the eternal horizon to the earthly. Real visions always point to the realm of the everyday, in which we encounter God, who is hidden beneath all the world's doings.

Genuine spirituality increases our tolerance for ambiguity. Ambiguity is graced by compelling signs and symbols of the unity and clarity that will one day be revealed. Jeremiah knew ambiguity—he could say, in the midst of visions and prophecies, "My heart is broken within me, all my bones shake"; Mary knew the ambiguity of seeing Jesus' seeming failure before her eyes. Despite the glimpse of dread and glory on the highway to Damascus, Paul lived and ministered in the midst of ambiguity.

It is in ambiguity that we receive and live out our visions.

HELEN'S STORY

Helen, a friend of mine who is Episcopalian, went through a time of powerful spiritual eruption around her fiftieth birthday. A professional woman, she cared for her husband, who was intermittently ill with schizophrenia. They had no children. She had let the pain of her life circumstances isolate her. As she turned fifty, she was afraid of living the rest of her life caring for a husband with a frightening and perplexing illness, and dealing with this without children or family or friends.

In her search for a pathway to hope, she began attending her church's daily Eucharist and the special Thursday night healing Eucharist. A vision developed in her. Each time she closed her eyes during the prayer of consecration, she saw Jesus gathering beautiful little children to himself in the front of the church. Then the picture changed. She saw herself standing by Jesus welcoming the children. For a while, the reality of that inner seeing became more vivid than all of Helen's other ways of seeing. Her life was filled with a growing sense of comfort and purpose.

She knew in her heart that God had a special calling for her. The quiet assurance gave way to overwhelming feelings. She told others of her visions. People responded with kind words, but their faces showed a blend of perplexity and incredulity. She could convince them, she thought. Having been so touched, wouldn't she now have near-supernatural gifts?

Helen became convinced that the vision about children meant that she would be able to tell the sex of the unborn children carried by the pregnant women in the church. She knitted a number of blue and pink baby shawls and handed them out to the prospective parents, telling them that God in prayer had told her the sex of the unborn child. (This was in the days before ultrasounds were regularly done to determine the unborn child's sex.) Patiently she waited for the births, sure that her special knowledge would convince everyone that she had been touched by God. The results were indeed remarkable, but not in the way she had hoped. Almost all the mothers to whom she'd given pink shawls gave birth to boys; almost all the mothers with blue shawls gave birth to girls.

Helen's world, which had been tottering before the uplift of the visions, began to crumble. Even divine assurance had failed her, or so it seemed. Helen was fortunate that her spiritual adviser, Linda, the parish director of religious education, was a wise and holy woman.

Linda listened as Helen told of how devastated she was at the failure of her prophecies. Linda was able to see how Helen's lonely life was influencing her sadness.

Then one morning, Linda surprised Helen. She looked her square in the eye and said, "I've lived with the story of your vision for weeks now. And I want to tell you—as a person who has been around in the real world and in the spiritual world for more years than I would like to tell—that the essence of your vision was real, real to the core. The heart and center of it were true as true can be."

Linda then told her of a dream she herself had long held—the dream of a special religious-education program for young people with disabilities. She envisioned it as an areawide effort that would help junior high and high school students with disabilities (such as deafness or cerebral palsy) receive religious education in an environment in which they could mutually support one another.

Linda asked Helen to coordinate it. The offer spoke right to Helen's heart. This was the call of her vision.

Helen turned it into a model program where people with disabilities could form links with one another and grow as God's children. In developing the program, Helen drew on the resources of her church and community, forming many lasting friendships. Her isolation was shattered.

Helen realized that at a time of crisis in her life she had mistakenly come to believe that she had a hot line to heaven. Her distress temporarily confused her, but the core of the vision was real. It was a calling from God to love and serve children. In doing so, Helen broke out of her isolation and forged lasting bonds with many others in her parish and community.

Helen's experience isn't unusual. Sometimes when the sacred emerges, seemingly out of nowhere, or when we move into a new and deeper dimension of sacred experiencing, we can be overwhelmed for a while. But with the quiet help of wise friends and the church, the flooding can subside and we can then see more clearly God's true summons upon our lives. Spiritual experiencing rarely comes in absolutely pure form, easy to discern and without any ambiguity. Our visions come in the midst of the struggles, desperations, yearnings, and imbalances of our lives.

It is easy for something genuine and real to throw us off balance for a while. We live in a world where the genuine and the real are in short supply. It is also a world in which we do not talk to each other about our visions. The ancient wisdom of how to live in balance with visions has grown dim. In the intensity of the moment, we forget that visions bring grace, not magic.

LET'S TAKE ANOTHER LOOK AT THE PAST

We can find this balance about visionary experience in the classic writers of the Christian tradition. Often the same writers who celebrated visions and wonders so passionately in their storytelling literature took a more temperate view in their theoretical writings. They told us that there are times to embrace our holy encounters with thankfulness. But they also said that there are times to step back from experiencing and reflect soberly. Both seasons are essential to living well with visions.

For instance, in the sixth century, in his *Dialogues*, Gregory the Great told of one miracle after the other with unbounded enthusiasm. Yet in other parts of the same writing he put it all in perspective. Outward miracles "can change the hearts of those numb to invisible truths, and they can encourage those whose faith is too feeble to penetrate deeper mysteries."[1] While he acknowledged the dazzling power of miracles to nurture faith, he made the point that good deeds, virtue, and holiness are far more important. For Gregory, "the proof of holiness is not to make miracles, but to love others as oneself. . . . For the true power is love, not in the showing of miracles. . . . The witness of heavenly discipleship is the gift of brotherly love."[2]

In the latter part of the second century, a crisis shook the church that was to forever define the role of prophecy and visions. A new movement called Montanism broke out like an earthquake in Asia Minor. Montanus and several other prophets claimed that a new out-pouring of the Holy Spirit had revealed the message of God. They prophesied that the world would soon end. The Montanist prophets claimed to be authoritative mouthpieces of God to the world. As one of the prophets, Maximilla, said, "The Lord has sent me as a partisan, a revealer, and interpreter of this distress. . . . I am compelled to make known the knowledge of God."

The Montanists' prophecies and visions were often frenzied and intense. After much consideration, the church rejected Montanus, but it did not reject visions and prophecy. The great Irenaeus cautioned the church about "driving true prophecy out of the church from anx-iety over the false." But in rejecting Montanus the church rejected the concept of one or more prophets becoming infallible mouthpieces of God to the whole world.

Instead, the church looked to the Jewish writings known today as the Old Testament and to the writings and teachings from the Age of the Apostles as the means by which revelation was transmitted. As a result of the Montanist controversy, the church made it clear it would never agree to a view of visions that made them revelatory in the same way that the saving mystery of Christ's life, death, and resurrection were revelatory. The church vested the authoritative, ongoing inter-pretation of the history of God's saving events in the community and the shepherds of the community. Visions could help supercharge that history, make it immediately vital, and connect its depths to the depths of people's inner lives, but in no way could visions replace that history.

The church fathers and mothers took a view of visions that Stephen F. Kruger, a medievalist who has studied the subject extensively, called "middleness."

Because visions played such a large role in the formative centuries of the church, the theories for understanding them are intricate and complex, based, in part, on the Greek philosophical ideas common to that time. Dreams and visions occupied a middle place between heaven and earth, a place of "middleness." In this middleness, dreams and visions often blended the divine and the earthly. They could contain the sublime, be filled with the healing resonance of God, and at the same time mix that sublimity with normal human thoughts and even with needs such as thirst or hunger.

Augustine put it this way: "Spiritual vision can be reasonably and naturally said to occupy a kind of middle ground." Augustine insisted on the imaginative quality of dreams, even those "that seem to involve visitations from the other world." "Angelic operations" sometimes work on our imaginations. But he stressed that even the highest dreams "operate within the intermediate sphere of the spirit."

In short, spiritual vision can be imperfect, even subject to outright mistakes.

Perhaps Gregory the Great gave the best description of the middleness of visions. He suggested that spiritual visions and dreams can be generated "by our thoughts combined with revelations." In speaking of Gregory's view of visions and dreams, Kruger stated, "Dreams thus stimulated stand between the wholly external and the fully internal."[3]

In summarizing some of the patristic view of dreams (and also visions, which the church fathers saw as "waking dreams") Kruger said, "The realm of dreams comes up poised between truth and fiction." Later on, in the twelfth century, St. Aelred of Rievaulx restated the position of middleness concerning dreams and visions. According to Kruger, "Aelred consistently stresses the dream's imaginative status— its position between body and mind . . . true and false."

This is a fundamental reality of visions: Visions are part us and part God, and this side of glory, we can't fully separate which part is which, nor do we need to.

VISIONS TAKE US TO THE HORIZON,
NOT BEYOND IT

One of the problems some people have with visions can come from a fundamental misunderstanding of who God is. God is not an object in our world like an apple or a tree. God is not an objective figure sitting in a localized place called heaven, communicating with us the same way we communicate with each other over cellular phones. As Avery Dulles suggested, the human mind cannot validly conceive of God as an object "spread out before its gaze." God, he said, "can never be an object, for every object is perceived against a more comprehensive horizon or background. Since God is all-comprehensive, he is non-objectifiable."

Most Native languages use words to describe God that are synonymous with the English word *mystery* Among the Algonquin-speaking peoples, God is *Gitche Manitou*, which means "all-encompassing mystery." For those of us of southeastern Native descent, God is often described as the Master of Breath. Our chant, our song, and our ritual around the sacred fire all draw us into a mystery toward which we can only point by singing and telling stories. We can invoke God, but we cannot define God.

Visions in their purest form are God's free gift, the gift of the holy mystery that borders our existence. They are the touch of the infinite, ever-expanding horizon that draws so intimately near in Jesus. Speaking as a Christian, I say they are the gift of Christ, the human one and the sacred one who united sky and earth and on whose all-so-human face the light of the sacred mystery fully shines. Christ came into our world, into a concrete and limited human existence and culture, and mystery became touchable.

In the same way, God touches and uses our imagination, which is the language of our inner heart. It's human to have an imagination that is earthly, bound to the earth, and the God who became bound to the earth in Jesus can touch and invade all our humanity—our imagination included.

Visions are pictures, metaphors, and feelings that we form when mystery intrudes. In one sense they are our stories because they are formed from our images, our personal background, our culture, our religion, and our history. Yet in another way they are also God's. Visions serve as symbols. On some level, they are always symbolic. As Avery Dulles said, "Mystical writers such as Dionysius the Areopagite and John of the Cross have favored a 'symbolic theology' in which the imagination is stimulated so as to evoke and invoke the presence of the spiritual world." In this view, visions are the stimulation of the imaginative, feeling, apprehending parts of our personality by the ineffable touch of God.

Visions are sent to us not so much to give us great revelations or a special hot line to heaven as to heal us, to pour over us the presence of the one who loves us. They convey presence far more than information. They are the embrace of God, not the dictation of God. They are sent to us to carry us up to the horizon.

I love to go to Jamaica and Florida and look out at the horizon of the sea. With my mind I know that there is another continent beyond the horizon, but when I look at the sun rising over the sea, it all becomes a mystery. My eyes go to what I can see. I see a setting sun or a rising sun and a sun inflaming a cloud with great colors, and I know I am in the midst of mystery. I know that something wondrous lies beyond that horizon. My whole being can go up to the horizon, but it cannot cross it.

This is my belief about visions and wonders. They carry us up to the horizon. They let us know that there are all sorts of new possibilities and realities that beckon us, that we cannot now comprehend, but that we will one day comprehend. But even in those experiences, intense though they may be, we do not see beyond the horizon. We are intrigued and tantalized but not carried beyond.

Visions are trips to the horizon. We stand before mystery that fascinates us, beckons us, and befriends us. But we do not cross the horizon. Visions serve as bridges between the sacred and the everyday arena in which we work, relate, breathe, live our lives, laugh, and cry our tears. They are conduits that enable the holy to invade our inside and outside worlds. God, like a magnet, draws our humanity into divinity. Visions are like mountaintops. They enable us to view the whole of our lives. Visions mix the holy and the earthly. They are both real and imagined. They hold not the truth of a newspaper or a computer manual but the truth of a painting, a piece of music, a kiss, an embrace. They present not so much objective truth as pathways—hiking trails into mystery. Eastern Orthodox icons hauntingly point beyond the colors and the figures to a wondrous realm beyond our picturing. So do visions.

Coming to the horizon can be like climbing a tower. As William Lyon Phelps put it, "the view halfway up is better than the view from the base, and it steadily becomes finer as the horizon expands."

Visions unleash our spontaneous religious imagination. Within each of us is a painter of sacred icons, a dramatist of inner mystery plays, a poet of hallowed verse. At the touch of the eternal, that natural part of us forms metaphors and stories that become bridges. The paint buckets of the icon painter, the stories of the dramatist come from the realities of the world we live in—our culture, our lives, and our time. Our inner visionary storyteller, hidden in our unconscious, draws from all stories of our lives to form our visions.

Marjorie How, turn-of-the-century scholar and poet, spoke of this interpretative role of visions, this naturalness, with poetic insight:

> Everyone who has studied the subject must agree, I think, that the form which the vision takes will vary in accordance with the mind of the seer. "All," says Miss Underhill, "probably borrow their shape, as apart from their content, from suggestions already present in the mind of the seer." The vision itself is a correspondence between something in the spiritual world, which cannot be literally expressed in our language, and

something in the material world, the significance of which our minds can grasp. It presents itself so vividly and so suddenly to the mind that its symbolic character is easily forgotten. The greatest mystics, however, one and all recognise that their visionary experiences are but modes of interpretation.[4]

Once in an adult education class on spiritual experiences, I held up a beautiful icon of Christ with a shining background of gold color and large swaths of blue. That icon, a favorite of mine, haunted, mesmerized, and intrigued while at the same time heralding the holy. I asked for a show of hands. "Is this icon true?" No hands came up. Then I asked, "Is this icon false?" No hands came up this time either. Then I played a short tape of Gregorian chant and asked the same questions, and again my only answer was the perplexed looks that came back to me.

We don't think of a sacred painting as true or false or of a holy music as true or false. Rather, we instinctively know that they point toward the hallowed. They gather up our imaginations, our feelings, and our thoughts and lead them into mystery. They are pointers; profoundly true, but true on a subterranean level.

This is what visions are like. They are not road maps or direct orders from heaven. But they are true in the way an icon is true or an old medicine person's chant is true. They transcend rational thought. There is a quality of "more." The images, the inner senses of visions, may mean what they mean, but they always mean something more than the most basic meaning. The word to describe this "more" is *transcendent*.

Our visions are fallible, as we are fallible. Mystery touches and intrudes through our fallibility. Visions are what we produce inside when we bump against the holy and are left inarticulate.

Visions are the natural way the presence of mystery enters us, weaving bright threads into our everyday existence. The metaphors and the felt memories that visions leave us become bottomless wells of meaning to fully plumb throughout our lives.

Telling visions to others becomes a means of transmitting mystery to others. Remembering them, telling them again and again to ourselves, touches deepening layers of their meaning, invoking still again the presence that gave them birth.

They are all moments, to use von Balthasar's words, when "the human is embraced by the transcendent Other," or in the words of John of the Cross, they are "the delicate touch which has the taste of eternal life."

The final goal of visions is to bring the holy into our everydayness, imbuing the ordinary and infusing it with mystery.

To use my grandfather's word, they make our whole lives shimmer.

v i s i o n   j o u r n e y

Most of us have encountered mystery. The holy meets us, and we have no words left. We could only allow ourselves to be grasped by it, pulled by it, into an unknown that was both fearsome in its awe and wonderful in its love. The following exercises will help you contact those experiences of God as mystery.

Writing

Quickly complete the following sentences:

"If I could draw a picture to describe holy mystery, I would draw . . ."
"The time I most felt God as mystery was when . . ."

We humans naturally form symbols. Different times in our lives have their own symbols—a picture, a song, a sound, a story—that hold reality that cannot be held in ordinary speech or ideas.

Complete the following sentence:

"The symbol that most conveys my experience of God is . . ."

Complete the following sentence three different ways:

"I experience a reality too overwhelming for words when . . ."

Different things in our lives trigger the experience of awe and mystery: nature, the resolution of a personal crisis, prayer, worship, the birth of children. List some of the activities that trigger this immersion in holy mystery for you.

finding the remembering spot

I AM A CONTEMPORARY MAN WITH AN ANCIENT HEART. I ZIP AROUND THE Internet. But the heart that beats in my chest was partly fashioned by the wisdom of long ago. So it is for all of us. We live in a society of rapid change and high technology, but beneath the surface we are people of the ancient times.

The challenge is to remember the forces that formed us. Each of us has our own remembering spot. This is a place that evokes our most powerful memories. Perhaps your remembering spot is your child-hood bedroom, a school playground, or a favorite family vacation site. Perhaps you have several of these special places. These places are charged with emotion. Events we hold as most hallowed often entwine around our starkest losses. When we return in memory to these special places, we tap powerful energies of transformation. We contact streams of awareness that can transfigure us and our whole world. Such remembering can push us equally into grieving and into the cloud of awe and holiness. We come to the root of our being.

Those bright memories are often the hardest to enter, because they are the memories most easily walled off with our pain. To contact the brightness, we also have to contact the pain. Remembering is the essential route to discovering again our rhythm of sacred experiencing.

THE CHILDHOOD PLACE OF REFUGE

From the time of my earliest memory, before the pain and confusion of school and the weight of my disability settled on me, I had a bright place of refuge. It was a street called North Gordon—a short, thin bit of pavement that ran right beside a huge cotton mill in Columbus, Georgia.

There stood the home of my grandparents and my aunt Lovey. Pop, my grandfather, was born in the Smokies of North Carolina. He was half Cherokee, and Granny had a little of the Cherokee blood in her. Most Native families away from the reservation like mine gradually lost all their identity. We were different. My great-grandmother Mary Alexander Ensley, above all else, held on to that which had been passed on. She was a healer, a medicine woman. She taught my father and grandfather to hold on to the traditions. They taught me that no matter what, I must remember. If we remember, we survive, we endure. If we forget, we vanish.

Pop, Granny, and Daddy told me the tragic story of my people and sang for me the old, sacred chants. They taught me to use an old gourd shaker and beat out the old rhythms that went with the chants. They taught me some of the Cherokee language and told me the sacred fables and stories that came from ancient times. They were people of ancient memory. From the time I was a toddler in their

home until Pop's last illness and death when I was thirteen, I experienced sacred times that seared themselves into my heart.

Of all my cousins, I asked the questions, so I was told the stories.
My father said my first word was, "Why?"

Pop took me to a special spot, just behind the power plant, on a
ledge overlooking the Chattahoochee, to tell me many of the old
fables and sing many of the old songs. He said it was a wonder spot,
a remembering spot. He said that if I ever returned to it, even fifty
years later, I would remember vividly, as if I had stepped back in time.

Like most people of ancient memory, my grandfather lived easily
with visions. I remember many things from my earliest childhood.
While some memories have fogged over during these forty-nine years,
others remain vivid.

I remember the Divine Mystery from those early days, in the bright
way very young children see God. God was like the wind that lifted
up and swirled the visible fall leaves—that unseen whirlwind lifted up
and supported the world I knew.

Below my grandparents' shack, the land fell steeply like the moun-
tainsides of the Smokies, the place my grandfather was born. Below
their house lived the angels, the *nunehi*, sent by the Provider from the
brightness above, Pop told me.

These were my angels. Most children see their angels. I was unusually lucky. I had a grandfather who saw them too. He called them the
Immortals. They had a lodge—a *nunehi-yi*, "house of angels"—under a
rock on the bank of the river. The pump house for the mill, which my
grandfather tended, rested on this rock. Each morning he followed
the old custom and went down to the river to honor the water, say
prayers, and absorb the brightness of the sacred. I would eagerly await
the first sight of his old, gray dress hat coming into view as he climbed
the cliff.

He would tell me that, as always, the angels were there. Sometimes,
it seemed, I could see the angels too, following behind him. I would

glimpse their light as they accompanied him to the top of the cliff and watch them as they returned to their lodge below to continue their dancing.

The wondrous formed just one part of the life I knew in the cotton-mill village. I found sacred seeing no more extraordinary than the bellowing from the mill whistle that shook the trees and leaves with its blast thirty minutes before quitting time and then again at quitting time. Or the regularity with which my grandparents, my father, and my aunt Lovey emerged from the back gate of the mill, a minute or two after quitting time, to gather me in their arms just outside the gate, where my mother and I waited for them.

My images of North Gordon began in wonder but ended in confusion and pain. Aunt Lovey died a dreadful death in a car accident. Pop, my grandfather, came down with cancer when I was nine and died a long, four-year death. I began to pull away emotionally from him before he died. I had to bury the thought of his dying, pretend it wasn't so. As I turned twelve and thirteen, the world of school, the world of books I devoured so hungrily, told of a world different from the world of Pop and Granny. It became almost easy to dismiss their ways as superstitious.

When I was thirteen and Pop was already hemorrhaging from the mouth, moving toward cancer's last stages, he told me to come spend days with him so that he could teach me all the old ways. But I did not go. It was more pain than I could handle. So I never fully learned all the old ways.

My memories of the early teaching grew dim. My soul froze.

My last memory of North Gordon is watching Uncle Henry, Pop's brother, smoking a cigarette beside the porch steps as the mortician carried Pop out to the hearse on a stretcher. I didn't cry at the funeral. I didn't cry for him until I was thirty, when I visited the cabin in the Smokies where Pop was born. I finally had to step through the numbness to begin recovering the center of my soul.

VISIONS AND MEMORY WORK TOGETHER

It took me thirty-five years, until I was forty-eight years old, to muster the courage to visit North Gordon again.

Through those intervening years I would often have to drive past the turnoff to North Gordon. I would place my hand as a shield over my vision as I drove past so that I wouldn't have to see where their house once stood.

When I was in Ontario leading a retreat for Native people, I saw some of the old men whose speech and manner reminded me of Pop. Their world was like Pop's world. I made up my mind to face the pain of my early mysteries and make the trip back to the street called North Gordon.

I tried once but met a wall of pain and had to turn back. Then I made a retreat weekend of prayer and rest and asked God's strength to help me walk down that street once more.

Soon after the retreat, I swallowed hard and headed for North Gordon.

I walked slowly up the hill to the bluff above the big river. My limbs wobbled with a blend of reluctance and anticipation, like an Olympic athlete walking expectantly toward the scoreboard, or a parent edging toward the nurses' station to see if a beloved daughter pulled through an operation. Dressed in my Cherokee longshirt, I was neither athlete nor grieving parent. I was simply a brain-damaged person of Native descent, returning for the first time in thirty-five years to the key spot of my childhood, where long ago my soul had been formed.

I knew that if I walked those several hundred steps, the world I returned to would forever change.

Often I had traveled to this spot in my dreams. I had nearly seen God's face in those dreams, or so it seemed, and I had felt dread. At times I had awoken from them moaning in pain; other times I had awoken with my bones trembling with sweet wonder.

Now as I edged toward the bluff overlooking the river, there was nothing tangible to fear. I was unlikely to encounter anyone. I anticipated no news, at least what we normally count as news, that would alter my life. Only the bluff, high above the white, foaming, muddy Chattahoochee River that swirled past rock islands with trees, waited for me.

I walked through a corridor formed by the old brick cotton mill towering on my left and wires that tied together big black transformers in the power station to my right. Once I passed through this space between the two industrial intrusions, I would see the wild woods and rocks and river below. But I was not there yet.

More awaited me than rocks, river, and clouds. More than you can see with eyes or hear with ears. Even now, though there remained many slow paces before the bluff, joy and dread had become kinfolk inside me. I started to remember.

Something huge rested on me.
Something that fascinated.
Mystery.
And remembering.

Walking toward the bluff thrust me into a reality different from the common reality in which we breathe our breath, cry our tears, laugh our laughter, and do our work. The world exploded all around me, and no words could name or tag what was happening. The only sure reality was that all things would now become different.

As real as any earthquake, the ground beneath me seemed to roll, as if a blanket were being spread. My body tingled, and I heard delicate, clear celestial sounds. My whole body became a listening station for the melodies that filled me.

Sounds of old-time Native chant blended with the heavenly sounds. I began to sing with them. Their bright heat filled me. From my pants pocket I pulled a shaker made of hide and stones and made rhythm with the songs.

Before I started my trip to the bluff, I knew I would have to stop at the empty lots where two stucco shacks once stood, the homes of my Cherokee grandparents and Aunt Lovey. In the small, wooded ravine separating the Bibb and Columbus Mills, my father had hunted rabbits with stone-tipped arrows that his own father, my grandfather, had chipped for him.

This place was the home of the many plants my grandfather nourished and summoned to become his medicine. I was facing it all now, facing it in one massive encounter. All the things I had for so long wanted to hold back now met me. I had come once before, weeks ago. But the nausea and resistance had enveloped me, and I had run back to the car, to a safe place. I had not been ready then for what awaited me at the bluff. It would be craziness to run with a raised golf club through a golf course in a thunderstorm. Yet by returning here, I had become a lightning rod for my memories, traditions, and ancestors.

But I was not crazy now. I had been crazy to let my heart ever leave this place. I had been crazy to try to erase North Gordon from my soul.

Tears now gentled the encounter into calmness.
Slowly and beautifully,
the voice I heard was that of the Creator,
the Provider,
in speech that transcends words.
I heard the same voice we all hear
when we walk past fear and come home.
The Provider whispered one message to me.
Healing. Mending.
Knitting lost parts together.
Reweaving the basket of living
in my heart, in the world's heart.

Letting the wind carry away the old bitterness.
Letting the sounds change groaning to song.
Coming home.
My home. The home of us all.
Through the terror into the tenderness
that alone makes all creation whole.

The Cherokee word *nowehtee*, which means "healing," came to me. It is a word that means healing above, within, and without. This word now so gently became the Provider's word to me. The tensions that had found their way into my body drained away.

I made my way now to the narrow ledge behind the power plant. So much had happened here long ago. Accepting the memories was a giving up I had long needed. The ledge behind the power plant, partly graded and partly covered with gravel and shiny, broken quartz, provided the surface on which I stood as I looked out over the river. I wore moccasins—what else could I wear on my first trip back? I felt the gravel and the quartz stone through the leather.

My feet began looking for the spot, the one spot they would never forget, the spot that, since Pop died, I had always avoided: the "remembering spot." Here Pop had told me stories, sang the old songs, and said the old prayers. He had told me that if I returned to that spot anytime in my life I would remember. It had taken me nearly thirty-five years to return and remember. The picture memories emerged like a 3-D film. My grandfather had taught me a different way of remembering, a remembering so complete that it brings the past into the present.

I saw the angels now dancing in the sky
(seeing angels was not new to me),
dancing that special dance
to heal the wounded of this earth.
These angels had always danced at North Gordon.

All the angels I had seen as a child
danced in the sky in one circle.
I knew why they danced.
They danced so that all who had been mercilessly killed
would be healed.
They danced so that this land—
this soil, these rocks, this water, and this sky
that make the world in which we live, our earth—
might have the healing salve put upon hurts
and be made whole.
They danced so that hatred would be transmuted to compassion
and that all which was lost would be restored.

Their dance was their prayer.
Their chant was their appeal.
They danced and chanted for restoration.
Their dancing and their singing were a keening, grieving cry
that came from reality's most basic center.
In the heavenly melody, joy and mourning,
keening and jubilation, blended into one sound.
The angels mourned for what we have lost
and what we are still losing.
Without pretense,
their voices embraced the anguish of stark loss
as they chanted of coming hope.
The dance and the prayer blended to drum in that hope,
to invoke it.

In the song,
I felt each molecule of my being
and each thread of this world
join in that yearning and hope.

Each breath of all that breathed
called in the remaking.

Part of our Cherokee prayer has been for the remaking of tobacco. Traditionally, tobacco has been sacramental, something holy to Native people, not something to be abused. The prayer of remaking sums up our yearning for renewal. Pop used to blow smoke from his pipe and wave the pipe until the smoke circled my head in blessing as he prayed a prayer for tobacco's remaking, which was really the remaking of us all.

Now it seemed for a moment that the whole world was tobacco, and we gathered in one chant for its remaking. The prayer came to me from the sky, the very stones, and my heart. I do not remember well the words of Pop's remaking prayer, but this prayer came to me on the bluff, and it is like his prayer.

"I am remaking tobacco,
I am remaking it with my own hands,
I am remaking tobacco,
I am remaking it with my own hands,
And I will be remade.
I am remaking tobacco,
I am remaking it with my own hands,
And we will be remade."

I chanted, I danced,
I sang until all this passed through me
and the stillness came.

My eyes turned to the water,
where a Native man emerged,
reaching from water to sky, like Tecumseh arising,
like the Iroquoian peace prophet Degandewidah emerging.

The figure of Christ,
as though newly immersed by John the Baptist,
bursting up from the surface
after he had gone under to honor the water.
Before me, filling all from water to sky,
was a face that spoke defiance,
defiance of all that enslaves and demeans,
and that blessed twin of defiance, compassion.
This comfort-bearing face
commanded in its firmness this saint's visage in deerskin.

Words for what I am trying to convey
are arrows that have no stone tip
and no guiding feathers.
They can never hit a rabbit dead in the center.
They will never hit a tree and stick in it.
You could shoot a quiver in a minute
and not stick and hit what you want to stick and hit.
All you can do is point in a direction with words.
You shoot off many, hoping enough will come near.
How close and familiar was that face.
How like home I found those eyes.
How well known were those injured palms.
How many times had I placed my hands in them?
Still, how could you know that face?
How could you touch those palms?
How far could you ever look into those eyes?
This face, so fully Native,
has graced the bare living rooms of so many
who had no other face to turn to for comfort.
Both face and prayer, jesu ducis memoria.
Some see the face as white,

sometimes as African,
sometimes as Asian.
I saw the face as Native.
I knew that face better than any other face,
and hardly knew at all.
That which was most Native
became that which is most biblical.
The face of the one who is the brother of everyone
was the most Native to me.

The light faded into a rose sunset in the west lands,
the place of saints and mystery.
I remained a long time.
The old stories and old mysteries blended into stillness.
This voice that speaks without words
gave me the message to give others.
What is the experience of the holy
but raw fear, mingling with raw comfort,
a mingling that consoles as it enchants.

On my way back from the bluff, back through the corridor to my car,
I stopped by the empty lot where my grandparents' mill shack had
once stood. I faced the river and said a prayer I had always known.

"I honor this water,
I honor this house,
I honor this soil,
where long ago my soul was aborning."

I said this four times, then seven, the number of invocation, and ended
with this prayer:

"You who live in the sunlands
envelop my soul in your sunrays . . .
you who live above . . ."

Like a young man who had just consummated his marriage with a long-awaited beloved, I had finally made my trip to North Gordon. I had long feared that trip, and I had long desired to make it. Finally, I had set up housekeeping with my mystery. Setting up housekeeping with another is a most fearful thing to do.

I had reached my remembering spot. I knew that after this experience I would have to speak, shy though I am, about things private and close. I knew I would have to tell of my pain, for pain and vision are forever entwined and mutually born from each other.

To do this, I needed more than the encounter with mystery on North Gordon. I needed a human voice to tell me it was time, the voice of an old man who also knew North Gordon's mysteries. He alone could confirm my memories. His voice alone could tell me when to tell this story. He died on Easter of 1996, two months before I wrote this book.

That man was my father. Before his death at age eighty-five, my father told me many of the old stories again, plus some I had never heard before. The telling was hard for him. When he recounted what was good, it meant that he had to remember again what was bad—the times when he was little and the boys taunted him and his grandmother, the time racists ran him and his family out of the north Georgia town of Arigon because of their less-than-pure-white pedigree. In the days just before his death, when he told me to get out the tape recorder and that he would tell me everything, I remember him tossing in his nightmares, mumbling the phrase the boys threw at him when he was little: "Dirty, rotten half-breed." Reliving the pain was his price for telling and remembering. Some scars remained until the end.

That's why we walk slowly into remembering, pace at a time. Even if we want it to, our remembering will not come in a flash.

Remembering is more like peeling an onion. One layer comes off, then another, until finally we come to the core. That kind of remembering is an extended work.

vision journey

This chapter and the following chapter take you on a long journey of remembering and experiencing. You may want to go through these prayer journeys and exercises many times, and each time you will likely give different answers and experience different scenes. You will seek your primary remembering spot and also those other remembering spots that contain the memories that shaped you.

Prudence plays a role in these journeys of memory. Pace yourself. Go through these exercises only as often as you are comfortable. You'll have an inner sense of the pace that is right for you.

Conversational prayer is the best companion for a journey of remembering. We can always talk to God, pour out our fears, give thanks for our joys, abandon ourselves to God's leading, ask for God's protection. We can always stop and converse with God in the midst of any spiritual practice.

Prayer

Dear God,
as I take these steps
on my journey of remembering,
I ask that you walk with me.
Take my hand in yours.
Guide my thoughts;
help form my feelings.
Remember with me.

You remember each of my breaths,
each hair of my head,
each hurt,
each joy.

When my memory is fogged,
remind me of my story,
for you hold the picture album of my life
in the depths of your bosom.
You are the keeper of my steps,
the holder of the picture album of my life,
the opener of my doors.

Protect me each moment of this journey.
Let your light, your holy angels, surround and defend me.
May your angels protect me, above, below, around, and inside.
Guide me at the right pace,
both into grieving and into the hallowed cloud of the holy
that is ever lit with your light.
Amen.

Guided Vision: Finding Your Own Remembering Spot

The following guided vision takes you to a special spot of remembering. Each time you pray this meditation, you may go to a different spot and have fresh insights. Eventually, you may find a central spot, a most basic place, and move into the core of all your feeling and knowing.

Put on some quiet music, and relax in a comfortable position. Let the chair or floor support your weight. Sense how the chair or floor holds you and grounds you. In that same way, God supports and grounds you. Sense how God, even now, supports your whole being, physical and spiritual. Have a sense that God's love surrounds you as a subdued and warming light. You breathe in the warmth and breathe out anxiety and tension.

It's time in your guided vision to talk to God. Name some of your anxieties, giving them a short tag such as "financial worry" or "relationship worry," whatever is causing tension. Actually enflesh your prayer, moving your lips gently.

Let the sense of peace that comes from giving over your worry to God surround you and carry you into that stillness that makes memory possible.

Now it is time to go to a place, a special place, where you know you will remember. That place is within you. It will come to you because it is part of you. Several images of places may float by; then one will come strongly to you. Let this happen.

When you settle on your place, go there in your mind's eye. Even if you do not picture vividly, just having a sense of it is enough. Knowing is more important than seeing.

Have a sense that Jesus—or, if you are not Christian, an angel or the presence of God—stands beside you at your remembering spot, touching your shoulder with a hand, making it safe to remember.

Remember whatever memories of the holy come to you at your remembering spot, whether those memories occurred at that spot or not. Being at the remembering spot helps all your memories emerge.

Remember those holy times. Let the sounds, the feelings, the smells return.

Stay with this part of the meditation as long as you remember.

Did any painful memories return? If so, slightly moving your lips, name them and tell them to the God of all comfort.

Did holy memories of sacred experiences come to you? If so, name them one at a time, saying, "I thank you, God" after each one you name.

Writing

You may want to start writing immediately—or later—after the previous guided vision. These are writing exercises you can return to often. You will be surprised at the different answers you get from using these tools many times.

Complete the following sentences three different ways. Write quickly.

"My remembering place came to be because . . ."
"My remembering place reminds me of God because . . ."
"The most vivid vision I remembered in this meditation was . . ."
"The most painful loss that came to mind was . . ."
"The most joyful time that came to mind was . . ."

remembering

visions

BURIED IN EACH OF US ARE TREASURES. WITHIN OUR HEARTS IS A MULTI-
corridored sanctuary of sacred art. In it we find statues, icons, sacred
music, sacred sights. These are the memories of a lifetime of sacred
experience. That sanctuary is a special place; the beauty of it can
transform our lives right now.

   To use these treasures we must first remember them. For most of us,
this is not easy. Many of the corridors of this sanctuary have locked
doors. Even in the corridors that are open, the paintings and icons
have drapes over them so that we do not see the sacredness of their
images. Inside this art sanctuary are sounds, but we've closed off our
ears to the music.

HOW A WOMAN REMEMBERED HER TREASURES

The elderly lady who sat by herself near the door of the retreat house where I led the weekend program did not need to tell me she needed someone to talk to. The pain and weariness etched on her face spoke loudly of that need. She might have been as young as eighty but in all likelihood was pushing ninety.

Her name was Nora. I made a point of going directly to her and speaking to her during every break. I sat with her at lunch. She said little, but finally she asked if I would pray with her during the afternoon break. She said she had a special need.

We went into the retreat leader's office. Once Nora started to speak, the words came out in torrents.

For ten years she had been a core member of her parish's Bible study group. She gave the teaching every third week and served as official greeter, welcoming new members, spending time with those who needed someone to listen.

Then the core group of the Bible study "retired" her from her positions. Her teachings were too spiritual, they said. They wanted intellectual and practical presentations. The parish was growing, young couples were joining every month, and the Bible study was growing. The core group wanted all the teachers to be younger professionals. They wanted a greeter who could appeal to all the new arrivals.

This shattered Nora. As she talked, it became clear that the Bible study had become her whole social life. She had never married. Though she once had many relationships, most of her cousins and friends had died more than a decade before. No one from the old times was left. No family was left. Her whole sense of belonging had been tied to the core group. The Bible study had become her place to love and serve. She had been needed, wanted there. Now she felt rejected and alone.

I wished that there was some way I could intervene and make her situation right, but I knew I couldn't change things. I couldn't prevail on the core group to reverse its decision, and I wasn't even able to give Nora any strategies to repair her friendships. All I could offer was my presence.

As I listened, it became clear to me what a tender and sweet soul she was. Her vocal intonations, even when she spoke of her hurt, carried tenderness and nearness to God in their rhythms and sounds. As she talked, her face grew mellow, almost beatific. I had no doubt that a deep and true holiness abided in her.

I told her what I felt: "Whatever problems you are having now, I see God in your eyes. Even in the midst of the mess you are telling me about, I can see that God loves in you richly. I just want to sit at your feet awhile and listen to some of the ways God has touched you."

Her face brightened at my words. Her voice grew motherly. She told me story after story of how God helped her through the lonely times, helped her care for her own aging parents years ago. She spoke of all the ways God had come to her in her prayers, her dreams, her visions.

As she talked, she lost any sense of self-consciousness. I'm sure she told me things she had never told anyone else.

She spoke of an abiding sense of God that would often bubble up in her as she did her housework. She told of how God filled her with compassion many years ago when she was still physically able to help with her church's soup kitchen.

She told of dramatic and wondrous visions. I was not surprised. She spoke of a time, five years before, on her annual retreat, when she woke in the night and saw Mary standing over her, smiling on her, pouring a bright and wondrous light around her. Her vivid meetings with the holy were many. Her practical wisdom about living came out in her conversation too.

In just listening to her, I felt I had made a pilgrimage to some holy, special place. I thought of what a treasure her core group and her parish were missing by moving her out of their mainstream.

And in telling her story, Nora had somehow moved away from her pain.

I pointed this out to her as we got ready to part after our time together. I told her that in our blessed and graced conversation she had reached a remembering spot. She had journeyed to a place near the horizon where she could see the treasures that God had scattered throughout her life. I reminded her that she could call up those treasures at any time. "Take time to remember with God. You never remember by yourself. God always remembers with you. And when you remember you make new pathways for God to touch you afresh."

I suggested she keep a journal and write in it every day to make concrete her scattered thoughts and feelings by writing of the ways God had been meeting her throughout her life.

Nora's situation was tinged with sadness. She deserved friends; she deserved people who would cherish her. She was a treasure that no one was looking to find. I couldn't fix it; I could only encourage her to remember—and to periodically allow God to take her to the horizon, where she could see the many blessings that had been showered on her.

WHY WE NEED TO REMEMBER

Nora is typical of most of us. Within our memories are many moments when God has come and offered us wonder, mystery, and beauty. But the chatter in our minds, the stresses of living, and the busy intensities of our days prevent many of those meetings with God from fully blossoming. Though God always knocks at the doors of our heart, we rarely open up fully, rarely let our visions be born, because we live on the surface of life.

Another reason our sacred experiences often fail to emerge completely is that the wonders we find all around us are repressed. We cannot tell our stories of wonder to others: our educational system discounts them, and our churches offer little opportunity to share our graced moments with others. Therefore, we stop telling them to ourselves. We push them under the surface and thus miss their hallowed help. God's light comes to us. Saints and angels touch our lives. But we all too quickly exile those emerging times of awareness into the shadows.

Older cultures were wiser. They considered taking time for memory a sublime spiritual practice. St. Augustine would often stop in the middle of his sermons and call on people to remember what God had done for them. Our ancestors understood that much of the healing effect of visions comes long after they occur. God delivered Israel from slavery in Egypt, and in the near-countless years since, Israel constantly remembers what God did. In the remembering, the full meaning continues to emerge and blossom into ever new understandings.

Visions energize us through memory. Remembering the visions of a lifetime helps link together God's works in our individual history, shows us God's healing ways in the present, and points toward our future. Memory can be subversive. When we recollect a hallowed past, when we invoke moments of timelessness, the sacred invades us afresh, subverting the stale present and opening possibilities we haven't even thought of. When we open ourselves to the mightiness of it all, we are able to overturn the constraints put upon us by a society that long ago abandoned the sacred.

Yet all of this remembering is very difficult for us. Our high-pressure jobs and full schedules cause us to stuff as much as possible into any one day, leaving us little time for memory. This modern shift into a high-pressure way of life has been dramatic. Many of us are just one or two generations removed from farm people who were close to the rhythms of nature. Their very work gave them time for silence, for remembering. Their way of life was much closer than ours to the world of the scribes who wrote the Bible—a world suffused by memories of what God did in the life of his people.

Remembering is a form of prayer. St. Bonaventure, the great Franciscan scholar, talked about sacred memory's power to draw us close to the eternal:

The memory is an image of eternity, whose indivisible presence extends to all times. . . . Memory has an unchangeable light present to itself in which it remembers immutable truths. And so from the activities of the memory, we see that the soul itself is an image of God and a likeness so present to itself and having God so present that the soul actually grasps him and potentially is capable of possessing him and of being a partaker in him.[1]

The reality we invoke when we remember visions is the reality that God's kingdom is breaking into our lives.

HOW TO REGAIN HALLOWED MOMENTS

We have all had times, I am certain, in the midst of a dream, in the midst of sleep, when the light of heaven flowed over us. We have at times been touched by stillness that is profoundly alive. There have been times when we were in anguish and a nurturing comfort, far beyond ourselves, comforted us.

Most of us, I believe, have tasted truly exceptional moments: perhaps vivid visions of Christ or one of the saints or angels coming to us in our sleep or upon waking. But we live in a culture that does not teach us to remember; instead, in so many ways it conspires to teach us to forget. We bury our moments of anguish and hide them, and we just as easily bury our moments that are sacred.

Rediscovering these treasures within us is part of our calling to experience our visions. This kind of remembering takes time and effort. It is helpful to keep several principles in mind as you proceed.

First, remembering requires a certain detachment. Often we can only appreciate the beauty of God's work in our lives with the perspective and distance that time gives us. The scenes of our lives are like pictures done in rough mosaic. The picture they form cannot be seen unless we stand some distance off.

In fact, the process of working with visions is similar to psychotherapy. Therapy involves a retelling of the negative aspects of our story until we trim them down to size—until the painful times no longer weigh down heavily and we can see our strengths. We tell the traumas to others and ourselves until they lose their fearsomeness and no longer overwhelm us. With detachment comes wisdom.

Second, our memories are meant to be integrated into our present lives. In societies closer to their sacred roots, the process of life healing means weaving the visions and transcendent moments into the course of life. That should be our goal too. Indeed, visions are part of the process of creating metaphors. Metaphors are stepping-stones, the way our inner heart (our psyche) provides powerful images, pictures, and sounds that help us move into the next phase of life. Metaphors are banners that remake our world.

Part of the process of remembering is returning to our childhood and recapturing the freshness of that forgotten world. The world of childhood is much closer to the spiritual world than is the world of adulthood.

A friend passed the following story on to me. A woman had just brought her newborn baby home from the hospital. She had a three-year-old daughter, who had anxiously waited for the arrival of her new sibling. The three-year-old made an unusual request. She wanted to spend some time alone with the new baby in the bedroom. At first the mother was hesitant, but then she agreed, leaving on the voice intercom in the bedroom so she could monitor what happened. When the three-year-old was alone with her sibling, she asked, "Please tell me about God, because I'm beginning to forget."

Many people who closely study young children find that the children are filled with sacred experiencing and vivid awareness of God, often sacred scenes they see inside themselves or outside themselves. Society breeds this awareness out of us. But inside, buried by years of repression, remain the bright traces and fragments of early, inborn sacred envisioning.

The best way to start remembering is to ask God's help. Asking God's help with honesty is the best beginning place for any phase of a spiritual journey. It is an absolute essential for a true vision quest. Asking means we need the help of God's Spirit. God holds every breath, every thought in the mind.

We cannot pressure ourselves to remember. Memory cannot be forced. Memory comes when we feel safe, when we have space, and when we feel secure, at ease in the sacred. Many of us have the illusion, fostered by pop psychology, that our minds remember literally everything that we ever experience. Actually, it's a bit different from that. Remembering and forgetting are two sides of the same coin. We fill our daily lives with so much data, so many bits of information: our breathing, traffic noise, all sorts of sounds, all sorts of movements. Our brains would not have the space or the energy or the time to remember everything. If we remembered literally everything—every honk of the horn in traffic, every time we rolled up the window, every time we tapped our foot—we wouldn't be remembering anything. We would just be flooded, every time we tried to remember, with disconcerting stimuli from every direction. Part of memory is forgetting— forgetting the nonessential and remembering the essential.

When it comes to remembering our sacred experiences, it's not as though each time we remember them the memory will somehow be the same. A sacred experience is not a onetime event; it's a seed planted within us. And each time we take out the seed, it has changed; it grows from seed to plant embryo, from embryo to seedling, from seedling to young plant. Each time we look at it, it develops more fully; new insights are born—just as insights from a four-thousand-year-old memory of slaves delivered from Egypt continue to emerge.

We never remember by ourselves alone. We remember with God, who holds each footstep, each heartbeat in memory. Whatever we forget, God remembers. In touching God, we touch God's memory— and God's memory of us, which God holds perfectly.

HOW TO DETECT FORGOTTEN VISIONS

When I lead seminars on sacred experiencing, I usually don't like to ask direct questions; that's a way of leading people. I open the floor and say, "Tell me about some of the experiences you might have had." I just sit back and let people speak.

It's remarkable how many people have maintained a conscious memory of experiencing God's love through the symbol of light. Last year, during a series of talks at my parish, I mentioned that in the early church it was common for people to experience their loved ones, gone to God, coming to them in dreams surrounded by light. At that moment several hands came up. More than one-third of the group had experienced sleeping or waking visions of sacred light.

Here are some other signs of forgotten memories.

Fascination. When you read or hear about a certain type of vision, when you see pictures of it in art, hear stories of that vision, you feel a fascination, an immense attraction to that particular vision, a fascination that comes from deep inside you.

At-homeness. Sometimes a description of a certain type of vision or mystical experience gives you a sense of homecoming. You say to yourself, "I've been there before." Your familiarity can be a clear indication that you have experienced a similar vision or have begun to experience a similar vision and blocked it. This happens with other kinds of memories too. Perhaps you see a TV special about the neighborhood you grew up in or you read a story about your alma mater, some place important to your life. Just seeing such a place or hearing about it calls up familiar feelings, a gut feeling that this place belongs to you and that you belong to this place.

In the same way, at-homeness may flood your soul when a sacred encounter is depicted that is similar to an encounter you once had. You may not be able to place it immediately, but you have the sense that you have experienced the same vision. This is familiar ground.

That familiarity relaxes and warms you even as it fascinates you. You have an interior homecoming.

Tip-of-the-tongue experience. Another sign that you have at one time experienced a certain kind of vision is what I call the tip-of-the-tongue experience. Something jars your memory, and there's the sense that something holy, long forgotten, happened in your past. It's on the tip of your tongue, as though you can almost remember it and what it was like, but it doesn't quite come to you. You recall just a fragment of memory, a sight or feeling, a tone or sound, and you can almost name it, almost call it up, but it eludes you. Perhaps at one time in your life you started to have a depth moment, a sacred encounter, and you repressed it. Sometimes when you begin to remember, the experience forms itself again, slowly in muted form, or perhaps in full form. The seed of it has always remained inside you, waiting to be uncovered.

Have you ever tried to remember the name of an old classmate or friend, perhaps the name of a town or other geographic location? But no matter how hard you try, it doesn't come to you? You forget about it for a while, relax, get a good night's sleep, and then sometime during the next day, unbidden, it comes to you in a flash. That's how it is with remembering visions. The memory can be almost there, but it just doesn't come immediately. Take some time, move on to something else, and usually you'll be surprised that the memory will surface on its own, a few hours to a day later.

Remaining fragments. Another way you can know that you have had certain kinds of spiritual experience is that fragments of it often bubble up from your deep memory. Spiritual experiences leave lasting changes and impressions in your soul. Sometimes a fragment pushes up to consciousness, and unbidden freshness and wonder burst into you. Its origins puzzle you, but it's a glimpse, a smell, a sight that once brought you eternity for a moment, and it now rushes to the surface. The world seems utterly new, and at the same time you are reminded of something long ago you can't quite put your finger on. The experience is completely real, but it has no apparent theme. Through prayer and remembering, the full memory will often surface, bringing some sort of help to you.

Visions you've always had. Let's not forget the obvious. You should spend sufficient time remembering and reflecting on visions you know you have always retained vividly. Often we give too little attention to those memories. St. Augustine spent a lot of time remembering God's sacred interventions in his life. In the permissive atmosphere of God's presence, he spoke out his pain, his sin, and vividly recounted God's many presences and their long incubations within his soul.

We so rarely give thanks for what God does for us. As you work with sacred memories, think of the love that is behind the memories. That love is still with you. Each of our experiences has its own personality, though ultimately there is one love that is the author of all our experiences. Take a moment to let God's peace settle over you.

Think of a time when love stilled you and comforted you. This love could be from God directly or from God through other people. It doesn't matter if it's a dramatic spiritual experience or one of those equally important quiet and ordinary times.

Perhaps your mind turns to family gatherings, early memories of the times others cherished you. All our loves truly come from the one Lover. All our loves participate in the one love that embraces creation. Allow those times of being loved to sweep over you and bring you to a great stillness. Think of the feelings you had. *Feel* the feelings. Carry yourself through the event in your life at the time it occurred. What was happening to you then? Relive, remember.

Look at your life after the experience. How did it change you? Take time for remembering.

GIVING THE PAINFUL TIMES TO CHRIST

As you take a journey in memory, you may remember some of your painful times. We remember the times God has loved us, the times

God has touched us. We draw close not only to our most joyful mysteries but also to our painful ones. Joyful and painful mysteries entwine around each other. When we remember one, we remember the other.

> The essence of Jewish religious thinking does not lie in entertaining a concept of God but in the ability to articulate a memory of moments of illumination by His presence. . . . Reminders of what has been disclosed to us are hanging over our souls like stars, remote and of mind-surpassing grandeur.[2]

In your imagination, stretch out your palms and allow Christ to place his palms into them. Close your eyes and have a sense of Christ placing his palms on your palms. Feel the love and comfort surround and heal you. If you need to let the tears come, take a moment. There is no need to hunt and search for the painful times; they will come on their own if they need to. For, often, when we are embraced in the comfort that sacred memories bring, deep inside we feel safe enough to let go of the hurts. Take a moment of silence, and if such times come up within you, do what the psalmists in the Old Testament did: Name your hurt and give it to God.

Within a courtship most couples experience timeless moments. Marriages can grow cold and nearly die if couples forget to remind each other about those special moments of first love. Recalling those times comforts them after an argument or during a season of strain. Remembering the times when togetherness opened into the everlasting and the world appeared charged with newness is essential for a marriage to stay healthy. Recovery together after a tragedy or a loss almost always entails memory, memory of obstacles endured or overcome, memory of tears and laughter.

Our relationship with God can grow dry too, when we stop remembering those moments of loving encounter. You will find that in remembering the times you've always remembered, and giving thanks for those times, you're opening the door to many more memories. The more we remember the past's holy perceptions, the more we attune ourselves and ready ourselves for those perceptions in the future, the more we become a finely tuned instrument, ready for the Master's hand.

v i s i o n   j o u r n e y

Our vision journey will be a trip into memory. You will find that your memories don't come all at once. Memory is a funny thing, for at the moment we try hard to remember, we don't remember, and then later on it just comes to us. You may find that you remember very little as you first go through these exercises, but a few hours later, or perhaps as much as a day later, you may find yourself flooded with memories. You may find that suddenly there is a bright smell, a bright taste, a bright bit of a scene, a fragment of a dream from the time God has touched you. Sometimes you will have full memories that will emerge as you are going about your day. Sometimes it will be just a fragment of what once was, a fragment that leads you to give thanks. But whatever your memories, they will be reminders to you of how God has always been with you.

Prayer: Remembering a Vision

Repeat the following prayer slowly. Actually move your lips to slow yourself down. If at any time a sacred quiet comes over you, pause, give in to it as long as it lasts, then continue.

God, in my busyness,
in the intensity of my living and my work,
I have forgotten many of the times
you have fanned me with your very breath,

the times you have comforted me,
letting me sink into your cushioning embrace,
the times the touch of your hand has sent warmth through me,
the times you have shown me a glistening horizon,
the times you have blessed me with hallowed mystery.

Guide me now on this journey of remembering.
Help me remember in a manner that is good for me.

Help me remember that which I have pushed down inside me,
that which has been clouded over, forgotten.
Dear God, sometimes I feel you near,
more present to me than I am to myself.
Other times you are a distant thought,
a barely conceived reality.
Whatever my feelings or my thoughts,
you have always walked close to me.

You remember each breath.
You hold in memory my every heartbeat.
You carry each of my sorrows.
You remember when I cannot remember.
Help me remember now.

Help me remember the quiet moments you stole upon me.
Help me remember the dreams long forgotten, in which your radiance
shone more clearly than all earthly brightness.
Remind my soul of visions in dreams mostly forgotten.
Guide my heart in this journey of recollection.
As I sleep this night, fill my dreams with remembering and
my morning with recollection.

Guided Vision: The Picture Show

Sit down and make yourself comfortable; you might put on some calming music, such as Gregorian chant, sounds of the sea, or other sounds from nature. Allow yourself to relax and rest in God's love. To prepare to experience God's love, think of some of the times you've felt love—God's love or the love of another person. Just let your mind drift back to those times.

Become aware of your breathing. Notice the breathing in and the breathing out. Sense God's comfort around you, like a blanket, a warmth that absorbs stress and fear and pain. It's time now to see and sense the soft, quiet light surround you.

In the comfort of God's touch you can begin to remember. When you see moments of God breaking into your life's story, pause and allow your senses to fill with the remembering.

Look at your life on an old-fashioned, drive-in-theater screen.

The Picture Show presents a scene from your infancy.
> Let the memory of a spiritual experience from your infancy emerge.

The Picture Show now presents a scene from your toddler years.
> Let the memory of a spiritual experience from your toddler years emerge.

The Picture Show now presents a scene from your grammar school years.
> Let the memory of a spiritual experience from your grammar school years emerge.

The Picture Show now presents a scene from your junior high years.
> Let the memory of a spiritual experience from your junior high years emerge.

The Picture Show now presents a scene from your high school years.
Let the memory of a spiritual experience from your high
school years emerge.

The Picture Show now presents a scene from your young adulthood.
Let the memory of a spiritual experience from your young
adulthood emerge.

The Picture Show now presents a scene from your middle-age years.
Let the memory of a spiritual experience from your middle-
age years emerge.

The Picture Show now presents a scene from your senior years.
Let the memory of a spiritual experience from your senior
years emerge.

Now picture that you're sitting in a beautiful field, a wonderful light
surrounding you. That light is God's presence. Christ comes to you,
and Christ is bearing a beautifully wrapped gift. You look at Christ's
eyes, and you know how much he loves you.

He presents the gift to you, and you know what the gift is: It's a picture of yourself after you have just experienced a sacred moment, a
sacred moment from your past.

Look at your face, at your eyes and expression, after you experienced this sacred moment. Now that you have seen the effect, let the
memory come fully alive to you. Recall the details. Go further now
into the stillness and hear these words as God's words to you, a prayer.
Read it while slightly moving your lips:

"My embrace has always encompassed you. I have always dwelled
in the innermost reaches of your heart. I have offered myself to you at
every moment as the comforter who quiets your troubles. I have
touched you with touches, unbearable in their tenderness. I created
the earth with its storms, its sunshine, the winds, and the changes and

undulations they carry in their movement, hints of eternity. I likewise inspire the undulations of your heart and come to you in the waves of your memory."

Writing

Write down ten of the most important visions of your lifetime, writing quickly to trick the inner censor.

We not only remember our visions but also work with them, uncovering their riches. You can use this exercise often, picking a different vision each time or, at times, working further with one vision.

Pick one of the visions you've already written down. Complete the following sentences three different ways:

"What I most learned from this vision was . . ."
"Recalling this vision enables me to . . ."
"Through my remembering this vision, God continues to say to me that . . ."

Writing: Dialoguing with Your Vision

Remember when we said that through writing we could dialogue with important symbols in our lives? We can also dialogue with events. In fact, the important events in our lives become symbols, as do the visions. The deliverance of Israel from Egypt was both an event and Israel's central symbol.

A good technique is to write up the dialogue as though it were a movie script, with lines for each participant in the dialogue. Of course, both parts of the dialogue are from you. At first it may seem strained, but keep the pencil moving. Soon that pencil will start moving swiftly as you contact that more hidden part of yourself that is both knowing and more in tune with God.

Here is a sample of my own dialogue with my vision of light as a junior high student:

Eddie: Vision, why did you come to me?

Vision: Eddie, I came to you because I heard you crying and I could not stay away. I had to let you know that God was near.

Eddie: Why didn't you make everything all right?

Vision: If I made everything all right, there wouldn't be room for faith. God wants partners who join hands with God in healing this world. If I made everything all right, you wouldn't be you. You wouldn't learn, decide, grieve, grow, and love. You wouldn't be a unique image of God. You would be like a motionless plant hanging from the ceiling. You wouldn't grow into being a partner.

Eddie: Was God in you, my vision, or did it just come from me?

Vision: God was in me, your vision. God built you, made you, to tune in to the nuances of God's presence. God really dried your tears in me, your vision. God really gave you hope. God really talked to you. And I, your vision, came also from you. God delights in mediation, and your humanity, your memory, your body, and your imagination mediated God to you in an unconscious way through me, your vision. Eddie, what do I mean to you now?

Eddie: You mean that no matter how much I feel like a failure, no matter how often I pull out an inner switch and switch myself for my failings, you tell me that God loves me and that God will make alive all that is worthwhile in me, if I will but let God.

In the same vein, dialogue now with the vision you have selected. Here are some suggested questions for the dialogue, but once you get going you will find that they spontaneously come to you. Go on with the dialogue as long as you like.

You: Vision, why did you come to me?

Vision: (Fill in the reply.)

You: What was the most important thing you taught me?
Vision:
You: What can you show me now?
Vision:

Continue with the questions and answers that come to you in the dialogue, writing your own questions and answers.

Ancient exercises like these journaling techniques help prime the pump and get the flow going within. Our capacity for vision has atrophied. We are getting the flow going with techniques so that the part of us that knows and senses God will come to life again and so that we can greet God's nearness through the varied moments of our day.

Prayer

Dear God,
thank you for touching me
in the sacred scenes I just relived.
Thank you for these times of intimacy,
these times of touch,
these times that connected me
with you and all that you love,
that connect me with your earth,
with your people, with life.

PART 3

the healing power
of visions

O gentle hand! O delicate touch, which has the taste of

eternal life!

—ST. JOHN OF THE CROSS

The capacity for visions that God placed in each of

us is one of our primary means of healing. Visions

heal the wounded parts of our spirits. They heal our

families. They heal our communities. Our ancestors

understood this. We need to learn again to let wonder

heal us, for it is God's way.

The vision way of healing takes a different path from most psychotherapy. Instead of emphasizing catharsis through experiencing pain, visions cause us to entertain memories of wonder and holy encounter. They allow us to spiral upward, to transcend limitations and enter the realm of unheard-of possibility. In the midst of the bright cloud of safety that wonder brings, we become strong enough to let go of our painful memories. The wisdom of visions places great emphasis on remembering wonder.

CHAPTER 1 0

god's therapy

VISIONS ARE NOT AN ESCAPE FROM LIFE'S HURTS. NOR DOES HAVING
visions preserve us from human flaws and failings—a point I will make
repeatedly in this book. They cause us to remember the past—including past hurts. Especially past hurts. As they do, they can speed our
healing by helping release us from the past's painful grip.

A vision did this for me not long ago. I didn't ask for it. I didn't
expect it. It happened at a time when things were going well in my
life. Ironically, a stupendous bit of good news hurled me back into the
grip of past hurts, and it took a vision to rescue me.

I had come home at the end of the day to be greeted with a note
to call a senior editor at a major publisher. I immediately knew what
that meant: They wanted to publish my book *Prayer That Heals Our
Emotions*.

I should have been thrilled. Instead, I felt a chilling fear, a nameless
despair. A raw and primitive grief emerged.

I called the editor and listened to him tell me that the publisher loved my manuscript and was anxious to publish it. He said he would be sending a contract. My voice breaking with hesitation, I said I would consider it.

In the weeks after this call, a nameless unworthiness overwhelmed me. I felt that there had been some kind of mistake. Something in me wanted to turn the publisher down. My friends prevailed, and in a few days I said yes and signed the contract. But a profound, puzzling melancholy stayed with me. Why? It made no sense to me. I had long dreamed of publishing my book. Why should I be afflicted with this sense of worthlessness at a time of great triumph? I was afraid, and I didn't know why. The fact that I didn't know why terrified me.

One night I knelt by my bed, hands folded in front of me, in the childhood posture of prayer. "Show me why, Lord. Show me why I am afraid." Out loud I described the confusing emotions of the previous two weeks.

I fell into a light sleep. I dreamed intermittently. One dream was a scene in junior high school when a group of football players ran over me in gym class. They pushed me to the ground and laughed at me. It was the kind of thing that happened to me many times in school. My way of handling the insult and mockery was always the same. I became numb. I didn't cry, didn't run away. I pretended that what was happening to me wasn't really happening.

But this time it was different. I woke up from my light sleep and began to weep. I let the despair come into my voice. It finally broke through the wall of numbness I had thrown up to defend myself.

Then a vision came in the midst of my dreaming.

Gently I fell into a deeper dreaming.
As I wept, a cloud gathered around me.
A cloud lit with brightness settled around me,
then slowly, gently lifted me, suspending me in the room.

There the cloud cradled and rocked me
as a mother rocks a young child.
The cloud warmed me, warmed even my bones,
for it contained the gentle heat of an eternity of love.

I breathed in the light of the cloud.
The subdued and comforting beauty filled my lungs;
my body's very cells tasted the peacefulness.
My breathing became deep and regular; my heartbeat calmed.
The light absorbed my tears,
drew out the hurt buried deep inside me.

And I heard this, with the heart's hearing:
"I warm you, I heal you, I comfort you.
As a father comforts, as a friend comforts,
as a brother or a sister comforts, so I comfort you.
Come to me always that I may comfort you
with the tenderness that alone can draw out pain."
Eased and rocked back into peacefulness,
I settled into a deep and dreamless sleep.

The vision helped me recall deeply ingrained ways I had come to think about myself. The rejection I encountered as a child had become more bearable when I rejected myself. If I joined in the rejection, no one could say or do anything that would surprise me. The sting of mockery was lessened. This way of coping got me through junior high school. But a profound self-doubt remained with me as an adult. Even though my life was often full of happiness, friends, and love, I felt unworthy much of the time. The despair that afflicted me when my book was accepted for publication was merely an intense manifestation of an underlying problem.

My vision in a dream of God's love coming as a bright, healing cloud pointed toward God's view of me—a man loved, nurtured, and affirmed because I was God's. Neither great success nor great failure tells us who we are. In my vision, I could see that only God could give me my true identity—my identity as God's child.

VISIONS CAN HEAL OUR SPIRITS

Visions have been part of my spiritual healing. Yet that healing has not been a smooth ride but a bumpy trip into the unknown.

Pop psychology and sometimes even Christian self-help materials are too quick to convey that our adult spiritual and emotional healing are clearly and completely understandable. Find the early traumas, deal with them using simple steps, and things should soon be in good order.

My own experience, and I think the experience of the tradition, is that the ways of healing are not that knowable or that much within our control. When it comes to spiritual and emotional issues, we often face unfamiliar territory at every turn. It's like the experiences you had as a child when you were taken to the doctor with an illness or an injury. Healing then was confusing and frightening. The doctor did mysterious things; some of them hurt you. You got a lollipop from the nurse and hugs and kisses from your parents. Then wondrously, in two or three days the soreness went away, and in a few more days the wound was healed.

Our spiritual and emotional healing are similarly mysterious. Healing comes to mean that something is wrong and that powerful others beyond us have to make things better. Hugs and lollipops and caring adults guide us through suffering's great unknowns and through healing that cannot be fully understood.

There is an unknowability to both our pain and our cure. In the midst of this unfamiliar landscape we can only trust, as we did as children, the other who is able to make things better. This other is the mysterious, untamed Comforter of Israel and all humanity. All we can do is give ourselves into God's hands, and much of that healing process will be as mysterious to us as were those childhood doctor visits.

To be in the midst of God's healing is to be in the hands of the skilled physician who knows fully the nature of our hurt and the route to our healing. All along the way, we can taste moments of embrace and assurance that the final word for us will be healing, wholeness, and the mending of heart, the knitting together of that which is broken. Visions can be part of that holy reassurance, the embraces that tell us that our walk in the middle of the painful, mysterious unknown is a walk with a mysterious lover, a mender who is both skilled physician and devoted parent. A walk into healing is a walk of not knowing fully the cause of pain, nor knowing fully the means of cure. It is a walk of trust, guided by mysterious, holy embrace and often illuminated for a while with the gift of vision.

Along the way there can be knowing, but that knowing comes only in relationship with God and after a time. The knowing—the insight—that bursts in is the fitting together of pieces, all coming as a gift. This insight also is vision.

Compassion, the forgetfulness of self, is the only pathway that heals. Visions plant God's compassion within us. They help us look at the whole of life from the perspective of eternity. Visions heal by smashing our isolation and connecting us with all of God's people and creation.

This banishes the sense of inadequacy that is the legacy of past hurts. We try to drive the pain away by attempting to become someone other than who we really are. We see ourselves through clouded lenses. We lose touch with our very soul. And so we need a cleaning of the lenses to see ourselves as God made us and sees us, and we need to let that God who sees us make us whole.

Many people today seek this clarity and release through psychotherapy. The insights and techniques of therapy are often valuable, but we should not, in our rush to embrace the new science of the mind, ignore visions and the older ways of healing. People's hearts were set straight, comforted, healed, and challenged long before the advent of modern psychotherapy.

Many holy figures in our history were healed by visions. Many of them had wounds that are familiar to modern psychotherapists. St. Francis of Assisi had a controlling and abusive father. Francis fled to the glamour of soldiering and warfare, but his dreams of heroism collapsed when he failed at combat and saw war's true nature. Dizzied and in emotional collapse, the young man haunted the caves of Assisi. "The caves reverberated with the sound of his screaming," Francis's biographers tell us. Slowly, visions of God's comfort soothed Francis's heart and filled his inner recesses with God. These vivid healing visions helped him grieve, let go of hurt, and spend his life for the poorest of the poor.

Degandewidah, peacemaker, pacifist, and founder of the Iroquois Confederacy, was a severely abused child. He was left abandoned on the ice as a toddler and suffered permanent brain damage and a speech impediment. In his anguish he turned to the Master of Breath, who comforted him in visions. Through a vision of the great tree of peace, Degandewidah received a call to lead warring tribes into peace.

Among the greatest visionary healers were the prophets of Israel. They gave individuals and society the tools needed to grieve, see afresh, and hope in a different future. Healing was not a lonely journey but one traveled with sisters and brothers. Through the prophets, the whole people of God experienced restoration.

In fact, the prophetic quality of visions is one of their outstanding healing characteristics. To heal, we need to see ourselves through a lens other than the lens of shame and inadequacy we create for ourselves. This clear vision comes when we are met by another who can see past the disappointments and failures to the unique, heaven-made, and God-fashioned us. We need the gaze of another.

That is the function of a prophet. Prophecy not only criticizes but also provides metaphors powerful enough to break through the numbness and articulate the anguish. The chief characteristic of prophecy is not anger but anguish—an anguish that is transformed into a vision of hope.

This kind of visionary healing prophecy is a stark contrast to the pop spirituality of the mall bookstores—the cheery, effortless spirituality of accomplishment, mastery, and success. Prophetic visions are realistic. They offer us symbols equal to the stark horror in our lives, bringing up the dreads and anxieties we have hidden away inside. In the great phrase of the theologian Walter Brueggemann, prophecy provides a way that "the stonewalling can be ended."

BILL'S STORY

Visions helped end the stonewalling for Bill, a friend I've known for many years. Bill was the consummate successful salesman. From the time he was class president in high school, he always seemed sunny and charming. He was always up. And his enthusiasm was contagious.

Bill's charm and energy made him a very successful salesman. He had many jobs. He typically started a new job with the thrust of a rocket blasting off. He would win national sales awards, making up to two hundred thousand dollars a month in commissions. Then, after earning these vast sums, he would lose interest and move on to another job. Bill always put a positive spin on these changes. Bill always exuded that upbeat attitude we Americans so value.

All was not well, however. Bill lived far beyond his means. His lifestyle—the large estate, the horses for each of his three boys, the expensive prep schools, the lavish family vacations—was financed in part by ever expanding credit. Then I heard that Bill had filed for bankruptcy and that he and his wife were in the midst of a trial separation while they sought marriage counseling.

I invited Bill over for dinner, thinking he might need some companionship. During dinner, he never mentioned his problems. Instead he spoke happily about his new sales position selling upscale lots of riverfront property.

After supper I suggested that we listen to a recording of Bach's "Jesu Joy of Man's Desiring." We turned off the lights, lit a vigil candle, and took time for silence. Somewhere near the middle of the music, I heard sobs—something I never expected to hear from Bill. After the music finished, Bill began to talk. Words poured out in a torrent. As Bill told it, behind the smiles and the success stories were dark, deep valleys of depression and addictions to mask the depression. He told a tale of addiction to pornography, vast sums bet and lost on sports events, and one or two extramarital flings. It was a common story, but one I never expected to hear from this man. He now appeared to be the opposite of the persona he had always presented: frightened and despairing instead of energetic and beaming.

I pulled out the Bible and read this verse from Jeremiah, long a favorite of mine:

> O, that my head were a spring of water,
>
> and my eyes a fountain of tears,
>
> so that I might weep day and night. (Jeremiah 9:1)

I told Bill that this place of brokenness could be a good place, a place where God could be found. I said that great people like Jeremiah could know God and still find themselves in seasons of great disloca-tion. Bill wrote the verse down and took it home. He memorized it and said it to himself every day. Like the suffering servant in Isaiah, he became well acquainted with his sorrows. Like Jeremiah, he learned to cry a fountain of tears.

Bill came over to the house often during the next few months. We would put on some sacred music and sit in silent contemplation, and then he could talk about whatever he wanted to talk about. Slowly Bill spoke of what he was discovering about himself during this season of lamentation.

Like so many seemingly high-energy people, Bill found that he was masking lots of hurts he carried from childhood, particularly a father who had used both alcohol and a belt in excess. In his therapy Bill learned that he had a problem with mood swings that might well have some physiological causes. Some mild medication helped. He learned of the need to admit weakness and helplessness. He learned too that depression does not excuse wrongdoing, and he named his addictions and the way he had hurt his family as sin he needed to admit and move away from. Bill's wall of numbness cracked; the pent-up regret and pain now had expression.

Bill's vision began growing inside him. He received symbols, like Jeremiah's image of the fountains of tears, to acknowledge his need and name his pain. After a few weeks, he began to have moments of God's fresh birth. Sunlight shining through the trees seemed like eternity itself breaking through. The sight of a bird foraging in the grass became for Bill a moment of seeing into the very wonder of God. Bright memories of his falling-in-love days with his wife began to surface throughout the day. Bill had been broken. Out of his brokenness, God fashioned a new way of seeing.

Bill gradually changed. He found less need to achieve worldly success. He and his wife reconciled and repaired their marriage. He became more involved in his parish, especially the church's ministry to the poor—a ministry he had always shunned before. Bill got off the roller coaster. He lived a balanced life, graced by the little visions, the daily grievings, the small repentances, and the hourly turnings to God that mark a life lived in the shadow of grace.

Visions like Bill's heal because they contradict hopelessness. The contemporary world not only numbs us to pain but also numbs us to hope. We cannot imagine a different future. Visions energize us with symbols of hope, creating a new sense of what is possible. They give expression to our unspoken yearnings and provide alternatives we never dreamed possible. They change reality.

As Walter Brueggemann said,

The prophet engages in futuring fantasy. The prophet does not ask if the vision can be implemented, for questions of implementation are of no consequence until the vision can be imagined. The imagination must come before the implementation. Our culture is competent to implement almost anything and to imagine almost nothing.[1]

Another Scripture in Isaiah, a vision itself, beautifully sums up this visionary prophetic process:

Even youths will faint and be weary,
   and the young will fall exhausted;
but those who wait for the LORD shall renew their strength,
   they shall mount up with wings like eagles,
they shall run and not be weary,
   they shall walk and not faint. (Isaiah 40:30–31)

VISIONS TIE US TO HISTORY

There's another reason visions bring healing. They tie us to a history. We are not alone in our pain. The visions we receive provide sentiments, images, symbols, and inner mystery plays that connect us to the history of our faith community and link us to the living past.

The pilgrims who journeyed to the great shrines of saints embarked on a journey back into the time when those saints lived. Since saints are imitators of Christ, the pilgrims who visited their shrines journeyed back into the time of Christ. They tied their affections to a saving history with each bodily step, each story exchanged on the road, each tear shed for themselves and others. They seized and appropriated that history as their own. When the grieving gave way to amazement, the story of their lives was tied together with a greater story.

The imaginative meditations so popular during the twelfth through fourteenth centuries pictured Christ's pain, his rising from the dead, and his glory. They tied the reader's inner and outer worlds—self, family, and community—to Christ's history in a passionate way. Visions provided a language that connected the eternal to the present moment and people's inner worlds to their outer worlds.

One key Old Testament passage reminded the people of Israel how they were lifted up and carried out of Egypt as though on eagle's wings. This was a startling reminder of the history these people were called to take into their whole being as their own. That fresh symbol tied them powerfully to their history while opening up to them a whole new future (Exodus 19:4).

Visions cause us to see our personal history differently. The joys, the terrors, the daily drudgery, even the sin are now seen in the light of that which is eternal, awesome, and holy. We see our own history differently as we tie it to the larger history of our faith communities.

Most visions fulfill many, if not all, the functions of prophecy. Visions don't have to be full of bells and lights to be prophetic. Many are like the vision of the great John Wesley. After spending his whole youth in religious struggle, Wesley felt his heart strangely warmed at Aldersgate chapel in London after hearing a homily on justification based on Luther's commentary on Romans. That warming of heart accompanied no great tapestries of imagination. But one predominant mood and metaphor—warmth—emerged. In that one moment the struggling history of Wesley's early life found resolution. A new future—preaching conversion of heart—opened up. All this was tied to a new understanding of his life. The moment of sacred touch tied him to the Scriptures in a new way, bonding him to a saving past. A simple, quiet vision not only changed one man but also changed the future of faith in both England and America. In that moment at Aldersgate we find nothing less than a prophetic vision in all its fullness.

Visions, like prophecy, come at the intersection of past and future, heaven and earth. They herald transformation, a new way of seeing. As Avery Dulles wrote, everyone who comes to believe experiences on some level the inner experience of the prophets. "A felt attraction toward the divine . . . is a necessary condition, I believe, for the prophets, the mystics. . . . In less conspicuous forms, this attraction is an ingredient in the religious life of anyone who comes to believe."[2]

HEALING COMES FROM THE HORIZON

I was very thankful to receive the healing dream of the cloud after the emotional crisis triggered by the promise of my book's publication. As I prayed, words formed in my heart, my own words, giving voice to the message that my encounter with God had planted in my soul. It was a message meant for others as much as for me.

The words came as a modern psalm of healing, and I think it is appropriate to share them here, as a message of visionary healing. It is the promise of God to heal all of us. These words are what I call words from the horizon—a message from that point in the distance where all our images and words meet an utter, eternal, and wordless knowing.

For my Cherokee ancestors, the common prayer of the healer was a prayer formed in the Creator's own voice. A person would go for a purifying dip in a clear stream accompanied by the healer. The healer would stand behind the person and repeat words of comfort as if God himself were saying them.

Read this prayer from the horizon in the same spirit. Imagine that it is God's own message to you, telling of God's nearness and healing touch. Read it slowly, slightly moving your lips, stopping for a moment if you are overcome by a graced quiet.

I am near as the air you breathe in and out,
solid as the earth that supports your feet.
I surprise you with my presence in the depths of your dreams.
In your waking moments I come to you
in the calm that overtakes you when you least expect it,
in the joy that makes your whole world

tingling and bright for a moment,
shining and shimmering for a moment—
with eternity.

I am near also
to the hurting that lies hidden, buried, walled away,
so far within that you forget it is there.
You cannot see or face
the pain of it all in one glance.
So I show it to you as you need to see it,
bit at a time,
in moments when you are ready.
I let you see your wounds
at the pace that is right for you.
At the time that is right for you,
I make it plain.

I am the one who fills your dreaming
with visions of healing,
brightening your dreams with my light,
nurturing you, in your dreams, with my own nurture.
With my comfort, my calm,
I cradle and rock your soul,
suffusing your whole body with an eternal caring.
I surprise you in the daytime with my peace.
I meet your fretting and your fear
with my tender mercy's quiet repose.

I come to you day and night,
stretching my hand to you,
absorbing your fears, your anxieties.
I am the healer who makes you a healer
by healing you.

I am the lover who helps you love
by loving you.
I am the comforter who teaches you to comfort
by comforting you.
I am the parent who dries your tears with my tears.
I am the herald of hope who teaches you to hope
by showing you a different future
in which to hope,
making your life a beacon of hope.

The imagery of my dream vision that preceded this prayer—the image of God's presence in a cloud—provides the basis for the guided vision I will share with you in the next section. The image of the divine cloud is a common biblical image. It tied my hurting and my healing to the history of faith that was my own. It also looks toward a future full of glorious hope.

Isaiah 4 uses the image of God's love as sheltering cloud. It speaks of that eschatological time, that time of consummation and wholeness toward which we all move and that can even now break into our world:

> Then the LORD will create over the whole site of Mount Zion and over
> its places of assembly a cloud by day and smoke and the shining of a
> flaming fire by night. Indeed over all the glory there will be a canopy. It
> will serve as a pavilion, a shade by day from the heat, and a refuge and
> a shelter from the storm and rain. (Isaiah 4:5–6)

Approach the guided vision as an opportunity to be carried through healing pathways. Allow it to prepare you for those spontaneous moments that fill us with wonder, that erupt unbeckoned in our lives.

Slowly repeat the following prayer, several times if needed, until a graced peace comes over you.

Dear God,
sometimes you seem absent,
sometimes present.
Sometimes I remember you well;
sometimes I forget you.
Whatever my feelings,
whatever my thoughts,
you never forget me,
you never run from me,
you are always near.

I give myself to you now.
I abandon myself to your great and good mercies.
I invite you now into my thoughts,
into the imagery of my mind's flow.
I invite you into the root of my being,
the root of my believing and thinking.
I invite you into this, my trip of healing.
I deliver myself over to your mending hands.
Amen.

vision journey

It is possible to find healing in the quiet with God. Here are a few thoughts to help you.

Guided Vision: A Healing Cloud of Love

If possible, lie down on carpet (a bed is too soft; you might fall asleep) with pillows supporting your head.

Allow God's love to bring stillness. Let God's peace flow over you. Have a sense of God as a warm light around you, soothing and calming you, communicating care.

As you rest in God's nearness, pause and sense the beating of your heart.

Attune your soul and your thoughts to your body's rhythmic flow.

Hear these words:

"My love is a salve that can soothe the scars of loneliness.
Sense the beating of your heart.
Listen to its sound,
and you will soon hear my own heart's beating,
for my heart always beats with your heart.
I am always as near as its pulsing,
for I am as close as your breath
and more intimate to you than you are to yourself."

Picture yourself lying down, cradled by carpet or blanket. Become aware of the floor supporting your weight. Just as God supports the weight of your life, the floor supports the weight of your living. Allow God's peace to settle over you, warming and healing you.

Notice your breathing. Each outward breath breathes out fear, negativity, anxiety. Each inward breath breathes in the Holy Spirit. Notice your breathing for a while, breathing out the hurt, breathing in the sacred presence.

After the breathing has begun to calm you, sense God's love filling your physical body. Your arms and your legs grow warm with God's presence. Your muscles relax.

Have a sense of a cloud surrounding you. It is a cloud fearful with God's holiness, yet comforting with God's nearness and protection. It is bright with a healing and subdued light. It surrounds you. You breathe it in. It fills your lungs, your body, with love. It comforts and warms you, bringing a great ease. The cloud gently picks you up, suspending you in the room, in your imagination.

Let your mind flow over your day.
Remember any fears you felt.
As you remember them, name them:
fear of loneliness, fear of failure, any fear at all.
Let them flow out of you
and into God's love as you name them.
Name the angers of the day (slightly moving your lips),
flowing out into God's love, which surrounds you.
Name the insecurities. Name the bitternesses.
Let the cloud absorb all of them.

It may be that deeper fear or insecurity (from long ago perhaps) has surfaced.

Don't reach for it; don't probe for it. Instead, recognize and name it as it surfaces on its own. It's important that your healing come at the right pace and the right moment.

Let the telling and the naming of the pain—and giving it to God— relieve you and take you deeper into God's peace.

Now let the cloud of light comfort you.
Let the light cradle you, rock you.
Rest in the comfort.
Perhaps words of God's comfort form in your heart
or come to your lips.
The cloud glows
with eternity's dazzling brightness
as you float and let the light brighten every bit of your soul
and every cell in your body.
Gently now, the light returns you to the floor

as you finish this guided vision,
this journey of imagination.

Rest for a while in the stillness.

After you have rested in the stillness, make a prayer of thanksgiving in your own words.

CHAPTER 11

the light

returns

WE TOO QUICKLY SEE VISIONS AS SUPERNATURAL WHEN THEY ARE AS ordinary as breathing and as natural as walking. Visions almost always come to us from our humanity, not as miracles—at least not the natural-law-breaking, stupendous, startling kind of miracle of popular imagination. But that does not mean that God is absent from visions. To the contrary, it is usually evidence that God is in them.

I learned this early on. The light that came to me as a boy did not leave me, but it began to speak in a different way, through the voice of fellow humans and through the ordinary circumstances of my life.

VISIONS HAVE DIFFERENT VOICES

There was my high school English teacher, who saw promise in my first essay for class and passed it on to the dean, Margaret Cox. Ms. Cox read it, ignored the messiness and near-illegible handwriting, and saw promise in it. She summoned me to her office, looked at me with a warm intensity, and said:

"When you grow up, you are going to write books that will affect many people. You are a big responsibility for us. You have a gift we need to nourish."

A flesh-and-blood human was speaking the exact same message spoken by God's presence in the brightness when I was thirteen. Those words of Ms. Cox changed my life. With special help and tutoring from her and her friend Helen Shepherd, my grades turned to A's and B's. The attention and love of these women followed me throughout my high school years and beyond.

The yearning to follow after the God who had opened up a pathway in my life grew into a determination to become a Presbyterian minister. I enrolled at Belhaven College, a small Presbyterian school in Jackson, Mississippi, to begin my training. Life blessed me with many close friends. We were a team.

Just when life seemed predictable, even comfortable, the light again interrupted my life. On the way back to school from my hometown of Columbus, Georgia, I stopped at a small Catholic church in Selma, Alabama. It was my first visit to a Catholic church. I sat in a middle pew in the empty church, and an exquisite peace washed over my body and my heart. My face felt the calm and sunshine of a holy nearness. This church felt like no other church I had ever entered, and a different sort of presence settled over me. As I looked at the tabernacle, it was as though Christ reached out from the Blessed Sacrament and kissed my heart. The stillness quieted fear and absorbed anxiety. I rested there for more than thirty minutes. I said to myself, "Eddie, if you don't get out of here soon, you are going to become one of those Roman Catholics."

Drenched in the peace of that moment, I slowly walked toward the back of the church. Just before I reached for the door, I turned and saw the face of a relaxed young priest with his collar undone. I blinked my eyes, and the image was gone. I heard a clear, soft message communicate, without words, this thought: "Here is the helper of a lifetime." A tremble passed through me.

Two weeks later, I met this helper at a youth meeting at Fondern Presbyterian Church in Jackson. A young Catholic priest, Father Bernard Law—now Cardinal Law of Boston—gave a talk on the civil rights movement in Mississippi. It was the first message I'd ever heard given by a Catholic priest. A quiet ease and a warm but solid presence came through this man's whole personality. Halfway through the talk, Fr. Law took off his collar. I was startled; his face was like the fleeting image of the priest I had seen in the church at Selma.

After the talk was finished, he came over to my table for coffee. I swallowed hard and introduced myself. Almost as though he knew what was happening in me, he looked at me with a reassuring steadiness and said, "Eddie, come have supper with me soon at the minor seminary."

The sacred presence, which had come to me in light when I was a young boy, called to me now through the earthly voice of a fellow human. I took Fr. Law up on the offer of supper, and we developed a close friendship. A man long sensitive to the many subtle textures of prayer and God's sacred touch, he became my spiritual adviser and my lifelong mentor.

After graduating from Belhaven, I transferred to Union Theological Seminary in Virginia, then to Austin Presbyterian Theological Seminary in Austin, Texas. As I explored the literature of the great Jewish and Christian mystics, I realized that my growing love of contemplation was leading me slowly to Catholicism. I loved and valued my Presbyterian heritage, and still do. Most of the time God wants us to bloom where we are planted, but in my case, there was a calling elsewhere. I struggled with the pressure of having to choose between two loves—my Presbyterian heritage and my call to the contemplative dimensions of Catholicism. Choosing between two loves is indeed a mighty struggle.

Even as my energy was sapped by this struggle, the weight of my disability bore heavily upon me.

At college, my friends and I were a family. Someone always helped with typing papers, giving me class notes, or guiding me through the perplexities of taking care of clothes, all the essential help I needed as a cerebrally injured individual.

Things changed in graduate school. I found myself on my own. Just taking care of clothes, much less typing papers and keeping notes, proved too daunting a task. My grades suffered, as did my appearance. I wore my clothes mismatched, sometimes backward and beltless, my hair was often uncombed, and my room became a confusing pile of clothes and paper. Bathing and dressing sometimes took hours. By the time I finished, it was, more often than not, too late to go to class. The helplessness of my boyhood returned. The isolation and desperation were even harder to bear since I had known so many years of sunshine in high school and college.

Even still, in the midst of some of the most distressing moments, God's presence as assuring light and love came over me, offering me the gift of unexpected stillness.

I kept in touch with Fr. Law, who had become Monsignor Law and the head of the ecumenical office in Washington, D.C., for the U.S. bishops. We wrote, talked on the phone, and visited often. I shared some of the personal ways God's love touched and guided me. Msgr. Law's wisdom helped bring balance to my spiritual experiences. With my permission, he showed my letters to some Vatican officials, including members of the Curia such as Cardinal Willebrands.

One particular evening, despair descended on me. This was a time before I had a full medical diagnosis of my disability. I blamed myself, as I had when I was young. That night I even started repeating my old mantra: "You're no good at all."

I collapsed on my knees and prayed, "God, if you are there, send me a sign, any sign."

I have found that, most of the time, God reveals God's nearness on God's own schedule, not mine. This time was an exception. I lay back in my chair, yearning for any sign of hope in my life but not really expecting it.

The phone rang.

Msgr. Law's voice greeted me. He and Cardinal Willebrands, the head of the Congregation for Christian Unity in Rome and the primate of Holland, were touring the States. They could visit me in Austin the next day. "Would that be OK?" he asked.

We met the next day, prayed together, and talked. Just before they left, Cardinal Willebrands, already versed in my spiritual journey, smiled a knowing smile and said in his crisp Dutch accent, "If the prophet will not come to the mountain, then the mountain will come to the prophet."

If two men so near to God could see promise in me, perhaps I could still hope. Cardinal Willebrands's cryptic parting words rumbled inside me for months. Was there a mountain that would come to me?

VISIONS CHANGE OUR LIFE'S COURSE

The issue of my life's course and calling weighed heavily in those days. My difficulties with my disability continued. My struggle isolated me. Unsure that I should follow my yearning to become Catholic, I took time away from school to work in a campus ministry in Austin in order to discern more clearly my path.

The light usually came to me in great tenderness, a warm nurturing other, a parent that cradled me and dried my tears. Usually my times of sacred meeting came as a surprise. Now it was different.

I had a gathering sense of coming eruption. Fear and awe, terrible mystery, pulled me toward a meeting. I felt like a child about to be squeezed through the canal in the rush toward birth and a barely hinted at life beyond.

One night I was on call at the ministry and made the waiting-room couch into a bed so that I could answer the door for any counseling emergencies. I fell asleep repeating the Twenty-third Psalm; then I dreamed.

As I prayed, my body began to tingle,
to vibrate from within.
Every part of me within and without.
The room that surrounded me
was slowly engulfed in invisible flame.
Then the unseen flame turned to visible flame.
Brightening until it blazed like a jeweled sun.
A molten fire of love filled my bones.

I was carried up and speeded through a vortex,
a whirlwind of compassionate fire, a tender heat.
I could experience with new senses,
like taste, touch, sight, but more.
It was as though I were a deaf man who could now hear,
a man who could not taste, who could now taste.

Everything became more vivid than normal experience.
Immense pain coexisted
with the joy of longing and love.
The pain was the cleansing side of love,
the pain of healing.
Wounded, closed-off parts of my being
opened to love.
I could "see," experience, "taste"
many times and many places and
many people at once.
I tasted eternity, timelessness,
place and time, in one instant.

I was shown a room
and told that this was the room of my soul.
I could view the wounds of my life in visible form.
I could see the parts that had closed off to love—
both God's love and others' love.
The wounded parts shined the brightest.
There the soothing light gathered to mend.

The flame spoke without words:
"This is love that knows no bounds.
I am fire and I will refine you.
I am love and I will mend you.
Lose yourself in my cherishing.
Lose yourself and you will be found.
For I am the jealous, eternal Lover,
and I love without bound."

Love showed me scenes of pain from my life.
Each time I viewed a scene,
love intensified.
The one who treasured me
felt each hurt more keenly than I.
Here was a love more intimate to me
than I was to myself.
The wounds began to shine like multicolored gemstones.

I heard the words:
"In your wounds your beauty lies.
From them flows the salve to soothe torn hearts."

I was shown the wounded hearts of countless people
all in one moment.
I saw their scenes of hurt unfold

all in one moment.
I saw God treasure and touch each.
I was told to touch others' wounded hearts with
my open palms,
an intimate act of touching an open, beating heart.
As I reached and delicately touched,
my being trembled with the dread of each hurt.
Each of these the Creator loved.
Then I heard the words:
"This is how I train people to love,
by touching the wounds that I touch."

For moments, the intensity of the scene would lessen;
the scene would change to the subdued light of an eternal stillness.
There is rest from cleansing,
refreshment after pain,
a peaceful hush after compassion.

Love spoke:
"I will show you the future of creation.
First I will show you the devastation."

Scenes of the pain of war,
discrimination, abuse unfolded.
"This is the future that is now.
This is the coming darkness that has come."

I asked:
"What is the way out of the horror?"
The answer came:
"My love, which takes on each pain,
bears each hatred."

I was then shown a beautiful, eternal meadow.
Flowers, light, water, trees, shade
spoke of new life. The light said:
"This is also the future, and this is also now.
If there is horror, there is also springtime.
Springtime is coming if people will but let it come,
if they yearn and long and wish and pray.
Your time can become a time of wonder."
I had a sense that this meant a return to spirituality
and a restoration of what has been lost.

I asked:
"How does the time of wonder come?"
"Through mysteries."

The first mystery was this:
"That which is absolutely free costs everything.
Anyone may touch my love without cost.
But when you touch it, you become different.
Love carries you into the crucible of change,
until you give away all that you are
to begin to love in the manner I love.
Open to that frightening, risky love."

The second mystery was this:
"That which is apart is tied together;
that which is truly free is truly bound."

I could feel the compassion move outward,
radiating through unseen cords to countless others.
The cords knitted us together.
We were each a universe of individuality,

yet we were also as one,
embraced by one love.
Each pain of the other was my pain,
each joy my joy.

"You are not redeemed alone,
you are not made whole alone;
you are healed together.
Yours is not a solitary questing,
but a questing with one another.
As you pray for others,
you are healed.
As you touch torn hearts of others,
your heart is mended.
Only as you forget yourself in love of the other,
only as you fall in love with my love,
will you then discover yourself."

The next mystery was this:
I looked in a room filled with huge treasure chests.
Gleaming golden treasure light came
through the cracks in the chests.
I opened one of the chests
and saw ancient scrolls and manuscripts,
each beaming with sacred light
that filled me with brightness.
I ate a scroll and tasted its sweetness.

I heard the words:
"You will be a finder of scrolls,
and you will tell people of their sweetness
and show them their brightness."

The old scrolls were the pathway to springtime.
Images of my writing and speaking
about the recovery of ancient spiritual heritage
passed before me.

After my vision in Austin, I knew more clearly my life's path and gave in to the desire that had been growing slowly for years. On one visit with Msgr. Law and his mother in Jackson, Msgr. Law received me into the Catholic Church at the Carmelite monastery.

I still treasure my Protestant heritage. The beauty of that heritage will always abide in my heart. There is a richness in the many different faith expressions, but to be rooted and guided, it's best to find a tradition and stay with it, be faithful to it, and let it shape the experience of the sacred. For me that place of grounding is the Catholic Church. The richness I celebrate there helps me appreciate and grow from the richness in other faith expressions. For all the Catholic Church's brokenness and scars, I find in her a seasoned and ancient love that entrances and intoxicates me, even after all these years. I believe her to be the one holy, catholic, and apostolic church, and I believe her to have the fullness of what Christ intended for his church.

VISIONS OFFER HOPE, NOT MAGIC

When I awoke that morning from my dream, life was just as difficult as it always had been. My undiagnosed disability did not disappear. As always, the visions had offered no magical solution to life. Still, my hope deepened.

Little bits of this vision of healing, purifying fire continue in my dreams, even now. Over the years I have come to see this vision as the same vision I had as a boy of thirteen. The vision continued to mellow, changing as I changed and growing as I grew. From time to time I still catch glimpses of it.

I developed a yearning to discover writings of the saints, the great spiritual giants of our heritage. Despite many odds, the way opened to publish books and speak to audiences about God's gift of love and prayer and tell them about the buried treasure of our spiritual heritage.

I have often thought about the glimpse of my vision that night in Austin. As I have lived with it, I have come to see it as a rich imagining from my soul, not a supernatural encounter, and in no way more special than other people's ways of knowing God. I am gifted with vibrant imagination; others are gifted in other ways.

I know too that the vision had long churned inside me until it became manifest that first time when I was a boy. It was born from my struggle with disability, from my search for a love that could understand my hurt and isolation, and from finding that love in God. The vision became the visible, imagined form of my desire for that love— a desire I pray will grow purer and clearer with time.

Imagination is far more powerful than we can know. When imagination gets mixed in with our yearning for God and God's yearning for us, fresh metaphors and inspired journeys happen. They are born from our nature, from our humanness. But our humanity and our nature are *graced* humanity and *graced* nature, finiteness that is built with longing for the infinite.

More and more people are beginning to see the humanness of the wondrous. I recall the movie *Phenomenon*, which was a surprise hit several years ago. It started off like a typical wonder story. George (played by John Travolta) sees a vision of a wondrous, seemingly holy light in the sky while he's walking at night. It transforms him from an amiable garage mechanic into a budding genius. More important, his experience endows him with sensitivity and compassion. He uses his gift to help people, even save lives. I thought this was going to be a typical miracle movie. The light was going to turn out to be a vision of God, an angel, or maybe even a benign alien spaceship.

But the cause of George's transformation turns out to be something natural—a brain tumor. George dies, but not before telling us that the compassion and other traits that had developed in his life are available to all of us, because they are located in the core of our human struggle.

v i s i o n   j o u r n e y

This vision journey is based on the account of Jesus' transfiguration on Mount Tabor. This is a vision about visions. It is a model for the way spiritual encounter can transform our lives.

All three synoptic Gospels depict Jesus taking Peter, James, and John to the top of a mountain that tradition identifies as Mount Tabor. There, according to Matthew, Jesus "was transfigured before them, and his face shone like the sun, and his clothes became dazzling white" (Matthew 17:2). The three men witnessed him talking with Moses and Elijah.

The disciples were dazzled by a transforming brilliance. Their first impulse was to build booths for the three sacred figures, to permanently capture this moment and to luxuriate in it. Instead, Jesus' plan for them was to go back into the more ordinary world of pain and hurt. Jesus wanted the memory to embed itself within them and lead them from that momentary glory into the task of bringing in the kingdom and, ultimately, walking with him through his passion and death as well as the resurrection that the glory on the mountain prefigured.

Spiritual writers through the ages have used this passage to remind us not to cling to visions but to take in the glory when it comes and then return to our mission in this ordinary world. We do not stay forever on the mountain of vision; we leave it in order to live and love in this world in the way that Christ lived and loved.

Even though we don't remain on the mountain forever, the memory of it can abide with us, helping give our whole life direction, infusing us with the new world that is coming. Peter explicitly referred to this passage as depicting the transfiguration, calling it "the prophetic message" and telling his readers, "You will do well to be attentive to this as to a lamp shining in a dark place, until the day dawns and the morning star rises in your hearts" (2 Peter 1:19).

Memories of our trips to the mountaintop can be that lamp shining in the dark places of our trip through life, reminding us of the time when all shadows will be illumined, all blank spaces filled in, and all creation transfigured in imperishable glory.

Begin by reading the account of the Transfiguration in Matthew's Gospel:

> Six days later, Jesus took with him Peter and James and his brother John and led them up a high mountain, by themselves. And he was transfigured before them, and his face shone like the sun, and his clothes became dazzling white. Suddenly there appeared to them Moses and Elijah, talking with him. Then Peter said to Jesus, "Lord, it is good for us to be here; if you wish, I will make three dwellings here, one for you, one for Moses, and one for Elijah." While he was still speaking, suddenly a bright cloud overshadowed them, and from the cloud a voice said, "This is my Son, the Beloved; with him I am well pleased; listen to him!" When the disciples heard this, they fell to the ground and were overcome by fear. But Jesus came and touched them, saying, "Get up and do not be afraid." And when they looked up, they saw no one except Jesus himself alone.
>
> As they were coming down the mountain, Jesus ordered them, "Tell no one about the vision until after the Son of Man has been raised from the dead." And the disciples asked him, "Why, then, do the scribes say that Elijah must come first?" He replied, "Elijah is indeed coming and will restore all things; but I tell you that Elijah has already come, and they did not recognize him, but they did to him whatever they pleased. So also the Son of Man is about to suffer at their hands." Then the disciples understood that he was speaking to them about John the Baptist. (Matthew 17:1–13)

Guided Vision

Take some time to let your mind and body grow still. You might put on a recording of Gregorian chant, sounds of the sea, or other nature sounds. Notice your breath—each breath in and each breath out reminding you of the breath of the Holy Spirit—carrying you deeper and deeper into stillness.

Let the stillness deepen by mentioning your anxieties one at a time to God. Use a short tag to name them, such as "financial fear" or "loneliness." Give them short names and then give them to God in conversational prayer. Keep mentioning these anxieties until the tension begins to leave and quiet begins to settle in. Naming our pain before God empties us and brings a God-given peace.

Let the peace continue to settle over you. Rest there for a while.

If your imagination is fuzzy today, that's no hindrance. Just having a vague sense of the scene to be imagined is enough to begin a significant redirection of your inner life.

In your imagination, you fall into a deep, profound sleep, like the sleep of the disciples in the Gospel scene. Feel the heaviness of it. Let the deep sleep ease your limbs, your heart, and your mind. Rest in this sleep for a while.

Like the disciples, you are now being awakened from your sleep. Before your eyes is a dazzling light shining with a celestial brightness. Let the warmth and wonder of it fill your eyes, your nostrils, your body. Wonder and amazement flow through you like a current. Your eyes make out three figures: Jesus, Moses, and Elijah.

You reach out and touch the hem of Jesus' robe, which is now white with a dazzling light.

As you hold the cloth in your hands, feeling its texture with your fingers, you begin to remember many of the moments when wonder touched your life. Let those memories flood you, one after another. Sense the smells, the bodily feelings, the sights, the sounds, the full grace of those moments.

Allow the brightness of those moments to join with the brightness that shines from Jesus. Your moments of glory join with his moment of glory.

Jesus speaks to you:

"You are very dear to me. My light, my glory, is always near you, always in you, hidden beneath each breath, behind each heartbeat, suffusing your life with unseen brightness. Hidden beneath your hurting is a glory that will one day fully mend the hurting.

"My light is a hidden light, utterly near, yet unseen. Sometimes the veil is lifted and you see my glory. This moment, this time, can be a quiet lamplight to remind you of the wonder. I plant in your heart now a new seed of hope, a seed of glory, that will warm you and light your way when the world confuses and perplexes you."

In your own words, give thanks for this moment of spiritual presence.

When you have given thanks, you see Jesus by himself, without the light or the glory. You know it is time to say good-bye to him for now, time for you to take up your daily life. But you will have the memory of this moment and the memory of all your own times of wonder that have fused with Jesus' glory. These memories will serve as a quiet flame to light your everyday journey.

Jesus takes your hand in his. You feel the strength of his hand. And before your eyes, your mission in the everyday world becomes clear to you. Scenes of new ways of loving, new ways of caring, new ways of bringing in the kingdom pass before your eyes. This is your work in the flatlands, for which your time on the mountaintop prepares you.

Jesus places both his hands on your shoulders, commissioning you to return to your everyday world, and leaves for a while this place of vision.

help for our
grieving

I HAVE REVIEWED HUNDREDS OF THE CHURCH'S VISIONARY ACCOUNTS. Ninety percent of them begin with the expression of anguish. The woman with the twisted limbs cries out at the shrine; her neighbors cry with her. Before healing dawns for a drowned child, the peasants throw off their shoes, kneel, weep for the loss, yearn, and make a pathway for healing.

The ever popular hymn "Amazing Grace" states, "'Twas grace that taught my soul to fear, and then my fear relieved." The stark fear forms as vital a part of the songwriter's vision as the comfort of relief.

The spiritual giants crafted the old meditations to first bring contrition. To draw out hidden wounds, the meditator was summoned to imagine Christ on the cross or Mary weeping at the foot of the cross. The meditation invited the sufferer to blend his or her sufferings with Christ's.

Converts in America's Great Awakening first underwent a cleansing—sitting on the "mourner's bench" to bring the inner terrors to public expression and weep for resolution.

Jonathan Edwards, the seventeenth-century New England Puritan, wrote of the prophetic-like meltdowns of numbness that mark true sacred experience: "Religious sorrow, mourning, and brokenness of heart are also frequently spoken of as a great part of true religion. These things are often mentioned as distinguishing qualities of the true saints, and a great part of their character. . . . This godly sorrow and brokenness of heart is . . . peculiarly acceptable and pleasing to God."[1]

VISIONS DON'T BYPASS THE HURT

A type of modern spirituality, often found in movies, mall bookstores, or TV programs, suggests that visions are a kind of heavenly magical rescue from the painful complexities of this world we live in. Many stories about near-death experiences or the apparitions of angels carry this magical spirit. Angels swoop in at just the right minute to rescue us from some of the messes we humans have made.

The implication is that we can bypass hurt and loss by miraculous spiritual formulas. Follow a certain set of spiritual rules, and you will escape hurt, and life will always have a wonderful rosy hue.

Such a view of spirituality robs us of our own responsibility for our lives and our world. It represses and denies the very real wounds of our existence. Biblical spirituality takes this world very seriously. Loss is real, death is real, and the hurt we inflict on one another is real. Some problems are so tangled that they defy ready or easy solutions. Abuse of the poor and the weak is real. Sometimes all that can be done is to pour out our grieving to God. Grief says that we care. Grief says that what was lost was of great value. Grief says that we need the mysterious help of another to build again. Grieving gives birth to astonishment.

In her middle age, my grandmother learned some of the rudiments of reading through an adult literacy program, though she never learned to write. She had a huge, white King James Bible. She would sit in her rocker and pick it up and read aloud from it, the only way she knew how to read. Her house was filled with her reading of Scripture.

One of the passages she turned to most often was Psalm 137:1–6.

By the rivers of Babylon—
    there we sat down and there we wept
    when we remembered Zion.
On the willows there
    we hung up our harps.
For there our captors
    asked us for songs,
and our tormentors asked for mirth, saying,
    "Sing us one of the songs of Zion!"

How could we sing the LORD's song
    in a foreign land?
If I forget you, O Jerusalem,
    let my right hand wither!
Let my tongue cling to the roof of my mouth,
    if I do not remember you,
if I do not set Jerusalem
    above my highest joy.

When she would read that psalm, it seemed that her voice and her whole being carried all the loss of a lifetime. She remembered nearly starving in the days after the Civil War, working in the mill twelve hours a day when she was six, just to survive, dealing with the recent death of her only daughter. She grieved not only her loss but also the loss of our Native people. Hearing her read this psalm, I felt the pain and the pathos. I found it a psalm that helped me feel my own pain, and somehow in that pain I could discover the vision of a comforting stillness.

Life not only has its seasons of well-being but also has its periods of suffering and hurt. This psalm and the other psalms of grieving call out raw emotions of resentment, pain, even rage. These poems and speech forms match the painful seasons of life in their ragged, painful disarray.

Psalm 137 is a way of praying through and processing the feelings that come with brutalization, not only for Jews, but also for individuals, cultures, everyone who has known isolation and exile. The psalm teaches a way of turning anger into grief and expressing it assertively to God.

We pay for hidden anger in many ways. When we don't acknowledge anger, when we pretend it's not there, it comes out in all sorts of ways that are destructive to others and ourselves. Anger can lead to helplessness and passivity when we turn it on ourselves. When we deny it and live in a pretend world, anger can become a hidden, unacknowledged poison within us that kills. We can act it out without full knowledge of what we're doing, and in our actions we can brutalize others.

The best place for anger is in our words, not our deeds. We can give voice to our anger and leave it at the throne of God. For God will transmute it into grieving, a grieving that collapses into hope and astonishment—and a vision of joy.

We must be honest with our deep grieving. Honesty before God with our grieving and with our anger renders us open to the surprises and the newness of life.

I often counsel people who have entrenched, unexpressed hurt. Perhaps they are recovering from divorce, a brutalized childhood, or another of the many hurts society can inflict that cause us to clench up inside in pain and rage. Our society teaches us to hide our wounds. But hidden hurt, especially anger that is unacknowledged, finds destructive outlets.

THE NATIVE GIRL'S STORY

It had been a long weekend. I had just finished a Friday and Saturday retreat in a Native American Catholic church after traveling two thousand miles to a large western Canadian city. The world looked blurry to me. Native elder and several traditional singers sang hymns to God to the rhythm and sweet beauty of Native chant. A smudge pot filled the church with the smoky smell of sweet grass. The pope had encouraged Native peoples to hold on to their old customs, as long as they were in accord with Christ, and in this church they fulfilled that request by celebrating Mass in a Native way.

My mind was so tired, I'm not sure that my talk at Mass was coherent. I invited people to the church for the evening retreat I would be leading. Then I turned things over to the priest.

After Mass, on my way down to the basement for coffee, a young woman stopped me and asked, "You are Native, aren't you?"

I assured her I was part Native. I could see her fear that no one other than her own people could understand what she would tell me.

I looked at her more closely. She had bandages wound around both wrists. Scratches covered her arms and face.

"They've taken my children." Her voice was shrill with desperation. "The welfare people have taken my children."

The long story emerged. Her husband, in the bottomland of alcohol, had beaten her and the children constantly. Her scratches were from his beatings. There weren't jobs available for young Native women. Her judgment clouded by the desperation that such a situation brings, she thought she had no options. She felt that her only choice, other than the street, was to stay with her husband. The authorities had chastised her for not removing her children from the home and used that as a reason to remove the children from her. Her love for them and her fear of never getting them back showed in her despairing appearance.

The scratches were from her husband, but the cuts on the wrists were her own.

I knew I didn't have long to be with her. Since, in her mind, I was a healer, she begged me to see if God would give an assurance that her children would return. I couldn't give her that assurance, but I held her bandaged hand tenderly in mine, and over and over again, with all the tenderness I could muster, I repeated quietly, while tears coursed down both our faces, "God loves you. God loves you."

I must have said it a hundred times. Finally I sensed a bit of calmness come to her.

I invited her to join the congregation for coffee.

The Native elder who had led the traditional chanting, who was also a leader in the Cursillo movement (an ecumenical movement that promotes deep change of heart) and AA, spotted her in the basement. He went immediately to her and said, "I want you to dance a dance for me."

The Native peoples of this area dance the fancy dance, a dance in which the body is bent and moved in rhythm. He did the traditional singing, and she danced her dance.

"Now," the elder said, "tell me what it means."

"I danced new steps in this dance, new steps that just came to me. So maybe I can step into a new time in my life."

After the dance, people embraced her, listened to her, and wept with her. Unlike many middle-class congregations, no one offered advice. It was enough to be there with her and let her know this was a place where she was wanted.

Talking with her later, I found out that this was her first visit back to church in many months. I urged her to come to the retreat that night.

After the night's retreat, I, along with some of the elders of the parish, prayed a healing prayer for each person that came forward. The elder who led the singing formed a team with me, holding an eagle feather over each person as we prayed.

The young woman was one of the last people to come to us. The elder chanted a Native song. I chanted "Guide Me, Jehovah" in Cherokee, a hymn long ago set to plaintive and gently beautiful chant. I knew that the young woman didn't understand the words but that the beauty of the sounds would slip into her, and after all, God understood the words.

The elder fanned smoke from sweet grass all over her as we prayed, symbolizing the presence of God surrounding her and summoning her into his presence.

"Breathe it in," he urged her quietly. "Breathe it in from deep down inside."

After she breathed in the sweet smoke for a while, we stayed there a long time in silence as the tears rushed out of her body.

After a long time she said, "I see a big light; I see a very big light."

The elder said, "I see it too. It is big and vast like the Mysterious One, the Spirit."

"I dance in it now. I dance in it; I dance in the light," her voice softly chanted.

"I knew you would. I knew you would dance in the light. That's why I had you practice your dance this afternoon in the basement. I knew that you would be meeting the light and that when you did you would want to dance in it."

I saw the light too. All three of us saw it together, utterly bright and utterly, totally restful for our souls.

We stayed with her for a long time in the stillness while her heart danced. After a little while, our hearts danced with hers.

Then, after we came out of the stillness, we talked some about the need for her to come to church every Sunday, to counsel with the priest, to stay close to the warm, human community of faith that was that parish. Much love and care waited at that church for her. But hers would still be a long and painful road.

The elder had known what he was doing when he had her dance, in her pained state, in the basement room where we all drank coffee. He was following God's lead and preparing her to dance in the light.

In some way maybe I had prepared her too, without realizing it, when I talked to her on the stair and told her over and over that God loved her. Really, everybody there was getting her ready for that dance in the light.

I don't know if she ever got her children back. But I believe, in my heart, that she stayed with the church, stayed with Christ, and followed his light.

The Native girl was able to begin grieving. The vision of the light was a healing light. The experience reminded me of something important about visions. We can't give heavenly assurance that things will always be OK. We can't offer magic. But we can ease people into God's light and prepare their hearts to dance in it.

We Christians can be so busy with words so prepared with words, so armed with words, so defended by words that we forget that we can bask in the light and take the hurting ones into the light with us. We can forget that for all of us the journey into the light is never just an individual, private journey, but always a journey of others leading us, readying us, guiding us. Never is this more true than when we are in a state of grief. We need others to help us walk into the light and then dance in it for a while

GRIEF—AND HEALING—FOR A COMMUNITY

We live in a culture that encourages people to swallow their negative feelings. The tragedy is that when we deny our grief and our rage, we become aliens to hope. When we don't acknowledge these negative things, we can't understand that grieving and raging before God can lead to hope. Yet this is a profound biblical and human truth.

Recently, about a hundred of us gathered at a family reunion at which we unexpectedly explored the depths of pain and found great hope. My ancestor Yancy had three wives. One was a Cherokee Native American like him, one was white, and one was African American. This was not at all unusual for southeastern Indians. Therefore, quite a diversity of people showed up for the reunion. Some of my relatives look African

American, some look Caucasian like me, and some look simply Native. Many look like a blend of all three. At the family reunion, perhaps 60 percent were as much African American as Native American.

We gathered together, and two elderly cousins, near ninety, told us again about Yancy. He was a young boy in 1838 when U.S. soldiers came with their bayonets to uproot the Cherokee people from their houses and send them into exile and diaspora in the South. Yancy lived to be over one hundred. Even though the destruction of the Cherokee nation took place more than 150 years ago, my elderly relatives remembered Yancy personally recounting this story to them.

The soldiers beat members of his family and raped some of the women. At the present-day reunion, the aging women of the family spoke the old words that had been spoken for over 150 years in our family—Yancy's parents' words to him when the soldiers came, "Run, Yancy, run"—as though the holocaust had happened yesterday.

My cousin Dhyani Ywahoo, who is a chant bearer, sang some of the old sacred chants in Cherokee. We closed our eyes as she called upon the presence of the Great Mystery to envelop us like the wings of an eagle flying above us. We remained in long silence after her prayerful chanting. A dignified, solemn grieving and yearning for what was lost took place in the silence.

Afterward at our tables we all told our stories of pain and hope.

At the end, Dhyani invited anyone who had something to say to come to the microphone and speak. Remarkably, no one came just to talk. Everyone who came sang or led a song. Most of the songs were black spirituals, and we all joined in with our very bones trembling and tears flowing. The last song, which a teenager came up and led, was "Precious Lord, Take My Hand."

Because we took our grief and rage to the Great Mystery, the Master of Breath, the God of Israel and of Jesus, hope has been tenaciously preserved and a vision of peace and renewal unfolded.

Do not hide from the pain and anger; name them, concretize them, and take them to Yahweh, who alone brings newness.

The greatest of visionaries knew how to mourn. St. Francis of Assisi hurt with the hurts of the lepers and the rejected. Long after celestial visions of wonder began interrupting Francis's life, grieving would still often overtake him. He cared, and caring means that we touch the wounds of those we care about.

Caring means that we get angry at those who cause hurt. The way out of this tangle is usually not a way we can find by ourselves. We need the help of another, one who will hurt with us and yearn with us in the place of our anguish, one more intimate to us than we are to ourselves, one who walks with us all the steps that we walk. The psalmists poured out their struggles to Yahweh, the sender of visions, the author of astonishment, who can send visions of hope that lead the way out of the tangle. Denial leads to unreality, but grieving paves the way to visions.

DEATH-RELATED VISIONS

We can't discuss visions and grieving without mentioning visions that have to do with death—our own near death or the death of a loved one.

Twenty-five years ago, the concept of near-death experiences exploded onto our cultural scene. Physicians began reporting—and taking seriously—a widespread phenomenon: heavenly visions of people who had clinically died and were then resuscitated. In the years since, this phenomenon continues to fascinate us. Most everyone has seen accounts on television in which people tell of leaving their bodies, speeding through a tunnel, and meeting a welcoming, warming light, or encountering deceased loved ones waiting in beautiful celestial meadows. Some people have had extended experiences and written what can only be described as travelogues of the next life. Some researchers see these visions as proof or near proof of an afterlife; others see them as the death throes of the oxygen-deprived brain.

Arguing, strongly, that such experiences should be given some degree of consideration are the long-term, positive transformations that seem to take place in the people who experience them.

Studies such as those of scientist and physician Melvin Morse compel us to take these otherworldly visions seriously. Dr. Morse has researched death-related visions extensively and describes these types:

- *True near-death visions.* These are the visions most publicized in the media. A person's heart stops beating, then he or she is resuscitated to tell a story of meeting a welcoming light. In some cases the heart does not stop, but the person comes close to death.
- *Deathbed visions.* Morse and others have found that dying children and adults often have dreams and visions of being taken to a heavenly place of light, long before they show signs of clinical death. Sometimes they see departed loved ones in their hospital rooms.
- *Bereavement visions.* In these visions, people see their deceased loved ones in visions after their deaths. According to Morse, as many as 60 percent of newly bereaved persons have this experience. One researcher, Dr. Therese Rando, found that 75 percent of grieving parents who had lost children experienced these visions. A certain number of these people have visions of departed loved ones so vivid that they see the person, as though alive—three dimensional—in the room with them. I have heard similar testimonies from numerous people I have worked with in retreats. Morse found two or more people having the same vision at the same time.[2]

Even when some people are not near death but are enduring physical or emotional distress, they can have visions that seem to be near-death. Christian and Jewish literature abounds with visions of warm caring light, such as the young man in Constantinople who was surrounded by enveloping light; or Benedict, who saw the world in a ray of light. The experience of light is a root visionary experience. Morse believes that "predeath visions, post-death visions, shared-death experiences (two or more people seeing a vision of a deceased loved one at the same time), and the host of other mystical experiences are all related."[3] Using scientific methods, with control groups, Morse gave a battery of tests to people reporting these kinds of experiences. He found dramatic results. People who had had these experiences were transformed in significant ways. They possessed less fear of death, possessed more clarity about life, and showed more zest for living. He found that those with mystic experiences were transformed as were those with near-death experiences: "Those who had had any sort of visionary experience of a loving light tested virtually the same as those who had had near-death experience."[4]

As convincing as these findings are, I could dismiss most of them were it not for this startling fact: All these types of death-related visions form a large, though nearly forgotten, part of the history of Jewish and Christian spirituality. Such visions fill up Christian literature, at least until the beginning of the scientific age.

Great Christian figures such as Pope St. Gregory the Great kept numerous accounts of death-related visions. Medievalist Carol Zaleski explored these accounts in depth in *Otherworld Journeys: Accounts of Near-Death Experience in Medieval and Modern Times*. Many of these accounts parallel the modern accounts. A person dies, leaves the body, meets a heavenly light, then returns to tell the story.

One account, in sixth-century Gaul, closely follows the pattern of our modern accounts. This report was recorded by Gregory, Bishop of Tours. He passed on the testimony of a simple-hearted holy person named Salvius. Salvius had worked as an attorney but in midlife became a monk. After the abbot's death, Salvius was chosen to succeed him. He became seriously ill. His fellow monks thought he had died and so went on with his funeral. On his death bier, Salvius awoke and said, "Lord, why have you done this to me, brought me back . . . ?" (English modernized.) Three or four days later he told the monks of his near-death experience:

"When you saw me dead four days ago . . . I was seized by two angels and carried to the heights of heaven." Salvius was then led to a place of "light unspeakable and unutterable space." Salvius's angel guided him until he came under a cloud "brighter than all light, from which came the noise of many waters." He smelled an "odor, of exceeding sweetness." Martyrs and saints greeted Salvius. After a while he heard a voice saying, "Let this man return to the world, for he is necessary to our Church." Salvius didn't like the idea, and said, "Lord, why did you show me these things, if I must be sent back from them?"[5]

This account shows many similarities with modern accounts: the loving, inexpressible light, meeting those gone before, and the reluctant return to the body.

Religious figures crafted meditations based on visionary meetings with the light. St. Cyril of Jerusalem guided catechumens through meditations that symbolically carried them through standard near-death imagery, meeting the light, the brightness of heaven. St. Bonaventure, St. Alphonse Ligouri, and many others used similar meditations.

The imagery from such experiences soothed and harmonized people, implanting in the center of their souls a hope that cannot be contained in words.

Even more common than near-death visions are reports of departed loved ones appearing in dreams or visions. A survey of personal accounts, from the time of the church fathers and church mothers— the time from the legalization of Christianity through the sixth century—seems to strongly indicate that visions of loved ones after their deaths were common, if not expected.

St. John Chrysostom, in a letter to a young widow who had just lost her husband, encouraged her to let out her tears, then to remember— and that in remembering, the nearness of her departed husband could be felt. Love and memory knit us together.

Grief is important (in fact, Chrysostom had waited for a time before even writing this widow, aware that she must spend time grieving), but so, too—after the first torrents of grief subside—is remembering that death does not separate us from those we love. Chrysostom reminded the young woman that often God sends visions of departed loved ones. In a passage that transcends time he wrote:

> For such is the power of love, it embraces, and unites, and fastens together not only those who are present, and near, and visible but also those who are far distant; and neither length of time, nor separation in space, nor anything else of that kind can break up and cut in pieces the affection of the soul.
>
> And if you find the trial very unbearable owing to its long duration, it may be that he will visit you by means of visions and converse with you as he was wont to do, and show you the face for which you yearn: let this be thy consolation taking the place of letters, though indeed it is far more definite than letters. For in the latter case there are but lines traced with the pen to look upon, but in the former you see the form of his face, and his gentle smile, his figure.[6]

Chrysostom writes in such a manner that it sounds as though bereavement visions were commonly expected; they appear to be part of the formative church's theology of grieving. Ambrose of Milan, who believed visions to be simply part of a believer's life, shared his anguish over the death of his brother Satyrus. Ambrose knew that grief must be expressed, even in public, if healing and cleansing were to come, and he wrote eloquently of his grief. But at times his brother chose to come to Ambrose and comfort him. Ambrose wrote:

> How excruciating it would be unless his image appeared to me as if here present, unless the visions of the mind represented him, whom physical eyes can no longer see. You are here . . . always presenting yourself at my side. . . . I embrace you, I gaze upon you, I speak to you, I caress you,

and I am aware of your presence, in the very quiet of the night or in the clear light of day, when you choose to come back to see me and console me in my grief.[7]

Gregory Nazianzen, who had visions interrupt his life on different occasions, also experienced visionary dreams of his departed brother coming to him. In a sermon of praise for his brother, Gregory talks about his own weakness in the face of loss, how difficult it can be even to muster faith in the period of grieving. Yet even in that time of grieving, comfort can come, and awareness of the one lost can intrude. In the midst of his very real human impotence in the face of death, Gregory looked to the time of the restoration of all creation, when he would see his brother in all his fullness, even as his visions and dreams anticipated that final seeing of the loved one who had departed:

> Why am I faint-hearted in my hopes? Why behave like a mere creature of a day? I await the voice of the Archangel, the last trumpet, the transformation of the heavens, the transfiguration of the earth, the liberation of the elements, the renovation of the universe. Then shall I see Caesarius himself, no longer in exile, no longer laid upon a bier, no longer the object of mourning and pity, but brilliant, glorious, heavenly, such as in my dreams I have often beheld thee, dearest and most loving of brothers, pictured thus by my desire, if not by the very truth.[8]

One remarkable aspect of Gregory's vision is that he seemed to understand that visions of departed loved ones are possibly partly from us as well as possibly divine—or a combination of the two. He said that in his dreams his brother was pictured "by desire, if not by the very truth." He acknowledged that even visions of his brother in heavenly glory, in part, came from his own wishing.

Whatever their source, those visions built faith in a final and ultimate reunion and tied Gregory's hopes to that final consummation for which all creation yearns. Gregory was mature in how he understood his visions of his brother. He seemed to live well with the ambiguity of visions. Even if the visions came in part from his desire, his desire gave form, symbol, metaphor, and image to an underlying, ultimate hope within him, a hope both profound and sure.

Gregory also told of his sister Gorgonia's final illness. Physicians pronounced her illness incurable. During a brief remission of her disease, she went before the altar in the sanctuary to pray with "a mighty cry" to "the Physician of all." Her healing was to be a spiritual one, not a physical one. Her "vision," as her brother Gregory called it, was a vision of the unseen presence of God, in which she was made aware of the day of her death. What was remarkable about this spiritual knowing was not that Gorgonia was correct about the time of her death but that she was overcome by the beauty and goodness of God.

Gregory's sophisticated understanding of bereavement visions sounds remarkably like what Dr. Melvin Morse has said about visions. In Morse's own research into death-related visions, he found that patients not infrequently had premonitions of the time of their own deaths.[9]

There are more and more accounts of death-related visions coming to us now from hospice workers who see patients transformed by such experiences. These workers hear accounts of vivid dreams that prepare people for their deaths. Patients talk to them of long-dead loved ones they have seen and of "visitors" who have come to help them prepare for death. Witnesses to the stories and testimonies of the dying are often quite convinced that something far beyond senility or drug-induced hallucination is going on. They see people who were not ready to die suddenly overwhelmed by peace. One hospice chaplain, Ron Wooten-Green, has observed patients even learning about their own ancestry what was not known to them prior to their visions.[10]

Death remains for all of us a great mystery. It symbolizes ultimate loss, the loss of the loves we have known, and the ending of hopes. A clear sign reads, "You have come this far, and you can go no further." Yet even as we near what can seem to be total loss, an unexpected comfort often comes, even without our beckoning, a comfort that declares to us that we do not die into death, but die into God. It is in connection with death—either the nearness of their own or the death of those to whom their souls were knitted—that most people have their most intense visionary experiences.

v i s i o n   j o u r n e y

When I ask people to name the first Bible verse that comes to mind, half of them say, without hesitation, "Jesus wept." Jesus wept for his friend Lazarus, who had died. Out of his grieving, Jesus entered into the depth of his sense of loss. That grieving led to his great miracle: "Lazarus, come out."

By entering into the world's hurt, entering into the grieving, we taste a helplessness that can only be given over to God's mystery of redemption. Jesus did not heal with a magician's wand. He healed by entering into the utter reality of the loss, naming that which was lost, valuing it, yearning for it with a most human yearning. Out of yearning comes the mystery of redemption.

Writing

On this vision journey we return to writing as a way of prayer.

Quickly complete the following sentence three different ways, writing the first thing that comes to your mind:

"If I drew a picture of comfort, I would draw . . ."

Finish the following statements, writing for as long as you need to. Remember to write quickly to get past the mental censor.

"The time I felt most comforted when grieving was . . ."
"Right now these are the things I most need to grieve for: . . ."

Quickly write a prayer, using the following words as a starter:

Dear Lord,
you always comfort me, always meet me with healing.
I thank you that you comforted me when . . .
Right now I give these hurts to you: . . .
Comfort me now by . . . Bring me to a place of healing resolution by . . .
Send me a vision of hope that . . .
Thank you for always hearing me. Amen.

After you have written your prayer, slowly read it, praying it quietly, slightly moving your lips, until you come to a place of stillness.

Read some of the earlier material you have written, letting it draw you close to God.

Now write.

"If God spoke to me now, I expect I would hear . . ."

visions to heal our wounded world

I GOT A SURPRISE IN 1965, A FEW MONTHS AFTER I ARRIVED AT BELHAVEN College. A group of the most popular young men on campus, the social "wheels," invited me to join the most prestigious men's social club. That night as I fell asleep, I thought about the boys who teased me in junior high because of my disability, and I contrasted those memories to this high token of acceptance. The light had promised me I would have a life returned in gentleness and warmth. I was tearful with gratitude.

My ego began to flow into this blessed moment—as I find it often does. The visions changed to all the beautiful coeds I would be able to date now that I was "in." Images of newfound popularity surrounded me. I could float through the rest of my life. The light smiled and communicated without words: "Don't get so comfortable yet."

Just as I was finally fitting in, the friendly light came to shake my life again.

THROUGH VISIONS, WE TASTE GOD'S FUTURE

For a while in high school, the racism that had swept the South as a result of the civil rights movement pulled me in, even with all my love of South African dissident writers Nadine Gordimer and Alan Paton. It seemed that everybody wanted to stop the encroachment on our southern way of life. While I was repulsed by those boys who drove through black neighborhoods shooting up houses with buckshot, I picked a genteel way of holding on to "our values." I became a proponent of states' rights against the federal government's encroachment. I even used the "n word" with the other boys, although I always felt a bit ashamed.

States' rights was a euphemism for segregation. What better way for a young man of questionable racial ancestry to feel at home than to jump on the bandwagon? I couldn't play sports with the other boys, but I could articulate southern nostalgia with my word skills. For a while, I looked on this as a ticket to belonging.

By the time I got to college, I had left most of that behind. I switched labels. Now I was an integrationist. I had finally begun to embrace the attitude of my favorite novel by Alan Paton, *Cry the Beloved Country*. But my embrace consisted mostly of words.

On the bus back to college from my first spring break, I noticed a middle-aged black woman sobbing in horrible emotional pain all the way from Montgomery to Meridian. The bus driver walked to the back at three different stops to brusquely calm her down. Fear ran through my heart. In my adolescent mind I imagined that I knew why she was crying—because she had to sit in the back of the bus. In the way that young people can quickly blame themselves, I thought it was my attitude that had done this to her. I wanted to go to the back of the bus with her. Maybe I could say something, do something, just be with her in her isolation. But in those days, going to the back of the bus was dangerous for a white man. Would people think I was a freedom rider? Would the driver order me off, leaving me stranded on the roadside? Would the young, white country types beat me up like they beat up the freedom riders? I just didn't have the courage to take those steps and cross that invisible barrier to her end of the bus.

Back at school I told my friend Helen the story. "She was crying because of the segregation," I said. Helen gave the more likely explanation that the woman had just had a death or other tragedy in the family. That night I had a vision as I lay awake in the early morning of my dorm room in Wells Hall, covered in sweat from the heat that radiated from the brick walls.

Suddenly I was back in the bus. I pressed the imitation leather seat with my hands to be sure I wasn't dreaming, and I felt its solidity. No dream could be this vivid. I looked in the back of the bus for the woman, but she wasn't there. In her seat I saw a stern Christ, his eyes fiercely glowing like the Son of man in Revelation. He looked right at me and with a voice that vibrated disappointment said, "I have come to you in your tears, but you didn't come to me in mine. Find me on this end of the bus, or you won't find me at all."

At that moment, thunder like the end of the world crashed through the bus, and I awakened in my bed to one of those booming, earth-shaking Mississippi thunderstorms.

I put the pillow over my head so that my roommate, Frank, wouldn't hear me, and I sobbed. I sobbed for not having gone to the woman. And only after thirty minutes of sobbing did some sweetness and relief come. I knew then that, if I wanted to meet Christ, I would have to do more than read theology and pray. I'd have to move to the back of the bus.

After this, I became involved with the civil rights movement. A center for the movement in Jackson was the Jewish synagogue I visited frequently. Rabbi Nussbaum introduced me to the writings of Abraham Heschel and to Jewish mystical literature. Locals tried to assassinate the rabbi, blowing up the synagogue that was a refuge to so many of us in the movement.

Afterward I took part in an anti-Klan march, became an ad hoc representative of my campus to the intercollegiate civil rights movement, and worked to fully integrate my own campus. My work was small and marginal compared with the great effort and sacrifice of so many during this time. But at least I no longer sat by watching while the Klan murdered and churches burned.

To fall in love with God means to fall in love with all that God falls in love with. Spirituality doesn't just bless and enhance our lives; it calls us to live different lives, lives in which we yearn and work and pray for the healing of our wounded societies—the lame and lonely, the forgotten and marginalized. Through visions, we taste God's future, and when we taste God's future, we find ourselves at war with society as we know it. We yearn for a coming consummation—the transfiguration of creation, when all will be made whole. We let God's future invade our present, our individual lives and our lives together as people of faith.

When we touch God, we touch infinite compassion—a heart that suffers with all creation's pain. Letting God's compassion touch us means that we become addicted to loving in the way God loves. We taste God's care for this wounded, confused world and set our feet on the pathway of living out that tenderness in concrete ways.

Karl Rahner expressed this same vision:

> Why are all those who love with great hearts humble and reverent as though they had been blinded by the splendor of an inexhaustible and indestructible mystery which they glimpse in the depths of the great moments of their love? . . . Is this not the great wisdom which we long for and venerate, and is it not the quiet splendor of the untroubled peace which can only reign in a person who has nothing more to fear?[1]

The great mystics and visionaries typically allowed their sacred encounters to lead them to spend themselves in caring, letting their very lives become a vision for others.

Visions from my own experience show the Creator's care for each human. To taste the Creator's love is to begin to love as the Creator loves. When St. Benedict saw the whole world in a ray of light, he saw the coming age, the eschatological age when all reality will be transformed. Benedict's vision is planted deeply within all people of faith. We see it in our different ways and at different times.

THE SWEAT LODGE GAVE ME A VISION OF PEACE

The time that this vision we all share became clearest to me was in a Native American ceremony called the sweat lodge. This ceremony is a way the Native people in North America open themselves up to the touches of God and God's visions. This particular experience of the sweat lodge expressed God's embrace of the world in a future whole-ness we do not yet possess fully.

The lodge had been built in the early 1980s by two people of Native descent: my dear friend Claire Dakota and her husband, Jerome. They owned a small farm at Standing Rock, not more than an hour and a half from my hometown, Columbus, Georgia. On their farm stood a hundred-year-old house, rickety and swaying on one side, several henhouses, and twenty acres of land overgrown with weeds. In the early eighties some of us of Native descent would go to the farm and spend most of the night praying together around a fire and in the sweat lodge.

I vividly remember one sweat lodge ceremony we celebrated there. We arrived early on a Saturday, gathered wood and stones, and helped rebuild the lodge. We worked together as a community to find twigs and branches and make them into a rounded semicircle. As we cut the branches, we said a prayer of thanks to God, who had created the earth and created the branches that were now giving themselves to us to become the frame of our lodge. We allowed handiwork in nature to remind us of God's mind, which could envision and fashion this beau-tiful world of ours. Finally, after many hours, the rounded dome of twigs was covered with tarps.

By this time a huge fire near the lodge was raging and hot. Under the fire we had placed stones that would be used in the ceremony.

Throughout the day we told some of the stories of our lives. I told the story of my grandparents and all they had taught me. Claire spoke of what her ancestors had taught her and passed on to her. We talked of the joys and sadnesses since we last saw each other. We also spent long times in silence as we built the lodge.

Finally, when night fell, we began the ceremony. In our first set of prayers we walked around the lodge, bowed our heads at the four directions—north, south, east, and west—and honored the one God, the Provider, the straightener of hearts, who came to us in each of the four directions. Then we entered the lodge dressed in swimsuits and towels, sitting upon the raw earth.

One of the men then brought the glowing hot stones to a pit in the center and closed the lodge flap. The darkness became near absolute, except for a mild glow from the rocks. Soon our bodies began to pour sweat. The sweat cleansed us of toxins and impurities. Our physical cleansing became symbolic of the cleansing of our souls. As the sweat flowed out our pores, the thoughts, fears, and mind chatter that pre-occupied us flowed out too. A solemnity of quiet surrounded us.

We passed a stick called a talking stick from person to person. Each person who held it might choose to hold it in silence as we all prayed in the silences of our hearts. Or that person might offer up a prayer, often starting in this fashion: "Creator, Great Mystery, we send up a voice; we pray for our own healing, our own cleansing, and the cleansing of all humanity and all the earth."

We drank water to refresh us as we sweated. I could feel the moist, nurturing earth beneath my bare legs. God was tied to this earth. I was part of this earth. I came from this earth; I would return to this earth. Yet I also came from the mystery that envelops this earth in God's embrace, as lover of the beloved. Some people poured water on the rocks, and blasts of hot steam enveloped us. And in the viscera of our souls we knew the mystery that is God was surrounding us all, like the steam that we heard blister and rise from the stones.

That particular night the temperature outside was down to twenty degrees, arctic cold for mid-Alabama. The wind blew fiercely outside the lodge. After each person had held the talking stick and said a prayer, one of the women led us in chanting a sacred song. Then we gathered outside by the fire, our bodies heated against the cold by the heat of the rocks, to cool off from the heat of the lodge. Clothed only in swimsuits and towels, we were refreshed by the cold wind as we stood gazing into the fire. The kindler of fire and of all creation kindled our hearts.

In coming to the lodge, we quested for vision, for seeing. The lodge became for us a pilgrimage, as surely as a pilgrimage became a vision quest for the faithful of the Middle Ages.

We returned for the second round, and a spontaneous, unbidden set of imagery unfolded in me.

In the eye of my heart I was carried back to my memory of a stream in the Smokies. As I sat sweating, my mind turned toward a beautiful wooded scene on this little mountain river. The crystal-clear, shallow waters rushed over rounded white rocks. In the middle of the river I saw a small island rock. The scene became as lucid as anything I see with open eyes.

I swallowed and turned away from the rock for a moment. Then when my gaze returned, I saw Christ standing on the rock, vested in deerskin. It was twilight. He lifted up his hands in the fashion of the medicine healer. Christ connected to this earth and united with eternity at the same time. His hands were stretched out as medicine, *nowehtee*, healing. His outstretched arms radiated an invisible but perceptible wave of healing that poured from his arms and swept over me. I breathed in the healing, healing like an invisible yet tangible substance entering my lungs and calming me, entering the very pores of my skin and the cells of my body, filling me with healing, with medicine—a medicine that comforted me, that took away fears.

I looked again, and I saw that I was not alone there on the banks of the mountain river. I saw animals, bears, deer, snakes, frogs, and people—all wounded—gathered in a circle around the rock. Some stood in the rushing shallow waters; some pressed against the trees on the banks. Some had been wounded by weapons. Some had been wounded by words. Some had been wounded by the hurts of a lifetime.

I saw a look of dejection on the face of a three-year-old, the pain of wanting to be loved and wanted and yet not being loved and wanted. Such a pain has its own look. Pain and tragedy filled the eyes of many. Each time I looked at a face, my soul joined in the hurting. Some carried physical scars. Some were bled white. Some faces contorted with physical hurt. Some of the trees gathered around the island had torn bark, withering limbs, or the mold of disease.

I saw Christ's eyes survey this multitude, which seemed endless. As Christ held out his arms, I could see a bleeding deer mend and run off into the woods. I could see the dejection on the face of a child change into the ease of a smile. I could see an elderly face creased with loneliness soften and beam. The physical wounds, the wounds of disease, the wounds of the heart—all began to heal as Christ, who took in the many wounds, held out his arms.

I told the people in the lodge of the vision. Some of the people in the lodge said that they could see it too. Then the vision changed. Christ's hands still remained outstretched, but the healing seemed to slow, nearly ceasing.

I said, "O Great One, O Gentle One clothed in deerskin, why is the healing dimming?"

And the reply came, "I do not choose to heal alone. I do not choose to work great medicine alone, but I call you, all of you, to work it with me. I call you to be healers, touchers, menders of souls, connectors of worlds."

Fearful, I waded into the water, stepping on the natural bridge of rocks, and stood by Christ. I stretched out my arms in the same manner Christ stretched out his, closing one of my hands around his outstretched hand. Christ said, "Join with me in the curing."

In a way I cannot express in words, in a way real and true, healing flowed from Christ's presence through my hand into the whole of my body, my soul, my memory. As my hands stretched out, the healing then flowed, bright and electric, from me through the rocks that supported my feet, through the air, and into the gathered multitude. But again I am putting into words the communication of the heart that has no words. Christ said to me, "For healing to continue you must join with me in the touching, in the mending, in this touching and being touched."

At that moment I felt some of what Christ felt. I looked out and saw a pained elderly woman and saw into her soul. No one had called her name with love for a great many years. All those who had loved her were now gone, and she waited in a waiting place for healing around the stone island on which Christ stood. I knew now what Christ meant by the touching and the being touched. It's as though the medicine, through the invisible rays of healing, poured out from Christ through me to the wounded.

It was a connection that went both ways. In return, I could feel the intensity and desperation of the elderly woman's loneliness. She touched me with her pain, and in turn I could touch her with the rays of healing that flowed from Christ through me.

I looked at a wounded rabbit whose spinal cord was broken, whose head now trembled and shook with fear. I could feel desperation, and my heart could pour out the healing touch with which Christ touched me. I looked upon wounded creation and wounded humanity, and I could feel just a little of what Christ felt in the touching and the being touched—the anguish, the pain, and the returning of healing waves of love, love that mended and healed and made whole. The multitude was endless and all visible at once, in such a way as can only be seen in dreams and visions.

Again, the seeing changed, and the healing diminished, nearly stopping. Christ said, "I will show you another lesson of healing. I will show you the helpers for healing."

I then saw those who had helped in my healing. My grandfather and my grandmother, who had so loved me as a child, joined me. My teacher Margaret Cox, who had helped rescue me; Cardinal Law; my dear cousin Dhyani—all the people who had loved me toward wholeness now gathered and stood behind Christ and me. I knew that all those whom God had used to help heal me were always in me to help me heal others. And with the strength of their love, the healing from me to others began flowing anew.

I could feel the love of my mother, my father, my aunt Lovey, those who had cradled me, and I saw so many others also who had cradled me when I was little, those who had dried my tears, those who had been my nurturers and healers. I could feel their love in back of me. I could feel the warmth of their medicine. I could feel their touch. I could remember all the goodness they had poured into me and all the presents with which they had gifted me. And because they loved me, the healing flowed again, with might.

Then the healing diminished once again. I heard the words: "I have another lesson of healing to show you, and it is a hard lesson. The lesson that you now must learn of healing is the changing of weapons."

WE MUST CHANGE OUR WEAPONS

The message puzzled me. "The changing of weapons"—what did this mean? Then in an instant I was standing there at the river and was yet in a totally different place, in the way such things can happen only in dreams and visions. The medicine that radiated from Christ carried me to a different place. I stood before a tree that reached high into the sky, towering so tall I could not see the top of it. I stood in awe of the tree and the image, and the symbol of the tree became clear to me.

I thought of that great tree of peace that Bonaventure spoke of in his visionary meditation, *The Tree of Peace*. His vast tree, he wrote, symbolized Christ, who came from the stump of Jesse. I thought of the Native symbol of the tree, the great tree of peace in Degandewidah's vision. The tree that Christ brought me to symbolized both. Under the branches, brilliantly shining, were what I can only call medicine stones, healing stones that gave off a dazzling, healing light that radiated the healing of the eternal God.

And Christ said, "I will teach you the lesson of the changing of weapons."

Christ then reached, as it were, to the place between my heart and abdomen, that place where we feel our feelings, and drew out of me a weapon, a stone war club.

Christ said, "Inside you hold many weapons. When you were a child, so much frightened you. The other face of fear is bitterness, the bitterness of weapons that would strike back, that would hurt others. Now reach in yourself and pull out the weapons."

I reached inside my heart and took out all sorts of knives and war clubs and arrows that came from me; the products of my hurt, the children of my fear, the weapons I used to strike back and hold off the fear. I drew them out of my vitals and placed them under the roots of the great tree. There they transformed into medicine stones that radiated great brilliance. I stood there for a season, removing the weapons from my soul and placing them in the roots of the tree of Jesse, the great tree of peace that alone can transfigure our angers and our furies.

Then in an instant I returned to the stone island in the middle of the river. This time I held a bright and shining medicine stone in the palm of each hand, and I could feel the warmth as my fingers gathered around the glowing stones. The glow of the stones flowed through my hand, through my limbs, through all of me as I stood on the rock with Christ.

This time the row of people in front of me had familiar faces. These were the people who, in my mind, had hurt me, the people toward whom I held unfelt and felt anger. Among those who stood near were a teacher who had made fun of me, students who had laughed at me when I was growing up, the people I would avoid if I saw them in a mall. All of them appeared before me now. My eyes wanted to turn away; I had held such weapons of harshness in me.

I tried to let my heart reach out to them and let the healing rays flow from me. My limbs weakened and wavered as I looked at all the people of my pain. I could not look them in the eye. I saw not only the people who had hurt me but also the people I had hurt. I saw that I too had inflicted wounds. I could look at them and see and feel what my words and actions had done to them. Visible in their faces were the scars of my withdrawing myself from them and saying hard things to them. I could feel it all, and I collapsed inside.

I spoke out with the language of my heart, standing near Christ, who stood beside me: "I cannot do this by myself. I cannot go through this alone. I can do this only with your help."

Then I heard Christ say in the heart's wordless communion: "These are your greatest teachers, these people of your pain. These are your teachers in becoming a healer."

I stretched out my hands. I could look them in the face now, and the healing again flowed not only to them but also to the whole multitude.

My mind and my heart came back to the sweat lodge. I sat there on the ground, which was now moist with my sweat. Sweat poured down until my eyes burned with the salt. Tears streamed from my eyes. Stillness like eternity filled the lodge. I then told the others of my vision, which is really the vision of all of us. It is the vision that in some way we all have if we will but stop a moment and see it.

I said to the group, "Let us now in silence all go to the root of the tree of peace and begin changing our weapons into medicine stones, for we are all called to be healers, and this is the pathway of healers."

After a long silence, we exited the lodge, letting the jolt of the freezing wind cool our heated, near-naked bodies. The wind quickly cooled us, and we gathered near the fire to warm from the cooling.

We entered the lodge for another round. I sat in silence. A few people prayed; some chanted. I sat in silence, and in the silence, without words, I heard Christ's message.

"You cannot be healed without becoming a healer. Gather in all the love that you have known—the love of all those whose gaze became my gaze—all the touches, all the love that met you in creation.

"The ways of healing are the ways of touching and being touched, feeling the pain in some way as I feel it. I heal by inhabiting the deepest places of the deepest hurts. My healing is my calling, my calling to join in the healing of earth and sky.

"Join me, all of you. Join me in the mending. I am the healer who loves and heals through many healers and the lover who loves through many lovers. Change your weapons, the children of your pain, into medicine stones. Look in the eyes of the people of your pain.

"I am the one who ties together that which has been torn and mends that which has been ripped and wounded."

The world changed for a moment, caught up in an eternity of light. It sparkled for a moment, and I dwelled in the eternity of its sparkling.

Each of us exited the lodge, returned to the old farmhouse, dressed, and began our journey home.

Hans Urs von Balthasar expressed this same scriptural vision of belonging to one another:

> Grace presupposes nature; it does not destroy it but completes it. . . . We are at the heart of the unfathomable mystery of the exchangeability of all spiritual goods in the household and circulatory system of the mystical body of Christ: "if one member suffers, all suffer together with it; if one member is honored, all rejoice together with it" (1 Corinthians 12:26). This is not only an external sense of the relationship of independent elements standing alongside one another, but in that mutual being for one another and ability for one another before God.[2]

Another great teacher from the Jewish tradition tells us:

> There is a divine dream which the prophets and rabbis have cherished and which fills our prayers, and permeates the acts of true piety. It is the

dream of a world, rid of evil by the grace of God as well as by the efforts of man. . . . God is waiting for us to redeem the world. We should not spend our life hunting for trivial satisfactions while God is waiting.[3]

The Scriptures indicate that the whole earth strains and longs for consummation. We yearn, not alone, but together before God. The Scriptures tell us:

"The LORD of hosts . . . will swallow up death forever. Then the LORD GOD will wipe away the tears from all faces" (Isaiah 25:6–8).

"For the first heaven and the first earth had passed away" (Revelation 21:1).

"Death will be no more; mourning and crying and pain will be no more, for the first things have passed away. And the one who was seated on the throne said, 'See, I am making all things new'" (Revelation 21:4–5).

vision journey

Our vision quest, our life journey, is not one we walk alone. Just the fact that you are reading this book—a book to help you draw near to God—means that someone, somewhere along the way, has enfleshed God's goodness in the way he or she loved you.

Visions are not just a journey of aloneness. We are accompanied by the love of all those who cradled us, believed in us, forgave us, delighted in us, and planted the seeds of our visions as surely as did Scripture and sacrament.

This vision journey is about the social dimension of visions. Sometimes another person can, in a sense, *be* a vision. Sometimes the veil is lifted and we see God's brightness in a very human person who reaches to us with God's reach.

Sometimes that other person becomes transparent and we see God lighting his or her whole personality.

Rabbi Heschel beautifully captures the way spiritual practice and prayer can lead us to visions that help us become God's partners in the healing of the world—the bringing in of the Kingdom:

> At the beginning of all action is an inner vision in which things to be are experienced as real. Prayer, too, is frequently an inner vision, an intense dreaming for God—the reflection of the Divine intentions in the soul of man. We dream of a time "when the world will be perfect under the Kingship of God, and all the children of flesh will call upon thy name." We anticipate the fulfillment of the hope shared by both God and man. To pray is to dream in league with God, to envision His holy visions.[4]

Writing

Quickly write the names of several people whose personalities transmitted God to you, people who, in a sense, became human visions of God's presence.

Those people have left something of themselves in your memory, in the shape of your personality. In a sense they are always with you. Pick a person from the list who particularly put you in touch with God. Quickly write three ways that person loved you as God loves you.

List some of the gifts this person gave you.

Write quickly to trick the mental censor. Repeat this exercise often, using the different people who have loved you with God's love.

We have been loved by God and loved by those God sent into our lives so that we ourselves might love with God's love, and love along with God. God does not choose to heal this hurting world alone but in company with those human beings with whom, through his Son, he is forever joined.

Guided Vision

Find a relaxing spot, lying on the floor or sitting in a comfortable chair. You might put on some relaxing music or nature sounds.

Let your breathing in and your breathing out remind you of the breath of God, the Spirit. Let the notice of your breathing bring you deeper and deeper into God's peace.

To journey even deeper into the stillness, name in a word or a short phrase any anxieties that now trouble you, letting them go into the presence of God, who absorbs our fears.

Now you are ready for a slow guided vision.

Gently, in your mind's eye, go to a place in nature that is safe to you, a place that feels at home with God. Look at the beauty of that place—the sights, the sounds, the smells. Stand there and take in the whole view.

As you stand there, you sense Christ coming up behind you. You do not look, but you know he is there. He puts his hand on your shoulder. Pause and feel the warmth of an eternal love pass from his hand into your whole body and soul.

He now moves and stands beside you. You drink in the light of his presence with your eyes. You see the light, you breathe it in. It warms you and you are lighted, everywhere within, with that light.

Others join you—relatives, friends, the people who have shown you God's love in their personalities. They place their hands on your shoulder, standing behind you, transmitting again the strength of their love.

You are filled to the brim with all this sacred caring.

Now the scene before you changes. One by one you see people who have been injured physically or emotionally, people caught in turmoil, people who are lonely. You do not have to strain for such images. They are already within you because of your participation with all of creation.

Together with Christ and in the company of all who have loved you, you begin to send out wave after wave of healing from your heart. You see the faces brighten. You see the wounds heal. You utter words of prayer for the healing of all.

You see light begin to brighten all gathered before you, a light coming from above, the light of the new Jerusalem descending. Let your own image of the new Jerusalem descending emerge from your depths.

Rest for a while in your unique view of the descent of the new Jerusalem. Now quietly return in your mind's eye to your room, your place of prayer. Let there emerge before your eyes one person you are called to love better. Now picture yourself loving that person.

Writing

While it is fresh, describe your own vision of the new Jerusalem descending. What did it look like? What was the feeling? How will that vision help you love better?

PART 4

the role of visions in life today

No man is an island, entire of itself;

every man is a piece of the continent, a part of the main.

If a clod be washed away by the sea,

Europe is the less,

as well as if a promontory were,

as well as if a manor of thy friend's or of thine own were:

any man's death diminishes me, because I am involved in

mankind,

and therefore never send to know for whom the bells tolls;

it tolls for thee.

—JOHN DONNE

Signs of a deep desire, a mighty yearning, for the

completion that only the sacred can bring, are found

everywhere in our society. People long for an end to

the isolation that is so pervasive. People are homesick

for God, homesick for authentic connectedness with

fellow humans. The thirst for visions we see every-

where is but a symptom of this wanting to come home.

To find our way home requires that we listen to the

voices of our ancestors. It means learning to walk in

balance with the spiritual, one step at a time. It means

finding sisters and brothers, communities of faith, that

are rooted and grounded, that can guide our searching.

walking in balance with visions

WHEN I WAS TWELVE, POP, MY GRANDFATHER, TOLD ME AN ENIGMATIC tale to help me cope with the varied changes adolescence would bring to my life. Though it could be an old Appalachian or Native story, I believe it was one he made up just for me, something he was in a habit of doing.

It went like this.

Once long ago, in a distant land of extreme cold, ice, and snow, only one place of warmth existed, a magical place where a group of people huddled around a large, self-replenishing fire. All the other inhabitants walked in barren coldness, apart from any warmth, isolated from one another.

Three men who wandered aimlessly in the endless cold heard a rumor of the fire, and they began groping their way toward it. Finally one night they caught sight of the fire's light. They spotted a group of people encircling the flames, chatting joyously as they warmed themselves.

One of the three men drew ahead of the other two and felt the first enticing sensation of warmth, the only warmth he had ever felt. Losing all control, he ran with abandon toward the fire. Never having seen fire before and having no knowledge of its danger, he dove right into its center. His agonized screams filled the night air. The people who were huddled around the fire pulled him out and bandaged his burns. He lived, found his spot by the fire, but carried scars from the burns the rest of his life.

Fear filled both his companions as they heard his screams. One fled in terror to the part of that land farthest from the fire, the coldest part of that cold land. The story goes that months later people found him dead, blue, and frozen solid.

The third man, seeing what had happened to the first two, chose a more difficult option. He elected to walk toward the fire slowly, deliberately, a step at a time, resisting both the fear that made him want to flee back into the deep cold and the fervent yearning for warmth that made him want to lose control and jump into the fire. Successfully fighting off both impulses, he eventually inched his way to the group huddled around the fire. The people welcomed him and helped him find just the right spot, where he lived out his days in the brightness, security, and warmth of the fire and in the caring companionship of the others who had found their places beside it.

As I grew older, I saw this story's application to spirituality. We don't jump right into the middle of spiritual experiencing, becoming seekers of ever-new thrills. Nor do we run in fear. Instead we approach slowly and deliberately, finding the place that is just right for us.

Our capacity for visions, like our capacity for sexuality, is a gift of relationship. And, like all of God's great gifts, it is not only capable of enormous good but also capable of harm, especially when put in the service of power. The most exquisite human gifts are the gifts of relationship and connectedness—gifts that relate us to others, relate us to our world, relate us to ourselves, relate us to God. Our speech, for instance, can enable us to communicate the varied richness of our humanity and the beauty of God's world. But we can also use our speech to berate, manipulate, or abuse others.

The attraction of woman for man and man for woman, our basic, physically built-in gift of relatedness, can bring priceless good. We can form family, allowing the love of husband and wife to pour over the new family being born. We can sublimate our sexuality, letting it fuel a powerful love and compassion for all our fellow humans. But we can also abuse our sexuality, using it for selfish gratification, manipulating others, using it as a means to dominate rather than a means to love and commit.

Even when we do not intend to hurt, almost all of us make mistakes in using our gift of relatedness when we are first learning to use it. Growing up, we have to learn through experience that our words can hurt. Experience should teach us when we are young that misusing our sexuality can cause harm. All our gifts of relatedness, creativity, and imagination are gifts that we learn to use by sometimes making mistakes and learning from those mistakes.

Likewise, because the human ability for sacred experiencing—for visions—can be misused and has been misused in the past, one of our responses to that gift has been repression. If something can hurt others or cause confusion, why not just suppress it and exile talk of it from civil conversation?

Unfortunately, by default, this has often been the response of educated religious people in the last century or so, at least on the local level. Basic human experiences of any sort can be raw and unwieldy at times. But as we all know, repression can lead to aberration.

Part of walking in balance is knowing that at times we will slip or stumble. We will get carried away and run toward the fire for a while, or we'll become afraid and run away from the fire. We learn to walk in balance by gathering the hard-earned lessons of the unwise times as well as the knowledge that comes from the wise times.

Today we face a major problem. Church and society have lost touch with much of the forgotten wisdom on walking in balance with visions. Most pastors know little of the subject. When we are over-whelmed with a felt sense of the spiritual, we often don't know where to turn.

Most of us have heard stories of sacred moments altering lives with their richness. But most of us also have known people who lost bal-ance because of following others' visions or visions of their own, becoming too spiritual for earthly good, forgetting about the critical commitments of their lives, even becoming obnoxious about visionary or wondrous happenings and trying to push the latest vision craze on friends and family. At times, I've heard stories of visions or fascination with visions, in the short run at least, confusing more than helping.

One chief reason for confusion is that we look on visions as heav-enly dictation, clear unequivocal messages. In short, we supernatural-ize visions. When we take visions as literal, rather than sacramental, chaos can result.

COMMANDER BOB'S STORY

One situation stands out clearly in my mind. Twenty years ago, a good friend from the upper Midwest, John, told me the story of a "vision-ary" in his parish. John took part in a popular Thursday night Bible study led by a retired naval dentist, Commander Bob, who was aided by a core group of several couples. Those were the days when the idea of small, intensive Christian communities rode a wave of popularity. The core group of the Bible study wanted close, intense relationships with each other. They shared meals, helped care for each other's chil-dren, wanted to become one larger extended Christian family. However much they desired that closeness, they faced one problem: they didn't get along well, especially when it came to decision mak-ing. Everyone wanted his or her ideas to prevail. Community meet-ings became a war of egos. The tension began to carry over into the Bible study.

Then someone appeared on the scene who appeared to offer a way out of the conflict. A thirty-five-year-old French-Canadian woman, Anne, began attending the study. One night during personal-witness time, she told of sitting in a field near her home late one evening, praying. She felt a warm, solid hand take her hand. A shiver went though her body; she knew that Jesus was beside her. As she narrated her experience, her words inspired everyone in the room, including my friend John. Her voice carried a clear note of purity and authenticity. John saw no sign that she made any of this up. He understood her experience as one of those graced, spontaneous, poetic, and imaginative experiences most of us have from time to time.

The leader of the Bible study, Bob, collapsed into sobs of joy. His voice trembling a bit, he declared that the group had just heard the story of nothing less than a miracle of biblical proportions. Now my friend John began to worry

After the study, everyone crowded around the new member. Commander Bob told her, his voice still trembling, that she must surely be a visionary sent by God to help the group through its impasse. He immediately asked her to join the emerging core group at their Saturday evening dinner and prayer meeting. Anne agreed.

John, though single, had been tagging along at these community meetings. Every Saturday night they met at Commander Bob's sprawling, custom-designed house, which was built in horseshoe fashion to accommodate his thirteen children. The children's bedrooms filled the north wing; the south wing contained the dining room, kitchen, master bedroom, and the only two bathrooms. A great room connected the two wings.

Excitement spread through the core group the first night Anne attended their community prayer meeting in the great room of Bob's house. All hoped her presence would move them beyond their misunderstandings. After the meal, Commander Bob said they would conduct their group discussion differently this time. Since God had obviously sent Anne to help the group through their impasse, since she had such a strong connection to God, Bob wanted to submit all the outstanding unresolved questions the group faced to Anne, who in turn would ask God to give her the answer. The first question put to Anne involved a dispute over whether the community meetings should be held on Tuesdays or Saturdays. Bob asked if Anne would close her eyes and ask God which night they should meet. Anne swallowed, closed her eyes, and became so religiously absorbed that she looked almost as though she were in a trance. Then her eyes fluttered open, and she said, "God wants you to meet on both Tuesday and Saturday nights." A chorus of awed "thank God's" came from everyone's lips, except John's. He fought an urge to run from the room.

The next question involved who would be members of the group. Anne asked God, and according to Anne, God wanted only the adults in the group to be members, not their children. Again came a chorus of assent. Finally, after a few more trancelike "communications with God," Anne laid out "God's plan" for the group. They were to meet twice a week. The community would be called the "community of the holy." The meeting place would be the great room at Bob's house, which now would be called the "place of the holy." All members should meet in the great room for private prayer as many of their non-working hours as possible. Only the members of the "community of the holy" could enter the renamed great room. This meant that non-members, including even Bob's children, could not enter the great room. John told me that tears of ecstatic wonder streamed down every face but his own.

Anne's plan for the community created an immediate problem for Bob's family. The children could no longer use the great room that connected both wings of the house when they walked back and forth from meals and the bathrooms, since they were not members of the "community of the holy." February in the upper Midwest brings deep snow and subzero weather. The children had to brave snow and freezing winds many times each day. Bob and his whole family immediately began the task of constructing a new outside hallway to connect the two wings of the house, since the children could not set foot in the "place of the holy."

John, who had a theological background and taught religion at the local Catholic high school, talked privately with Bob and some of the couples, who dismissed his concerns about their new visionary as a lack of faith on John's part. For several weeks, this "community of the holy" continued with great zeal.

John dropped out of the Bible study and the community after that Saturday. He talked privately with the pastor, and the two of them began weighing the best way to intervene in the situation. Then one Monday night, around midnight, John received a call from Bob, begging him to come over to his house immediately. Bob was sobbing, fear on his face. His fifteen-year-old son had screamed at him, saying, "What do you need to turn our living room into a chapel for? The church and the Blessed Sacrament are just two blocks away." Somehow these words from a child had provoked a much needed moment of insight for Bob.

Something was wrong, very wrong. *The Exorcist*, the movie, had shown just a year or so earlier, and demons were still on people's minds. Now Bob feared that his whole house and all the people involved had been possessed by demons. He asked John and the pastor to conduct an exorcism of the house. John, like me, believes that personalized evil exists, though it is far less powerful than some would like to think. We humans can create enough confusion and do enough evil on our own, in most cases, without having to frequently turn to the devil as an explanation for our predicaments. John told Bob he would be glad to pray for him, but he was not going down the road to another supernatural explanation with him. Soon after, the diocese and the pastor intervened, removing the core couples from leadership of the Bible study and asking John and the priest principal of the high school to direct it.

Judaism and Christianity have lived with visions for thousands of years. The types of misunderstandings that cropped up in the core group of the Bible study have cropped up numerous times. In all likelihood, Anne's first experience, which she recounted for the group, could have been life-giving had it been properly understood. While out in nature, eternity broke through for a moment, Anne's spontaneous, unconscious imagination became involved in the sacred moment. Understood in those terms, the experience could have benefited others when Anne retold it.

VISIONS OUT OF CONTROL

This is not an isolated horror story. As visions have grown in popularity in our culture, so has the abuse of visions.

Two of my friends, highly educated professionals who aren't affiliated with any church body, were introduced to some New Age videos by some friends. On these videos, a man channels a "wise" spirit who supposedly reveals the secrets of the universe and how to live a happy life through positive thinking. Incredibly, my friends have recruited a large circle of other professionals, including physicians and psychotherapists, all enthralled with the videos. I listened to one tape, and to me the "message" sounded like disjointed, self-help gibberish presented as visionary-channeled communication.

My friends take every word as absolute truth, altering their lives according to the messages channeled by the visionary. They invest these words with more authority than what fundamentalist preachers give to the Bible. I ask them why, and they say that the person who does the channeling for the wise spirit sounds so spiritual and sincere that he can't be faking. After all, it's a vision, isn't it?

It's sad that, in too many instances, the literal interpretation of bogus spiritual messages can lead to destructive cults that demean people and rob them of their humanity. This view of visions makes people subject to leaders who claim spiritual hot-line connections to heaven.

Such imbalance is not particular to contemporary times. Spiritual experience has always had the potential for being abused. Martin Buber once told the story of a man who sought spiritual honors. He went to Rabbi Bunam and told him of a vision he had in a dream over and over again, in which his father came to him and told him he was destined to be a great leader. The rabbi listened to him and then paused in a long silence and said, "I see that you are prepared to become a leader of men. If your father comes to you once more, answer him that you are ready to lead, but that now he should also appear to the people whom you are suppose to lead."[1]

Within Christianity there can also be abuse. I recently came across a pamphlet about a South American Catholic visionary who receives "direct revelations," as the pamphlet put it, from Jesus and Mary. The pamphlet said that hers were likely the greatest prophetic experiences since Moses saw God face-to-face.

In a similar manner, visions from sites of spiritual activity—which might be ultimately healthy and worthy of belief—can be used in uplifting ways or in ways that lead to confusion. As a Roman Catholic, I think particularly of approved Marian sites such as Lourdes or Fatima. Here the church is cautious. It never requires belief in such postbiblical visions, and it can only say, after thorough investigation and a lapse of time, that they are worthy of belief for those who choose to believe. Visions from such sites can never be validly seen as the equivalent of Scripture or the authority of church teaching. Such sites have touched and transformed the lives of millions of people. My own visit to the shrine at Guadalupe in Mexico forever changed me. Most people allow the inspiration of these sites to aid them in living whole, balanced spiritual lives.

Other sites that are yet to be approved, such as Medjugorje, have profoundly influenced the lives of millions. Everywhere I meet scores of people whose lives have been turned around through visiting Medjugorje or hearing inspiring stories from there. There is a powerful healing energy of love from that simple Bosnian village that has touched people throughout the world. I don't know what the church will ultimately decide about Medjugorje, but I believe there is a real possibility, from the good fruit that has been born, that the church's verdict will be affirmative.

Most people let the visions from Marian sites help them grow closer to Christ and the whole message of biblical faith in a balanced way. But some do not. Some treat the messages and visions from the sites as though they were part of the Bible. I've read pamphlets that present the messages of Fatima or Medjugorje as though the words carried weight equal to, or even greater than, the Gospels.

I read one pamphlet that suggested that priests' ability to celebrate the Eucharist would grow weak, and that the elements they consecrated would grow weak and ineffective, unless they supercharged their priestly energies by a visit to Medjugorje. The same pamphlet suggested that failure to visit Medjugorje was the same as consciously failing to meet Jesus if you were alive at the same time he lived and had the means to visit him. Visiting the site would be just the same as journeying with Christ and the apostles in Palestine in the time of Christ's death. Such assertions run blatantly against church teaching and the teaching of Scripture. Of course such pamphlets aren't coming from the actual visionaries and church people on the scene at Medjugorje and are by no means approved by the priests in charge in Medjugorje.

Even a wonderful visionary event can be misused. Any true, authentic expression of the holy can be misused. As we all know, the Bible can be misused and misapplied.

HOW MUCH AUTHORITY SHOULD VISIONS HAVE?

The central problem is the implied belief that visions or messages carry the authority of Scripture or the teaching ministry of the church. It doesn't have to be stated outright, but when people treat those messages in the manner of the examples I've cited, they are ultimately claiming this kind of authority for visions.

During the Montanist controversy, the church long ago said a loud no to any individual or group acting as an unmediated visionary mouthpiece for God. For those of us within the Christian tradition, God's revelation in Christ has an absolutely unrepeatable character. Even if the recipient of a visionary message is a canonized saint, theologian Benedict Groeschel warned, that person "may indeed make errors in understanding that revelation or in reporting experiences which are not authentic revelations."

Scripture itself, the heart of revelation, is not primarily a book filled with hot-line visionary and prophetic messages coming from on high. Rather, Scripture presents the drama of God's acting in the history of a particular people, leading them, guiding them, and redeeming them from bondage in Egypt. The prophetic and visionary parts of the Bible interpret and make real this action of God in history and ultimately interpret the presence and activity of God in all our lives.

For those of us in the Christian tradition, God revealed God's fullness by becoming a human being in Jesus, living our life, dying our death, and delivering his humanity to the Father, who raised him from the dead. The visions and wonders of the New Testament played an essential deepening, interpreting role, supercharging the whole drama of God's taking on our humanity with wonder. But the visions weren't the story; they highlighted the story.

Karl Rahner, one this century's preeminent theologians, made the same point:

> Any given private revelation is always—as experience shows, in Scripture and in the Church—a synthesis in which the character of the recipient, as determined historically (theologically, culturally, etc.) and psychologically, is fused with the mystical or normal grace given to him in the depths of his existence. Hence one cannot exclude the possibility of illusions, misinterpretations and distortions, even where there is genuine private revelation.[2]

Of course, most of our visions don't rise to the definition of "private revelation" but are rather the blending of inner images and thoughts with the gifts of grace that God gives to all God's children.

The ordinary visions we all have and the visions that come to the attention of the broader church, such as those of saints or from sites such as Lourdes, are always a mixture of human subjectivity, the stuff of people's lives, the stuff of memories and inner images, as well as the religious training a person has received. Mixed in with this can be a true encounter with the holy. And really, this side of glory, we cannot separate one from the other, nor do we need to.

VISIONS POINT US TOWARD GOD

The better route is to allow the visions that receive wide attention, as well as the ordinary visions we all have, to be inspiring pointers to God, in the way sacred chant or icons point us to God, rather than as sources of concrete information. Instead of becoming substitutes for or additions to Scripture, these moments, rightly appropriated, open our eyes wide to new depths in Scripture and church teaching, making them vibrantly alive. Used rightly, such moments ultimately point to the God who is always coming to us in every event of our lives.

What about all the visions that predict things that come true, visions that have about them the quality of the supernatural and the extraordinary? Some of the visions from my own life seem to have that quality at first glance. For instance, when I was a thirteen-year-old struggling with brain damage and isolation, a vision gave me hope and a promise where none seemed to exist before.

But there's another way of looking at these experiences. Deep down, I likely knew that I had untapped strengths and abilities. And eventually, my teacher Margaret Cox, Cardinal Law, and others saw the strengths and abilities in me and called them out. Mixed in with all this was a mysterious, holy element that came from God's beyond.

That holy element comes to us all, *but it's always mixed with the stuff of our being.*

Sometimes—and this is a mystery we will likely never grasp—truly remarkable happenings can occur when God touches us. We are healed or witness some otherworldly occurrence. But even these remarkable events get mixed in with our inner images and even our illusions. Groeschel highlighted the case of St. Catherine Labouré. She had a visionary experience in which she foretold the bloody massacres at a French commune forty years before they happened; she predicted the exact date. She made some other predictions that turned out wrong. When confronted about this, she just admitted she was "getting it wrong." As Groeshel put it, "This admission of simply 'getting it wrong' on the part of this simple visionary is something one should never forget."[3]

When venturing into the area of prediction or the realm some call the paranormal, even highly inspiring visionaries, whose messages touch us profoundly, can often end up like St. Catherine Labouré: "getting it wrong." Those of us within the Christian tradition must always check to see whether our religious experiences or the religious experiences of others square with Scripture and church teaching. If an experience is not in line with church teaching, we should reject the experience. The same goes for talk about visions. If pamphlets or books treat certain visions with the authority only the Bible should receive, we can be sure that the pamphlets or books are questionable.

Discerning visions not only means squaring our visions with the teaching of our communities of faith. It means squaring our visions with the moral teachings of our faith communities. For me as a Roman Catholic, that means not only that visions not contradict Church teachings but that they be in accord with Church moral teaching. For instance, a spiritual experience suggesting that it's okay to steal or express racial hatred must be rejected immediately.

I recently read a book on mysticism and ecstasy by a well-known spiritual writer from what I call the nonattached segment of spirituality (nonattached meaning that it is not rooted in an established religious tradition). Normally I shy away from spiritual books that don't come from a valid tradition, but this one seemed different. At first I thoroughly enjoyed it. She quoted Teresa of Ávila and other Christian and Jewish mystics on ecstatic experience. Then, after telling myself for page after page that this book was different from all the free-floating, individualistic books on spirituality, I hit a stone wall. The author said that she had learned to follow the highs of her ecstasies no matter where they led her and that real spiritual highs need physical release. She then described the spiritual ecstasies that led her to have an affair with a married man and eventually leave her husband and daughter (her daughter would be better off with the husband, she said). I threw the book into the wall, thinking, "That's what's wrong with non-attached spirituality." Adultery certainly doesn't square with Scripture and tradition.

DISCERNMENT AND VISIONS

Walking wisely with visions means embarking on a journey of education. It means gaining a thorough knowledge of our faith. It means being intimately familiar with Scripture and church teaching. To fully plumb the riches of our spiritual encounters, we need to plumb the riches of the church's theology. For those of us who are Roman Catholic, excellent tools for learning church teaching, in addition to the Scriptures, are the Catechism and the documents of Vatican II. The richer our total understanding grows of the whole broad drama of redemption as handed on in Scripture and interpreted through church teaching, the richer our visions will grow. That growing, expanding understanding of the wonderful wisdom and mysteries of the faith provides lots of paint for our visions, and our spiritual experiences in turn make alive, vivid, immediate, and present this rich, holy, and ancient teaching of the church.

Most of the complex discernment rules for visions common around the turn of the nineteenth century were for visions that claimed to be highly supernatural messages to the church or world or that professed to be extraordinary happenings in the midst of an individualistic, highly mystical inner journey. Very few of us will ever experience those sorts of visions. Three simple questions can help us discern the health of our visions, going to the core issues of discerning visions: Do they help us love and serve better? Do they line up with the teachings of Scripture and our faith tradition? Are they consistent with our faith community's moral teaching?

I am often shocked at how many people follow one visionary after another, centering their lives on marvelous happenings and seemingly wondrous messages from visionary sites, without even a basic knowledge of their own faith tradition.

One friend, a physician, journeyed to most of the purported sites of Marian apparitions, both approved and nonapproved. Every night before retiring he read messages from those visionaries like others read the Bible. I asked him once if he had ever read any of the documents of Vatican II. He replied, "No, they are too boring." I asked him if he had ever read the Chalcedonian Creed and the early faith statements of the church. He looked puzzled; he didn't know what I was talking about. He possessed a brilliant mind, yet he was working out of nearly complete de facto ignorance of basic teachings, such as the humanity and divinity of Christ, the Trinity, and how those teachings developed.

Eventually, he enrolled in a summer program at a Catholic college and got a master's degree in theology. That education, more than following visions, turned him around and helped him grow into a great asset to his parish and diocese. He kept his openness to visions, but they served to make alive the rich, solid, broad faith he now held. The messages and experiences of visionaries, instead of being the near-total content of his faith, now became inspiring pointers that enlivened the vast and holy landscape that comprises the faith handed on to us by the apostles.

TALKING ABOUT VISIONS

By now, perhaps, you are wondering if it is OK to attribute anything in our lives to God, since our experience of the holy is so mediated by our inner and outer worlds. You've probably noticed the many times I have said that God came to me, touched me, and changed me through my spiritual experiences. You've heard me quote inner words, inner knowing, in a way that suggested that their origin was in God's activity. You've heard me tell how others have also been touched by God's interrupting their lives with infusions of the holy. The spiritual literature of the faith abounds with the language of God's communicating to us, God's coming to us, and God's acting in us. When and how can we speak of God's speaking to us?

There is a way we can speak of God's communication, a way we can tell of the divine nearness that sometimes leaves our souls trembling. That way is to use the language of poetry, the language of devotion, a language that is, finally and ultimately, the language of those in love.

God always comes, always speaks, always communicates, in the inmost part of our souls, through God's footprints in nature, through remarkable and mysterious happenings in our lives. The problem is that we do not yet see clearly, see fully. We see through that mirror darkly, as St. Paul reminded us.

Yet we need to speak of God's communicating in our midst. We need to hear others speak of God's doings and speak of God's speech. How, then, can we speak of this discourse and conversation that we feel so intimately but do not yet fully grasp or fully see or fully hear?

The age-old wisdom is that there is a way, there is a language. That language is the language of poetry, of devotion. It is not a literal speaking, an absolute speaking, or a revelatory speaking, in the way only the Bible speaks. It is not an interpretation, in the way only the church interprets. Rather it is the wonderfully imprecise language of being caught in love.

In terms of human relationships you might, at a special, intimate time, tell your mother that she is the whole world to you. You might tell a spouse, "You are the moon and the stars." You aren't talking in literal language. You don't mean that your mother is literally the universe or that your spouse is the big, round rock that circles the earth. You use the language that flows from you, the language of poetry.

In that same way, throughout Christian and Jewish history, people tell of God's speaking and God's coming using the language of poetry. We just need to step back from that language and know that it is not absolute language, not the language of revelation, but speech laden with the wonderfully imprecise, humble, "not fully knowing" language of poetry.

Recently my pastor gave a sermon on his decision to become a priest. When my pastor was twelve, a priest spoke at his school. The priest quoted Frost's poem about the "road less traveled" as a description of the priesthood. Looking back, my pastor now says that God was speaking to him through that priest's words, through that poem. My pastor was using the language of poetry, the language of devotion.

We may all speak of God speaking to us, God acting in us, God coming to us. In fact, try though we may, we could not really hold back from such speaking. But it is the language of lovers, not absolute language. If we know it for what it is and don't confuse it with revelation, it is a right and wonderful way to speak of the holy.

spiritual

emergencies

MOST OF THE TIME, GENUINE SPIRITUAL EXPERIENCES LEAD TO BETTER overall emotional health. Even scientific studies, as we have seen, clearly demonstrate this. But most of us know people, maybe even ourselves, whose lives have been thrown off balance when flooded by spiritual sensations and ideas. In the older traditions, such periods were called "spiritual inebriation." They were seen as passageways to greater growth, times of temporary imbalance that led to the transformation of the whole personality.

Today many psychotherapists call this kind of flooding experience a "spiritual emergency." It is an emergency in the obvious sense that it can be a time of great distress that calls for quick remedial action. But it is also an emergency in the sense that it's an emergence. Something new is being born. The whole personality is coming alive to God.

Tumult, imbalance, and a flood of spiritual feelings are characteristics of a spiritual emergency. Everyday reality, responsibilities, and commitments fade into the background as intense, unfocused reality surges in. There is a temporary loss of steadiness in life, and sometimes a temporary loss of common sense.

One psychologist-researcher, Kristin Watson, at the University of Victoria in British Columbia described spiritual emergency in poignant words: "One is bombarded and consumed by tumultuous inner experiences that challenge beliefs and one's relationship to . . . reality." At times, Watson said, the body can even be affected: "Forceful energies streaming through the body . . . and the psychological, visionary manifestations may leave one sounding and feeling incomprehensibly overwhelmed by unconscious, mythic material."[1]

While not all spiritual emergencies have all these symptoms, they share one characteristic in the short term: They destabilize. The early biographers of St. Francis of Assisi described the early period of his conversion as a time when to others he seemed crazed, like a person drunk with love. His spiritual emergency was a needed experience en route to an eventual wholeness and balance drenched with God. Francis had the advantage of living in a culture familiar with the flows of the spiritual life, including periodic emergencies of the kind he experienced.

Sometimes renewal retreats, such as Cursillo, Marriage Encounter, or charismatic retreats, cause participants to experience a type of spiritual emergency. Usually the leaders of these movements have lots of experience in shepherding people through these spiritual breakthroughs to a balanced, richer walk in life. Occasionally they fail in this regard. Discovering the beauties of contemplative and meditative prayer can sometimes trigger an emergency as the person's new spiritual life emerges. Similar feelings of overwhelming spiritual experience can happen when people hear about major scenes of visions, perhaps purported appearances of Mary or major revivals such as Brownsville in Pensacola. Their lives begin to lose balance for a while, and they are consumed by the spiritual realities they hear about and are flooded by spiritual feelings.

EMERGENCIES AND ADDICTIONS

Many people who continue to grow in the spiritual life have periods of "emergencies." Sometimes they can be quite distressing, but they are temporary phases.

This was true for me. When the light came to me when I was thirteen, I thought I had been touched by magic. When I was flooded by spiritual memories of my grandfather on my first trip as an adult back to the site of his cottage, I was thrown into a state of spiritual emergency. I returned every day to the bluff, remembering old chants and stories. I was flooded by a sense of God and memories of Pop—memories I had long repressed. I lost track of some of my responsibilities. I swore I would always wear some form of Native clothing wherever I went. I showed up in church one day in a bright red Cherokee long-shirt and moccasins—just fine for a day celebrating different cultures but not for an ordinary Sunday Mass.

My father gently helped me keep things in perspective while not denying the powerful recovery of my spiritual past that now so entranced me. My friend Robert took me aside and gently but firmly brought me back to everyday reality. My cousin Dy, a well-known Native spiritual elder, stayed on the phone with me, an hour every day, it seemed, for a couple of weeks. She didn't dismiss my experiences or give them undue gravity. She said that when people were flooded with vision in the old days, they were watched carefully and were not allowed to make important decisions. They were released from that watchfulness only when they could laugh at themselves for their excesses. Then they were ready to integrate their new insights and experiences with their lives.

After two or three weeks of friends keeping me grounded, I finally could laugh at myself for walking around town in moccasins and even wanting to go out in public with medicine paint on my face and feathers in my hair. (Fortunately, friends had talked me down before I emerged with paint, feathers, and beaded shirt.)

But overall, the trip to the bluff was one of the most needed experiences of my life. I was changed for the better by seeing Christ at the bluff, letting the sacred and Native realities of my grandfather fill me up, and once again owning my beginnings. I was lucky to have friends and family around who could gently guide me back to common sense so that I could, in due time, fully appropriate all the new insights and realities. I'm lucky. I am surrounded by many wise friends who know me inside and out.

Because people going through an intense spiritual experience may feel that God is speaking directly to them, they are prone to make unwise decisions about their life's course. They should postpone decisions until their lives settle. The good effects of spiritual awakening can come only after the tumult has died down. People going through spiritual emergency need kind and gentle help from others to manage the passage safely and move to the place of good growth.

One reason mistakes happen during spiritual emergency is that we lack knowledge. The basic wisdom for living with vivid spirituality is often missing at a time when people everywhere are returning to spirituality. We no longer have the communities we once had, hundreds of years ago, which had innate, organic knowledge of how to live well with visions. We no longer have such wisdom passed along to us.

Anne and the members of Commander Bob's community, whom I described earlier, were stuck in a group spiritual emergency and weren't open to the help available to guide them through it. Many of us have known individuals and groups that seemed stuck in a constant state of spiritual emergency. These situations and people can give spiritual experiences a bad name.

For a few people, spiritual emergency becomes a way of life rather than a stage to pass through. Some quit their jobs to center only on the spiritual. Many badger friends and fellow church members to share in their transports of enthusiasm. Others leave spouses, even families, who don't share the high-decibel intensity. They can become downright obnoxious to others in demanding that they share the fervor.

When spiritual emergency becomes a constant state of spiritual imbalance for an individual, or even whole groups of people, a state of spiritual addiction can develop. Intense experiences can flood our bodies with endorphins, morphinelike chemicals that our bodies produce naturally. People can become addicted to these emotional states. We see that happen with people who become addicted to the adrenaline rush that anger brings, becoming "rage-oholics," constantly losing their tempers in order to keep the adrenaline rush. It is possible to become experience junkies, treating spiritual experiences as new highs. Rather than integrate the initial breakthrough experience and move on in their journey toward God, spiritual addicts can attempt to replicate the initial intensity by moving from one new spiritual interest to another.

The truth is that we are not constructed for a state of constant spiritual tumult and intensity. Graced moments, quiet visions, and extraordinary spiritual events may be part of our lives, but they are not constant companions. They are meant to help us. We can channel them into our everyday living and let them help us fulfill our life's commitments. But becoming addicted to spiritual experiences will destabilize our lives.

JEFF'S STORY

Jeff, a friend of mine, is a priest who was recently appointed pastor of one of the largest parishes in his diocese. More than twenty years ago, Jeff had a spiritual experience that developed into a full-blown emergency.

At the time of his crisis, Jeff was a senior in high school, and his life seemed to be going nowhere. He was a classic underachiever. Aptitude tests put him in the upper 5 percent, but his grades didn't show it. Despite coaxing and pushing from his parents and teachers, he coasted by on a C-minus average. Neither was he particularly interested in sports. He loved to spend full days cycling through the countryside by himself or with friends. Introverted and shy, Jeff was gentle for a teenage boy, but he grew distant from his parents, communicating little with them except for a few quiet grunts at the dinner table when they asked him questions.

Jeff's rebellion was quieter than that of many teens. He was caught once in the presence of a friend who was shoplifting. But other than that, he was fairly well behaved.

He rarely broke his parent's curfew. He began to date in his senior year, and the girls he went with were quiet and wholesome like him. All in all, Jeff was a good kid. Considering all the things that could go wrong in a teen's life, his parents felt that they at least had some blessings to count, even if they wished for more direction in Jeff's life.

Then Jeff attended a weekend retreat offered by the local ecumenical teen movement. Like many youth retreats, it was emotional. On retreats, young people, who live so much on an emotional level anyway, open up to the spiritual in an emotional way with each other. In the midst of peers they open up their secret hurts, cry, laugh, have fun, talk about God, and together feel the inrush of the holy.

This discovery of spirituality was a jolt for Jeff. The Sunday night he returned home from the retreat, he rushed in the door, brightness twinkling in his eyes, and hugged each of his parents while saying, "Praise the Lord" over and over. Without further conversation, he retreated to his room and locked the door.

Jeff was as noncommunicative as ever with his parents over the next weeks, except for the hugs and the "praise the Lord's."

Many of the teens in the group were Protestant, and Jeff visited their churches with them. This was his first experience in non-Catholic churches. He particularly liked the music at the black Pentecostal church. Visions are a common part of prayer and worship in the Pentecostal tradition. So are exuberant prayer and the body movement known as holy dancing. Jeff tried out all of this.

Instead of spending so much of his time cycling, as he used to, Jeff stayed locked behind his bedroom door a great deal of the time, except for school and meetings with the teen ecumenical group.

His parents' apprehension grew. When they asked their son what was wrong, a beatific smile and faraway look would cross his face, and he would say some pious phrase like "God is love." Then one day his parents knew they had to intervene. Jeff had forgotten to lock his door, and his mother saw it slightly ajar. She saw Jeff, his hands lifted toward heaven, his eyes open and ecstatic, and tears coursing down his cheeks. He was moving his body in rhythm as he quietly chanted, "Hallelujah, hallelujah."

His mother briskly entered the room, grabbed Jeff by the shoulder, and said in an uncompromising tone, "You are coming in here and talking to your father and me about what's going on."

Tears of worry trickled down his mother's face as she asked him over and over if he was on drugs. His father cried too.

Jeff finally opened up. He spoke of having visions of becoming a priest or a monk. He told of all the teens at that church praying over him and having visions that God was calling him to a special purpose. To his parents, who knew only Catholicism, his words were incoherent.

His father swallowed hard and asked him, "Do you have visions, Jeff?"

Jeff said that he did. In his dreams, angels had told him that one day he would preach.

HOW TO HANDLE A SPIRITUAL EMERGENCY

Jeff was exhibiting some of the classic signs of a spiritual emergency. In my experience, five signs are most compelling:

- You have a sense of spiritual flooding, of being overwhelmed with spiritual sensations for more than a day or two.
- The feelings are disorienting or have a tumultuous quality to them.
- For a period of a week or more, you lose interest in reality: daily responsibilities, small pleasures such as taking a walk or relaxing with a newspaper, fun times with family or friends.

- Because of these spiritual impulses, you feel a consuming need to stay constantly engaged in spiritual practices.
- Because of emerging spiritual realities, you feel an overwhelming urgency to make major life changes, such as taking on a new vocation, forming new relationships, or joining a new church.

Whenever emergence turns into emergency, it's an occasion for guidance.

The first and most important thing to remember is that spiritual emergence, even if it turns into an emergency, is an invitation to grow spiritually. God is issuing you a summons to come closer, to open up more doors of your personality to God. The newness of all these realities is just temporarily destabilizing. In the long term, the experience means more growth. If you are helping someone in a spiritual emergency, remind him that what he's experiencing is likely the sign of a great spiritual good that is emerging. St. Francis of Assisi passed through spiritual emergency, as did many of the great saints. Creativity, new insight, fresh love, and fresh wonder can all emerge on the other side of a spiritual emergency. They can be, as Emma Bragdon said, "gateways to higher functioning."[2]

Another important step in dealing with spiritual emergency is, as psychologist Watson put it, "temporarily discontinuing active inner exploration." This doesn't mean that the person must stop praying. It does mean temporarily ceasing intense inner spiritual practices such as contemplative styles of prayer, meditation, the reading of mystical and contemplative writers, and any journaling that involves intensive inner probing. Avoid for a time excessive use of the rosary or similar meditations. Avoid all intense prayer. All this is a temporary expedient until the person gets on an even keel again, until the emergency turns back into emergence. After things become steady, the person can resume these practices with even greater benefit than before.

Conversational prayer is a great help during a spiritual emergency. In the midst of this rediscovery of different prayer forms, we can forget one important core truth of spirituality, one that we've always known: We can talk to God in conversational prayer! Using conversational prayer in the midst of a spiritual emergency grounds us in the reality that our God is immediately personal. We can tell God all our feelings, all the newness, all the sensations, in our ordinary, human words. God is personal. Talking to God is the most basic form of prayer we learned as toddlers. As adults, we can and should pray that way. Even better, we can actually pray out loud.

People going through a spiritual emergency should be encouraged to talk regularly to someone else, perhaps a minister, priest, counselor, or family member. Pick someone noted for gentleness, someone who will not disparage the spiritual experience but will just listen. The most important qualification for such a listener is common sense that is grounded in everyday reality.

I would also recommend engaging in ritual and liturgical prayer, such as attending Mass or saying the daily office. The church's prayers are grounded and tested; their steadiness can slow us down, calm us, bring us back to common realities. If the person is in the habit of journaling, he or she can continue but should avoid inner exploration, concentrating instead on the stuff of daily life, such as work or school commitments, family, and ordinary events.

Jeff received the guidance he needed. His parents took him to the local mental-health clinic for evaluation by a clinically trained pastoral counselor. For a week, Jeff came in every day for psychological testing and counseling. The counselor even took a blood sample to screen for drugs.

When he spoke to Jeff's parents, the counselor was reassuring: "After thorough counseling and spending hours talking to Jeff, I can assure you that your son is suffering from only one condition: adolescence. He tests within normal range on most clinical measures. He's a little shy for his age, but otherwise normal. He's had some powerful spiritual experiences lately, but lots of kids do. He's been around some churches with a different prayer style than what you are used to."

Jeff's dad asked, "Then what's happening?"

"It may be something good. I think he's thinking about his direction in life and might be interested in the priesthood. It could be a phase, but why don't you have him talk to someone at your church."

His parents followed through on that suggestion. Their pastor referred Jeff to the vocations director for the diocese, who was stationed at a nearby parish. The vocations director was wise in dealing with the exuberance of youth. Jeff wanted to leave for seminary immediately. The vocations director slowed him down, spent time with him, counseled and befriended him.

He helped Jeff understand that he was going through a flooding of spiritual experience that people often go through when sacred break-throughs happen in their lives. He told Jeff to postpone definite decisions about the priesthood for some time, until the flood tide subsided.

He got Jeff involved with more grounded ministries in the church, such as helping out with the ministry to the destitute. Jeff took part in a three-week, church-sponsored mission trip to Mexico.

With counseling from the vocations director, Jeff's life took on direction. The director said that they would consider Jeff for seminary only if he completed his first year of college with a B average or better. Jeff buckled down to solid studying for the first time in his life and ended the year with an A average, then transferred to college-level seminary, where he received a well-rounded formation. Then his bishop sent him to Rome to complete his theological education.

Jeff at eighteen had gone through a spiritual emergency. He was touched by the holy in a way that was temporarily destabilizing. But it was a temporary imbalance that led eventually to a much greater balance.

THE IMPORTANCE OF BEING GROUNDED

The most important step you can take to deal with a spiritual emergency is grounding. The essence of being grounded is to become present to everyday reality. A person going through a spiritual emergency should be encouraged to pay attention to his or her body, to exercise, to go out in nature. A person in this highly charged spiritual state should force him- or herself to get back into everyday routines, to stop and do a life inventory, to look at commitments, and to do fun things with people—activities that do not involve spirituality.

In today's culture, it's good to encourage spiritual activities with spiritual people, but sometimes it's good to take a break from the spiritual and do fun, earthy things. Take a trip to the beach. Work in the garden.

Grounding is also an important activity for the spiritual life. We need to remain grounded in daily realities whether we are in the midst of a spiritual emergency or not. It's a good preventative; it helps keep spiritual emergences from turning into emergencies. It puts this world right before our eyes, this world that Christ forever graced by joining with creation and humanity in incarnation.

Our spiritual experiences are for the sake of our living; we don't live for the sake of our spiritual experiences. Keeping the commitments, the tasks, and the earthy joys of our lives is central to the truly spiritual life. Our visions make the everydayness of our lives godly and holy. Leave out the everydayness and we eliminate an important reason for visions—the transfiguring of this all-too-real world of ours. If we leave out the earthly realities, we become too spiritual even for incarnation.

Another important step in dealing with spiritual emergency is catharsis. When we are flooded with spiritual emotions, we need to express them. We need to get the feelings out as we feel them. Some of that can happen in conversational prayer with God. But it also needs to happen with another human being. If you are having intense visions, find someone who listens well without judging, who can just let you express all the new feelings.

Also, avoid making any major life decisions until the time of spiritual emergency has passed.

HOW TO INTEGRATE BACK INTO LIFE

The last task in dealing with spiritual emergency is what Bragdon calls "integrating back to life."[3]

In many respects, the exercises in this book have been designed to help you integrate your spiritual experiencing back into the flow of your life. Integrating all these new perspectives, feelings, and insights can come only after the crisis phase of spiritual emergency has subsided. If you have friends who can be understanding and accepting of your experiencing, talk it over with them.

Keep before your eyes the vividness of the spiritual experience you have just passed through and all the varied incarnate realities of your life. Look at your relationships, work, church life, family, reading, hobbies, and so forth. Gently and very slowly begin to look at how your spiritual experiencing can affect all these areas. If you have access to a spiritual director, a minister, or a therapist (who accepts your faith), by all means talk to that person.

You may want to alter some of your life's directions. Maybe you are called to form some new and more edifying friendships. Perhaps you are called into a new ministry in your church. Maybe you are called to more intense spiritual practice. Perhaps, even, you may be called into a career change. If you are in fact heading for change, be sure to go slowly. Looking at these possible changes, large and small, can take place only after the intensity has subsided. Any major changes should be in consultation with the important people in your life. Most of all, they should be tested with common sense. As one friend always reminds me, "If it doesn't make common sense, it doesn't make sense." Still, there are those rare times of holy foolishness that defy common sense, like Mother Teresa's call to help the dying of Calcutta. But those are the rare exceptions.

Vocations to priesthood, to vowed religious life, or to marriage can all become clear in the wake of spiritual emergence or emergency. St. Francis of Assisi began his community, his life of heroic service, only after the initial intense flooding had subsided and then only after he had talked it over and received the approval of Guido, his bishop.

A sense of calling to serve the church in a fuller way, even in a full-time way, involves more than the intense feelings that come with spiritual awakening. It involves the church and the faith community validating that call, saying yes to it. Too many times, intense spiritual emergency has led people into individualistic ministries without the church's recognition or guidance. Yet the wildness of spiritual experiencing has been responsible for some of the most heroic and wonderful vocations in the history of faith.

HOW TO HELP SOMEONE IN A SPIRITUAL EMERGENCY

The first step in helping someone through a spiritual emergency is to stay grounded yourself. Avoid getting caught up in the excitement of the person's intense experiences. Keep your life's commitments and daily realities in perspective as you help. Journal about your feelings as you help. In prayer, ask God's help.

You may also find yourself frightened or repelled by the intensity of the person you are helping. Don't ignore those feelings; acknowledge them to yourself. Then try to be as nonjudgmental as you can in listening to your friend. Let the person get it all out. Never discount his or her experience.

As much as possible, stay at ease with what is happening. Reading about visions and other spiritual experiences can be helpful if you are going to be helping people in the grips of spiritual emergency on a regular basis.

Carry people who are in spiritual emergency through the steps we mentioned earlier. Suggest that they leave off intense spiritual exercises until things calm down. Encourage them to use the church's prayers and conversational prayer. Remind them that much good can come from what they are going through. Most of all, help ground them in the everyday. Be sure they pay attention to the ordinary pleasures of work and family life. Be a gentle presence to them. After the floods subside, help them integrate their experiences with the rest of life. Try to involve them with a wider circle of people who can support and guide them and keep them grounded. Keep in mind that great good can come to the person and to others through their journeying through this passage of spiritual emergency.

You may need to directly intervene if your friend wants to make sudden life changes in work, relationships, or vocation. Ignatius of Loyola said that important decisions should not be made in either times of great spiritual consolation or times of spiritual deprivation. The in-between times are the only times when wise choices can be made.

Don't hesitate to refer to the clergy or a therapist if you become overwhelmed. Don't let your own life become destabilized by the temporary imbalance in someone else's journey.

Be watchful for other kinds of imbalance. If you work regularly in spiritual direction or pastoral counseling, you may encounter people afflicted with self-inflation. An experience of the infinite can lead us to perceive that we are infinite. We center on self, rather than on God and God's world. Worse still, those with self-inflated spirituality can use spirituality's charm as a tool of power to entice others to follow them, robbing the followers of their own uniqueness.

Another danger is allowing our capacity for sacred experiencing to be triggered by something other than the sacred. Visions, as Luke Timothy Johnson, Scripture professor at Emory University, reminded us, concern that which is ultimate. Many things can masquerade as the ultimate. We have seen how race, ideology, politics, and a sense of self-righteousness can call out to that intimate part of us meant for responding to God. Hitler was good at arousing people's capacity of sacred experiencing and centering it on something other than the ultimate, something that was destructive. We need to give that holy part of ourselves over only to God.

In the intoxication of a flood of spiritual encounter, it's easy to forget that God comes to us in many ways besides our felt experience. God comes through our logic, through handed-down tradition, through other people. Visions are not the whole, just part of the whole. They are transitory, leading to the ultimate reconnecting of our broken hearts, our broken world, our broken communities, the eschaton, the new Jerusalem, the healing of creation. The key is to seek the experience of God, not the God of experiences. It's all part of learning to walk in balance with the sacred.

CHAPTER 16

visions and the
new millennium

Upheaval. Prophecies. Renewal. Great catastrophes. To grab an audience, the media constantly hype the idea that earthshaking change goes together with the coming of the new millennium. Yet little suggests such a change, at least on the surface. Y2K, the millennial computer bug, received quite some attention, but it hardly turned out to be the world-disrupting event a millennium ought to bring.

There isn't even an impending bogeyman anymore. Now that Communism is the preserve of geriatric Russian pensioners, Moscow can't be cast as the great villain. We rush into the next millennium without the gargoyles of apocalyptic catastrophe staring at us from every side.

Yet beneath the calm surface, a sense of impending change rumbles within the tectonic plates of our world. A hunger, a deep wanting, rumbles around in the hidden places of our individual hearts and in the one heart of our shared humanity as well. Ironically, that yearning has little to do with the millennium, little to do with the addition of one more year to the calendar. This hunger is due partly to something we suppressed a few hundred years ago.

The change of century in 1900 was marked by promise of massive change brought about by new technology and scientific inventions. Then everyone stood on tiptoe to see the marvels that technology would surely bring. The twentieth century more than fulfilled those expectations. With computer technology, the changes and discoveries that will come in the next century should be even greater than in the last century. Yet technology doesn't carry the same fascination now as it did in 1900. Few stand on tiptoe with wonder at the new science the way they did a century ago. We now know that no matter how massive the technological changes, science and technology will not fill what we most hunger for: the completion, filling, and mending of our souls.

Today we hunger for something far more human than the wizardry of scientific change. We hunger for a part of our very humanity—our capacity for visions. We hunger for what is subtle, deep, resonant, and basic to our living. Several hundred years ago we lost something priceless, as priceless as our emotions, our art, and our drama. We lost the very stories that bind us together. We partly lost the right to embrace openly our sacred envisioning. We lost the right to let sacred seeing gift us with a vision of the holy that could mend us, unite us, and tie heaven and earth together.

Soon after Communism's old iron walls collapsed, people in Eastern Europe complained that they had been guinea pigs for seventy years in an artificially conceived utopian experiment that failed. We in the Western world are beginning to sense that we too have been part of a failed experiment—the experiment of living without the sacred. The ability of sacred envisioning is built into the marrow of our souls, into the raw cells of our physiology. For countless tens of thousands of years, our ancestors lived with visions, were enriched by visions, met the nameless mystery that loves through visions, and were healed through visions. When that went underground, we lost not just a part of our heritage but also a part of ourselves. We are at the end of a failed three-hundred-year experiment. It repressed much of our humanity in the same way that Marxism repressed people's humanity. And just as people in the former dictatorships of Eastern Europe are struggling to reconnect with their roots, we are struggling to once again draw life from those who have gone before us. We are struggling to reclaim an authentic spirituality. Another wall begins to come down.

We live in a time of the changing of worlds—not because of the millennium, but because something vitally human can no longer be ignored and pushed deeper than our memory.

I have, in earlier chapters, mentioned the signs of hunger for a renewed and authentic spirituality. I've spoken of new interest in visions and the wondrous, in new sightings of Mary, in religious movements among the poor that have moved across continents.

I've also spoken of the many people whose spirituality is unattached to historic religious communities. We can see the abundant crop of spiritual books in the bookstores. On television, the History Channel, the Learning Channel, the Discovery Channel, and other solid educational channels devote a significant portion of their airtime to stories of wonder and the paranormal. Serious science takes up the study of near-death visions and the physiology of spiritual experiencing. Top medical journals run articles on the healing power of prayer, meditation, and spirituality. I worry about this nonattached spiritual questing, which is divorced from the religious communities and the community memories that bring balance and health to visionary experiences. Yet I still rejoice that people search for the sacred.

The thirst is just as intense in traditional religious communities. The reports of appearances of Mary are just the most obvious sign of a desire to touch and see the holy. Revivals involving hundreds of thousands of people break out in places like Pensacola, Florida. Theologian Kilian McDonnell said that if current trends continue, the Pentecostal body of Christianity will be the largest body of Christians in the world at the end of the next century. At many large metropolitan synagogues, people have to sign up months in advance to get into classes on Jewish mysticism and spirituality, a development not even imagined two decades ago.

These accounts of visions and a desire for the sacred are not signs of millennial hysteria. They are signs of homesickness, a gnawing hunger for an essential reality. They are the astounding resurfacing of ancient subterranean streams from a long history that always flowed beneath the surface of our collective life. As we awaken to this rediscovery, we will find that we have a different history from the one we've been taught.

Another sign of impending change is the pain that spreads out before us in spite of unprecedented prosperity. The sight of well-raised, well-educated, pampered middle-class youngsters turning to violent shootings tells of vast inner deprivation, even among our most educated and most prosperous.

A loneliness covers our land thicker than the smog that still fills our cities. Isolation spreads into homes rich and poor. A hunger for home, long-forgotten, aches in our souls. The massive changes our world has undergone have broken up our natural neighborhoods and communities. The natural human ties that held our ancestors to place and history were long ago severed by our mobility. Rich and poor alike find themselves cogs in a nameless, impersonal economic machine. We disseminate libraries of information over the Internet in a flash, but we are losing the ability to touch.

We may not be able name the home we have lost, much less conceive of a pathway back, but we know that something monumental has been lost. The loss of home weighs down on us more heavily than did the threat of thousands of now-rusting Soviet missiles.

WISDOM OR FOLLY?

The question is not whether the next millennium will see a rebirth of visions. That question is easily answered. Suppression won't work any longer; an era filled with visions is unavoidable. The question is whether we will live wisely, or unwisely, with our visions.

Living unwisely with visions means treating them as holy hot lines and therefore starting lots of competing, even warring, sects, cults, and movements that lack the rootedness to truly transform and heal. Living unwisely with visions means embracing them without looking to the ancient wisdom that fills our long-neglected history of spiritual experiencing. Living unwisely with visions means letting self-serving leaders gain control over others, using the ecstatic and the visionary as their claims to power.

Living wisely with visions means entering the cathedral of the sacred an inch at a time on our knees, with the humility that comes from knowing that we ultimately belong not to ourselves but to a holy and loving God who gifts us with our every breath. Living wisely with visions means humbly seeking, learning, and appropriating again the near-forgotten ancient wisdom about spirituality.

The same question is asked everywhere—by the nonattached spiritual seekers at mall bookstores, by the poor turning to Pentecostalism in Latin America, Africa, and Asia, by Catholics searching for Mary. That question is, How can we see visions and dream dreams again? How can we enter into an authentic, transforming spiritual life that can change a culture?

Yet that question is rarely taken up by theologians, whose job it is to answer such questions. Except for a penchant among some theological writers to keep up with the politically correct cause of the moment, theologians are answering outdated questions, all too often for audiences who no longer exist or care. The predominant issue addressed by many theologians remains making faith understandable to the critically oriented people of today's world. This small audience can be found primarily in vanishing pockets of university faculties.

The methods, the forms of speech, and the norms of theology are borrowed from the disciplines of the modern university. Ironically, these disciplines themselves are changing drastically as many of the brightest at our universities realize that the old critical methods no longer work. They announce the death of modernity and the birth of a new postcritical era.

Theology was once woven into the fabric of the whole. It shared in the tears, the anguish, the amazement of human communities. Augustine helped resolve conflicts, prayed for the sick to be healed, let himself collapse into the anguish of those he cared for. He opened wide "the mouth of the heart" as he put it, to take in astonishment's transforming dimensions. He listened to people's visions and comforted their disappointments. At the same time he was an eminent scholar, conversant in all the thought forms of antiquity. Thomas Aquinas, whose monumental synthesis can awe us even now, fell on the ground with tears in the same prostration of prayer shared by the sick seeking visions at shrines. He opened wide the vital parts of his humanity to the synthesizing touch of visions. Mighty medieval women like Hildegard of Bingen and Julian of Norwich laid out a tapestry of visionary knowing that mended hearts and tied worlds together.

In contrast, our theology, our formal telling of faith's history, too often comes not from the community of the faithful but from the scattered community of the university and for the scattered community of the university.

The modern approach to history and the ancient approach to history differ greatly. Modern historiography and, to some degree, theology approach history from the point of view of an unbiased observer, an unattached outsider. Modern "reconstruction" tends to be "naturalistic, empiricist, and agnostic, at best, toward the claims of anything 'real' lying behind the limits of the natural world," according to Walter Brueggemann.[1] It misses the whole dimension of divine presence and is not open to the astonishment such presence brings. God is expelled from the process of making history.

In contrast, sacred history evokes the presence that lies behind events. Secular history is history from the outside, whereas sacred history tells the world-creating story of the remembering community,

carrying on the mystery that inspired the telling and the remembering and the retelling. As Raymond Van Dam said in his masterful
study of shrine visions and miracles in late antique Gaul, "The saint's
miracles at his tomb marked not only the convergence of past and
present, but also the intersection of heaven and earth."[2]

So-called secular history also has an agenda. In a sense, it is "history
from above," a history of those with power. History is all too often
written by the powerful, those with power at the academy, those who
have a vested interest in keeping things the way they are.

Sacred history is the history of those who are powerless. The
laments of bereaved women, "the protests of raging prophets, the cries
of the poor," the laments of those in anguish make this history full of
imagination. It is the voice of the marginal. The Bible and the classic
writings of Christian spirituality are full of this kind of voice.
Brueggemann called this sacred history "the desperate rhetoric of the
powerless and marginal [who] will have no access to public, formal
power." They therefore must rely on the fierceness, imagination, and
poetry of their speech in telling old memories in such a way that they
make a world and create astonishment. Sacred history, to paraphrase
Brueggemann, is counterhistory. It comes from below.[3]

Powerful symbols, phrases, and stories can say something to one
generation and then through divine inspiration mean something different to other generations and sustain belief and hope over many
generations. Jugren Moltmann said, "Sacred history is pregnant with
the future." The telling of history is the hope in God's future. It allows
us to minister to a world of lost horizons. We are pulled by the future
of God's promise and God's goodness. Sacred history always has an
outward reach.[4]

Sacred history is central to the life of the church. The health—even
the viability—of many historic communities of faith depends on
answering the question of how we can have visions and dream dreams
in our day. This is the question of religious experiencing. The central
task is the recovery, the restoration, the full-hearted repossession of

near-forgotten old memories, the recounting again of another kind of history for the sake of a different kind of future.

VISIONS AND THE CHURCH

If visions are to truly heal, truly reconcile, and truly give hope, they need to take place in a community of human beings—a community with all the nuance and depth that history gives. Our visions are never ours alone any more than our lives are our own. Our visions have meaning only as they are nurtured by community, shared with community, and discerned by community. Visions come for the sake of us all, to unite us in the subterranean strata of our collective humanity.

For me that community is the church, more specifically, the Roman Catholic expression of the church. Visions gift the church enormously. Most priests, ministers, religious, and full-time lay workers are called to their ministries through some form of religious encounter. The movements that bring spiritual vigor to laypeople—charismatic renewal, Marriage Encounter, Cursillo, contemplative prayer, and others—all provide a permissive atmosphere for experiencing the sacred.

In the last few decades, theologians have championed "theology from below." By this they usually mean looking at the stirrings of insight and understanding that later developed into the major doctrines of the faith rather than starting "from the top" with the doctrines. The phrase also has come to mean listening to the poor, the dispossessed, and the marginalized. Theologians should pay more attention to the "theology from below" that is going on today. The unprecedented upsurge in the interest in miracles and Marian apparitions, though not always balanced and often an embarrassment to theologians, is a powerful voice from below. The rapid spread of Pentecostalism in the developing world among the poorest of the poor is a voice from below. African American congregations, which have always had room for visions, emotions, and wonder, are a voice from below. Hispanic Catholics, who have always ceded a large place to wonder, who decorate their homes with colorful and sacred pictures of wonder, are a voice from below. Native American Christians like me, who come from communities that have never lived without visions, are a voice from below. A loud voice resounds from below. Let us heed this voice.

Many religious educators and theologians dismiss this voice with a broad academic sneer. But we must remember that the issue of visions is being pressed most vigorously by the unsophisticated and the marginalized—the people whom the Gospels say are so dear to God and, in their poverty, so close to Christ.

At the same time, the simplistic interpretations of visions that so many enthusiasts latch on to need the moderating influence of tradition. In today's world, scholars hold important keys to the old wisdom. Enthusiasts for visions need these theologians and scholars to bring balance. For their part, theologians and scholars need to hear the loud voice of those touched by visions to help restore rapture and astonishment to their own thinking. Their scholarship needs to catch fire in the same way Augustine's and Ambrose's thought caught fire—in living memory, among ordinary people.

During the controversies that led to the Nicene Creed, the common people called the theologians to orthodoxy and to central Christian realities. In the same way, their loud voice can be a call for theologians to take up once again the issue of religious experiencing. The viability of historic communities of faith depends in large degree on this happening.

Hundreds of millions of people are turning to Pentecostalism in the Third World, tens of millions visit Marian shrines, and the numbers of nonattached religious experiencers are multiplying exponentially. If ever there was a cry from below for guidance, this is it.

Addressing issues of religious experiencing in religious education, at all levels, is also an essential task. Pastors need help in creating a safe place for amazement. Religion teachers miss a great opportunity when they fail to incorporate the ebb and flow of religious experience on the local level. If people do not find space for religious experience in the church, they will find it outside the church.

The reality that we humans are built for visions challenges the way theology is done. One theologian who has thoroughly grasped this is Hans Urs von Balthasar. He called for a kneeling theology—theology to be done on one's knees.

For too long, theology has followed an attitude that is almost enslaved to the ideals of the eighteenth-century Enlightenment, which mandated that everything be critically doubted. It gave rise to what Avery Dulles called the "hermeneutic of suspicion"—a means of interpreting faith by starting with doubt, from the viewpoint of an outside observer. That critical framework is in retreat everywhere. Replacing it, Dulles suggested, should be a hermeneutic of trust. Since we now know that it's impossible to be unbiased observers, we have to pick a stance. Even an electron changes when observed. We should opt for a stance of trust, rather than doubt, in the passed-on wisdom of our faith.

Too often, the theology tied to the Enlightenment answered questions posed by the academy for the academy. Theology needs to maintain its dialogue with all philosophies and answer the questions of philosophers and thinkers. But at the same time, to truly serve the church, theology must come from the heart of the church. It must be sensitive to the questions that come from the heart of the church, from the common believer. Theology must be sensitive to the moves of the Spirit among the lowliest and answer the questions that come from them. Theologians of the academy should realize that, in its power to mold minds, the academy holds the power to make worlds. As Brueggemann constantly reminded us, the academy wields enormous power as it speaks from above.

The voices of local bishops and religious leaders are essential resources for theologians; these voices should serve as guides to the leaders at the academic level. The pastoral leaders of our churches, who, as Dulles put it, "draw on their tacit sense of faith, and on that of their faithful," dry tears, mediate conflicts, listen to stories of wonder, and live in the heart of their people. These local leaders and ministers are closely attuned, in a special way, to the voice from below. Their very commission to guide and lead comes from the center of real church communities.

Our task is to, slowly and with care, inch back to the Enlightenment and behind it. We need to find new, subtle, and rich ways of seeing, tapping again the long-neglected streams of heart and life. Someone as great as Thomas Aquinas could prostrate himself in tears in his cell, seeking a vision to help him synthesize his theology, like a peasant seeking a vision and cure at a shrine. Yet this same Aquinas maintained the rigors of fully educated, critical thought.

At the same time, this discovery of some of the richness before the Age of Reason should be a careful rediscovery. In an attempt to correct the excesses of the Enlightenment we must be wary of a thoughtless embrace of all that preceded it. While we can never be totally critical or objective, we do need to learn to distance ourselves at times. The lessons of the Enlightenment were not all bad. Who would want to believe once more that the world is flat? We are learning again that beauty, poetry, passion—and visions—can be part of our theology, but distance and objectivity, as much as possible, still have their role.

Augustine, Ambrose, the Cappadocian Fathers—virtually all those responsible for the formation of the church's thought life—had visions and celebrated the visions of others, blending head and heart, cognitive thought and visionary experience. It must also be remembered that the greatest female theologians of the church, Hildegard of Bingen, Julian of Norwich, Catherine of Sienna, and so many others, thought and wrote primarily in the literary medium of visions.

The collapse of the idea of a neutral, nonattached observer, so central to Enlightenment thought, leads to another kind of theology, a theology in which the theologian is not just scientific observer. In this beyond-Enlightenment theology, the theologian is entranced, caught up in the beauty of what is seen. While not for a moment neglecting the rigors of scholarship and the times of reflective detachment, spiritual life today calls for nothing less than a theology of adoration, a poetic theology of metaphors, intelligibility, and depth that can again brighten and fire a world that is desperately hungry for the ultimately beautiful.

THE TRUE ROAD HOME

The true road home is always a slow road. This wonder craze, which shows little sign of abating, is a major indication that we are in between the times. One time is gone forever; the coming time isn't here yet. Some of what passes as wonder and spirituality, especially the nonattached spirituality, is merely a brief pause on the way home.

With my own ears I heard old Native stories. When I was a young man, the fire of love in my vision told me that that which is old is that which is new. Carefully and slowly, tasting and absorbing, we need to hear the old stories again and let them work their hidden meaning and transformation in our lives. For me it was Native stories and, later, Christian and Jewish stories. Where did you come from? What have you lost? If we go back a generation or two, many of us find our ancestors in synagogue or in church. We might not make the stories our own, at least not all of them, but we need to hear what they are. Otherwise we will never know who we are.

The uncovering and processing of the wisdom of the near-forgotten stories is a task for generations. We slowly sing and dance their words as a Hasid sings and dances upon new insight. We quietly taste their sweetness. We walk slowly, one foot in front of the other.

And it may well mean we will make the knock on that church or synagogue door that we never thought we would make. Without ancient community and family, visions cannot heal.

We can learn to dream again, to have visions. Together, we can dream a dream of redemption, a dream of justice, a dream of taking the leper into our home. We can touch again the inebriating fire whose gift is totally free—and totally costly. Images and metaphors will help us grieve again and stand mute in the amazement of hope that is from beyond us and always a gracious gift from God.

In short, we will dream again God's dream. For we are never alone in the visions we dream, no matter their middleness and humanity. Dreaming with us is the Lover of Israel, the God of Jesus, the Creator, the Great Spirit, the Master of Breath, who knits together all creation's doings—the one alone whose dreams are the dreams that heal.

NOTES

CHAPTER 1:
We All See Visions

1. Northern California Jewish Bulletin, 15 November 1996.

2. Abraham Isaac Kook, *The Lights of Holiness*, trans. Ben Zion Bokser, The Classics of Western Spirituality series (New York: Paulist Press, 1978), 212, 208.

3. Robert Lee Hotz, "Religion," *Los Angeles Times*, Saturday, 8 November 1997, sec. B9.

4. George W. Cornell, "Spiritual Experiences Defy Scientific Beliefs," *Daily News Los Angeles*, Saturday, 10 January 1987, Valley section, p. 18.

5. Greeley quote drawn from Cornell article.

6. National Opinion Research Center from Cornell article.

7. When I say that visions are natural, I mean that there is a natural—built-in bodily and psychologically—way that visions come to us. In a sense we are made for visions. When I say that visions are rarely supernatural, I mean *supernatural* in the popular understanding of that term, referring to stupendous events through which God is intervening in a direct, paranormal, unmediated way in the world.

   Supernatural is used differently in theology. Here it means that God is elevating our nature through grace in gifting us with faith, love, and hope; God is orienting our humanity toward himself. As von Balthasar puts it, paraphrasing St. Thomas, "Grace presupposes nature; it does not destroy it but completes it" (Hans Urs von Balthasar, Medard Kehland, and Werner Loser, eds. *The von Balthasar Reader* [New York: Crossroad, 1997], 22).

   When the Holy Spirit gifts us with faith, love, and hope and unites us with God, a type of supernaturality, in a theological sense, is present. When visions are a means by which the Spirit orients our natures toward God and gifts us with grace (or another manifestation of that orientation), a type of supernaturality can be said to be present, as it is in all the many varied ways God gifts us with grace.

8. Phillip Berman, *The Journey Home: What Near-Death Experiences and Mysticism Teach Us About the Gift of Life* (New York: Pocket Books, 1996), 168.

9. Ralph W. Hood, "Personality Correlates of the Report of Mystical Experience," *Psychological Reports* 44, no. 3 (1979): 804–6.

10. Melvin Morse, *Parting Visions* (New York: Villard Books, 1994), 88–89.

CHAPTER 2:
The Light Makes a Promise

1. David O'Reilly, "Revelations in the Brain Physiological Processes Linked to Some Visions and Enlightenment," *San Jose Mercury News,* Saturday, 21 February 1998, Religion and Ethics, 2E.

2. Robert Lee Hotz, "Seeking the Biology of Spirituality: Is there a biochemistry of belief?" *Los Angeles Times,* Sunday, 26 April 1998, Home edition, A1.

3. Melvin Morse, *Parting Visions* (New York: Villard Books, 1994), 71.

4. Denise Despres, *Ghostly Sights: Visual Meditation in Late-Medieval Literature* (Norman, Okla.: Pilgrim Books, 1989), 26.

5. Abbot Suger, quoted in Eddie Ensley, *Prayer That Heals Our Emotions* (San Francisco: Harper & Row, 1988), 28.

6. St. Cyril of Jerusalem, *The Cathechetical Lectures,* "Procatechesis," paragraph 15. The Nicene and Post-Nicene Fathers Second Series, vol. 7, Church Fathers section, CD-ROM edition, The Theological Journal Library 3.0, Galaxie Software, no pagination. English modernized. (Readers can also find an on-line electronic version at Christian Ethereal Library hosted by Wheaton College: http://www.ccel.org/)

7. St. Ambrose of Milan, *Two Books Concerning Repentance,* Book 2, chapter 8, paragraph 66. The Nicene and Post-Nicene Fathers Second Series, vol. 10, Church Fathers section, CD-ROM edition, The Theological Journal Library 3.0, Galaxie Software, no pagination. English modernized. (Readers can also find an on-line electronic version at Christian Ethereal Library hosted by Wheaton College: http://www.ccel.org/)

8. Despres, xi.

9. Eugene d'Aquili and Andrew B. Newberg, *The Mystical Mind: Probing the Biology of Religious Experience* (Minneapolis: Fortress Press, 1999), 210.

10. Abraham Heschel, *Quest for God* (New York: Crossroad, 1982), 28.

CHAPTER 3:
What Are Visions?

1. Samuel H. Dresner, *Zaddik* (New York: Schocken Books, 1960), 125.

CHAPTER 4:
The Medicine Stories of Christianity

1. R. C. Finucane, *The Rescue of the Innocents: Endangered Children in Medieval Miracles* (New York: St. Martin's Press, 1997), 1–2. Finucane's book is an excellent introduction to the thousands of medieval depositions depicting wondrous events and visions. His work includes translations of actual depositions.

2. Ibid., 109.

3. André Vauchez, *Sainteté en Occident aux derniers siècles du Moyen Age: d'après les procès de canonisation et les documents hagiographiques* (Rome: École française de Rome, 1981; Paris: Diffusion de Boccard, 1988), 518–23. "In the first canonization processes (trials, examinations), one finds in fact almost all the methods and rituals of healing attested for the High Middle Ages, which go back to the pre-Christian era if not to prehistory. The majority of those who experienced miracles recovered their health after having gone to the place where the remains of the saint were and slept nearby, for it was believed that their therapeutic value worked with more efficacy during sleep. The incubation was accomplished, in the best cases, by a vision or apparition of the intercessor whose help had been implored, followed immediately by the healing. A light invaded the church and when the beneficiaries of the miracle belonged to a group of *contracti* (paralyzed or paraplegic, etc.), who made up the main body of the clientele of the sanctuaries, a great noise was heard of bones and sinews being put back into place. The departure of the evil was sometimes preceded by the appearance of an abundant sweat that covered the sick person during the night, after which he awoke at dawn, fresh and fit. Yet it was rare that the miracle would occur on the first day. As a general rule, the pilgrim had to stay for a rather long time in the sanctuary—at least nine days (a novena), sometimes two or three weeks—before obtaining satisfaction."

   This excellent book details the common practice of "incubation" of visions at shrines, the group experience of visions at shrines, and the relationship of therapeutic visions to healing. See also D. Mallardo, "L'incubazione nella cristianita medievale napoletana," Anal. Boll. 57, 1949, 465–98.

4. Finucane, *Innocents*, 122–23.

5. Benedicta Ward, *Miracles and the Medieval Mind* (Philadelphia: University of Pennsylvania Press, 1982), 2. Ward reiterates this point in the concluding remarks to her book: "Perhaps the first conclusion that can be drawn is that the records of miracles in the Middle Ages are not merely bizarre sidelights to the religion of the period. They provide, rather, a way to approach the ordinary day-to-day life of men and women in all kinds of situations and in all ranks of society, and serious historians must take them into consideration" (214). In addition to Finucane's excellent work in *Innocents*, Benedicta Ward deals extensively with shrine and pilgrimage related miracles (Ward, 10–131).

6. Ibid., 215–16.

7. Bob Keeler, "The Power of Faith," *Newsday*, 21 December 1993, 61.

8. Melvin Morse, *Parting Visions* (New York: Villard Books, 1994), 49–50.

9. Larry Dossey, *Dreams and Healing, Alternative Therapies in Health and Medicine*, vol. 5, no. 6, electronic edition, no pagination.

10. Reynolds Price, "Jesus Then and Now," *Time*, 6 December 1999, 94.

11. Augustine material drawn from Augustine, *Confessions*, trans. Albert C. Outler, 1955, Christian Classics and Historical Works section, CD-ROM edition, The Theological Journal Library 3.0, Galaxie Software, no pagination. (Readers can also find an on-line electronic version at Christian Ethereal Library hosted by Wheaton College: http://www.ccel.org/)

12. In his old age, Augustine celebrated and made popular the many miracles, especially the physical healings he believed he witnessed or had credible information concerning, in his diocese of Hippo. Peter Brown summarizes Augustine's view: "A God whose generosity had scattered so much purely physical beauty on the earth could not neglect physical illness. . . . These reliefs were some slight hint, like thin rays of sunshine entering a darkened room, of the final transformation, the glorious resurrection" (Peter Brown, *Augustine of Hippo* [Berkeley: University of California Press, 1969], 417). Brown also gives an excellent overview of Augustine's belief that miracles flourished in the church on pages 415–18 in the same book. Augustine discusses miracles at length in *City of God*, The Nicene and Post-Nicene Fathers Second Series, vol. 7, Church Fathers section, CD-ROM edition, The Theological Journal Library 3.0, Galaxie Software, no pagination.

13. St. Cyril of Jerusalem, *The Catechetical Lectures of St. Cyril*, Lecture 5, "Of Faith," paragraph 11. The Nicene and Post-Nicene Fathers Second Series, vol. 7, Church Fathers section, CD-ROM edition, The Theological Journal Library 3.0., Galaxie Software, no pagination. I modernized the English on this quote. (Readers can also find an on-line electronic version at Christian Ethereal Library hosted by Wheaton College: http://www.ccel.org/)

14. St. Gregory Nazianzen, Oration 18, "On the Death of His Father," paragraph 12. The Nicene and Post-Nicene Fathers Second Series, vol. 7, Church Fathers section, CD-ROM edition, The Theological Journal Library 3.0, Galaxie Software, no pagination. English modernized. (Readers can also find an on-line electronic version at Christian Ethereal Library hosted by Wheaton College: http://www.ccel.org/)

15. Ibid., paragraph 31. English modernized.

16. St. Gregory Nazianzen's quotes found in Morton T. Kelsey, *God, Dreams, and Revelation* (Minneapolis: Augsburg Publishing House, 1974), 138. Kelsey's book is an excellent survey of the wide extent of visions in all parts of the church during the first few centuries.

17. Morton T. Kelsey, *God, Dreams, and Revelation* (Minneapolis: Augsburg Publishing House, 1974), 138.

18. Ibid., 193.

19. St. Athanasius, *Against the Heathen*, part 2, paragraphs 31.f and 33.3. The Nicene and Post-Nicene Fathers Second Series, vol. 14, Church Fathers section, CD-ROM

edition, The Theological Journal Library 3.0, Galaxie Software, no pagination. English modernized. (Readers can also find an on-line electronic version at Christian Ethereal Library hosted by Wheaton College: http://www.ccel.org/)

20. Bernard Gui, *The Life of St. Thomas Aquinas*, ed. and trans. Kenelm Foster, O.P., contained in *The Life of St. Thomas Aquinas: Biographical Documents* (Baltimore: Helicon Press, 1959), 37.

21. Ibid.

22. Ibid., 43.

23. Ibid., 38.

24. Ibid., 39.

25. Ibid., 46.

CHAPTER 6:
Seeing Life with New Eyes

1. Bernard Shaw, preface to *Androcles and the Lion* (New York: Brentano's, 1916), xxxviii.

2. St. Gregory I, (Dialogos), *Life of St. Benedict*, (St. Pachomius Library) electronic version, chapter 35, no pagination. http://www.ocf.org/OrthodoxPage/reading /St.Pachomius/Saints/

3. Benedicta Ward, *Miracles and the Medieval Mind* (Philadelphia: University of Pennsylvania Press, 1982), 216.

4. George B. Wilson, "Dissent or Conversation Among Adults?" *America*, 13 March 1999, 10–12.

5. Ward, 2. Ward later reiterates this point in a powerful statement: "Our usual definition of 'miracle' as the direct intervention of God in the normal running of events is a narrow and modern concept, which had little meaning before the sixteenth century at the earliest. A cause-and-effect universe, with its exclusive interest in 'how' things happen, in the mechanics of events, is then recognized as only one way of thinking about reality. A more subtle and varied understanding of the world and the place of man within it—and of the relationship of all creation, including man, to God—is there for rediscovery. Certainly the records of medieval miracles can suggest a new approach to the records of miracles in the Bible, an area in which demythologizing long ago reached a dead end" (214–15).

6. Ibid., 3.

7. Ibid., 4.

8. William McIntosh, "A Theater That Transforms Us," *Parabola*, winter 1997, electronic edition, Northern Light Database, no pagination.

9. Thomas Aquinas, *Summa Theologica* 1.105.7, quoted in William C. Placher, *The Domestication of Transcendence: How Modern Thinking about God Went Wrong* (Louisville, Ky.: Westminster John Knox Press, 1996), 135.

10. William C. Placher, *The Domestication of Transcendence: How Modern Thinking about God Went Wrong* (Louisville, Ky.: Westminster John Knox Press, 1996), 135.

CHAPTER 7:
Trips to the Horizon

1. Quotes from Gregory the Great found in Carole Straw, *Gregory the Great* (Berkeley: University of California Press, 1988), 68.
2. Ibid., 93.
3. Stephen F. Kruger, *Dreaming in the Middle Ages* (Cambridge, England: University of Cambridge Press, 1992), 45.
4. Marjorie N. How, *Dreams and Visions in English Poetry* (London: The University of London Press, 1916), 62.

CHAPTER 9:
Remembering Visions

1. St. Bonaventure, *The Soul's Journey Into God,* found in Ewer Cousins, trans., *Bonaventure: The Classics of Western Spirituality* (New York: Paulist Press, 1978), 80–81.
2. Abraham Heschel, *I Asked for Wonder* (New York: Crossroad, 1987), 102.

CHAPTER 10:
God's Therapy

1. Walter Brueggeman, *Prophetic Imagination* (Philadelphia: Fortress Press, 1978), 44.
2. Avery Dulles, *Assurance of Things Hoped For* (New York: Oxford University Press, 1994), 216–17.

CHAPTER 12:
Help for Our Grieving

1. Jonathan Edwards, *On Religious Affections* (electronic version at Christian Ethereal Library hosted by Wheaton College: http://www.ccel.org/), no pagination. English modernized.
2. Melvin Morse, *Parting Visions* (New York: Villard Books, 1994), 48–52, 74–79, 216.
3. Ibid., 89.
4. Ibid., 88–89.
5. Marcus Dods, *Forerunners of Dante* (Edinburgh: T & T Clark, 1903), 177–79. English modernized.
6. St. Chrysostom, *On the Priesthood: Ascetic Treatises, Select Homilies, and Letters.* "Letter to a Young Widow," The Nicene and Post-Nicene Fathers, vol. 9, Church Fathers sec-

tion, CD-ROM edition, The Theological Journal Library 3.0, Galaxie Software, no pagination. I modernized the English on this quote. (Readers can also find an on-line electronic version at Christian Ethereal Library hosted by Wheaton College: http://www.ccel.org/)

7. St. Gregory Nazianzen and St. Ambrose, "St. Ambrose, On His Brother Satyrus: I," *Funeral Orations*, trans. Leo P. McCauley et al., The Fathers of the Church series (Washington: Catholic University of America Press, 1953), 190–91. English modernized. Sequence rearranged for clarity.

8. St. Gregory Nazianzen, *Panegyric on his brother, S. Caesarius.* Oration 8, "On His Sister Gorgonia." The Nicene and Post-Nicene Fathers Second Series, vol. 7, Church Fathers section, CD-ROM edition, The Theological Journal Library 3.0, Galaxie Software, no pagination. English modernized. (Readers can also find an on-line electronic version at Christian Ethereal Library hosted by Wheaton College: http://www.ccel.org/)

9. Morse, 98–99.

10. Ron Wooten-Green, "The Symbolic Language of the Dying: Metaphor and Meaning," *America,* 16 October 1999.

CHAPTER 13:
Visions to Heal Our Wounded World

1. Karl Rahner, *Foundations of Christian Faith* (New York: Crossroad, 1986), 438.
2. Hans Urs von Balthasar, Medard Kehland, and Werner Loser, eds., *The von Balthasar Reader* (New York: Crossroad, 1997), 22, 420.
3. Abraham Heschel, *I Asked for Wonder* (New York: Crossroad, 1987), 55.
4. Abraham Heschel, *Quest for God* (New York: Crossroad, 1982), 19.

CHAPTER 14:
Walking in Balance with Visions

1. Martin Buber, *Tales of the Hasidim—Later Masters* (New York: Schocken Books, 1948), 254.
2. Karl Rahner, *Sacramentum Mundi,* vol. 5 (New York: Herder and Herder, 1970), 358.
3. Benedict J. Groeschel, C.F.R., *A Still, Small Voice: A Practical Guide on Reported Revelations* (San Francisco: Ignatius Press, 1993), 34.

CHAPTER 15:
Spiritual Emergencies

1. Kristin W. Watson, "Spiritual Emergence: Concepts and Implications for Psychotherapy," *Journal of Humanistic Psychology,* 34, no. 2 (spring 1994), 25–26.
2. Emma Bragdon, *The Call of Spiritual Emergency* (San Francisco: Harper & Row, 1990), 16.
3. Ibid., 206–7.

CHAPTER 16:
Visions and the New Millennium

1. Walter Brueggemann, *Abiding Astonishment* (Louisville, Ky.: Westminster John Knox Press, 1991), 37.
2. Ibid., 134.
3. Ibid., 41–45.
4. Jugren Moltmann, *Theology of Hope* (New York: Harper & Row, 1967), 108.

CONTACT THE AUTHOR

Eddie Ensley and his associates are nationally known speakers. They are available for parish missions, conferences, retreats, days of renewal, leaders' days, catechist training workshops, liturgical meetings, lay ministry formation, and clergy days. For more information, contact Eddie at 1-800-745-4416 or 706-322-8840. E-mail him at: yahula@worldnet.att.net, or write:

Contemplative Brothers
Box 8065
Columbus, GA 31908

Eddie is collecting stories of people's visions and sacred moments. He would love to hear from you. Mail your accounts to the above address.